D0794515

THE INTERNATIONAL KITCHEN

Forthcoming Titles in *The International Kitchen* Series

THE INTERNATIONAL KITCHEN

Europe, the Mediterranean, the Soviet Union, and Scandinavia

IRWIN GELBER

VNR VAN NOSTRAND REINHOLD
New York

Copyright © 1991 by Van Nostrand Reinhold

Library of Congress Catalog Card Number 90-44224
ISBN 0-442-31936-3

All rights reserved. No part of this work covered by the copyright hereon may be reproduced or used in any form by any means—graphic, electronic, or mechanical, including photocopying, recording, taping, or information storage and retrieval systems—without written permission of the publisher.

Printed in the United States of America

Van Nostrand Reinhold
115 Fifth Avenue
New York, New York 10003

Chapman and Hall
2–6 Boundary Row
London, SE1 8HN, England

Thomas Nelson Australia
102 Dodds Street
South Melbourne 3205
Victoria, Australia

Nelson Canada
1120 Birchmount Road
Scarborough, Ontario M1K 5G4, Canada

16 15 14 13 12 11 10 9 8 7 6 5 4 3 2 1

Library of Congress Cataloging in Publication Data

Gelber, Irwin, 1933–
    The international kitchen. Europe, the Mediterranean, the Soviet Union, and Scandinavia/Irwin Gelber.
        p.   cm.
    Includes bibliographical references and index.
    ISBN 0-442-31936-3
    1. Cookery, European.   2. Cookery, North African.   I. Title.
    TX723.5.A1G45   1991
    641.59—dc20   90-44224
                                                                        CIP

CONTENTS

PASTA, RICE, POLENTA, AND PIZZA 61

SOUPS   93

FISH   123

POULTRY   157

MEATS   193

VEGETABLES AND SALADS   247

DESSERTS   277

PREFACE

This initial volume seeks to provide the professional chef and the serious student of culinary arts with a useful repertoire of dishes reflecting the rich culinary heritage of Europe, the Mediterranean, the Middle East, the Soviet Union, and Scandinavia. Subsequent volumes will deal with the foods of Central and South America, and Asia. Dishes are designed to be used as "specials" or for "special occasions."

Rooted for the most part in the cuisine of the common folk, many preparations that are quite similar in concept and content appear in a number of different cultures. These are attributed to the land of origin, whenever possible. In many cases, pinpointing the country of origin was very difficult. In addition, the number of menu items available from this geographic area is very large. For the most part, the included dishes are ones that were developed over the years by numerous cooks in homes and in local restaurants who relied extensively on the availability of fresh, local, seasonal products. Some of the traditional preparation methods, influenced by local custom, product availability, or perhaps by the inspiration of a particular chef, have been reformulated to conform with current culinary practices. Throughout the text there is a basic devotion to the use of fresh, easily obtained ingredients and to a straightforward, uncomplicated style of preparation. It is hoped that through the use of the recipes in this volume, contemporary chefs, cooks, and students will be able to offer a greater variety of menu offerings.

ACKNOWLEDGMENTS

I would like to thank the countless cooks from many lands, who, over the centuries, experimented, refined, and ultimately inspired the various food preparations referred to in this volume. In deference to their efforts, I would hope that these recipes are not viewed as the final word in what has been one of humanity's longest-running endeavors, but rather, as a guide that may serve to further the work of those who preceded us, and in doing so, keep alive the flame of culinary inspiration. That being said, I would like to express my thanks to a number of people who helped me in preparing this book. First, my thanks go to Myriam Gelber, who served as my research assistant, and Margaret Bachelder, who offered valuable editorial assistance and constant encouragement. To my colleagues, Chef Charles F. Leonardo, C.E.C., assistant director of dining services at Northeastern University and president of the Epicurean Club of Boston, and Chef Donald E. Carlson, executive chef, The Inn, Northern Arizona University, two gentlemen who truly love the culinary arts, and Chef Esther Press McManus, whose culinary artistry has left an indelible imprint on the restaurant renaissance of Philadelphia, my everlasting gratitude for their willingness to share professional expertise and for their enthusiasm and interest in this project. A very special thanks to Chef Kurt Scheller, executive chef, Ramses Hilton, Cairo, Egypt, and president of Les Toques Blanches, Egypt, for his generous spirit, for his assistance in providing materials from that part of the world, and for his friendship.

I also would like to acknowledge the following chefs and culinarians who responded to my inquiries and generously shared their knowledge with me: Mr. Kurt Weid, chef de cuisine, president of the Sveriges Kokschefers Forening, Uppsala, Sweden; Mr. Viacheslav M. Kovaliov, expert on Russian cuisine, 'Ekonomika' Publishing House, Moscow, USSR; Chef Helmut L. Kahlert, culinary arts instructor, Boston, Massachusetts; Mr. Karl Brunnengräber, culinary author, Frankfurt, Germany; Chef Karoly Ungar, president, Association of Hungarian Cooks, Budapest, Hungary; Chef Fritz-Edmund Dorweiler, Hauptgeschäftsführer, Verband der Koche Deutschlands e. V, Frankfurt, Germany; Chef Dumetru Burtea, president, The Romanian Association of Cooks, Bucharest, Romania; and Mr. G. van der Veen, chairman, Dutch Hotel and Restaurant Association, Gravenhage, The Netherlands.

And lastly, my thanks to several people at Van Nostrand Reinhold: Judith Joseph, Pamela Scott, and Cynthia Zigmund, whose example taught me a dimension of "patience" that I never knew existed.

INTRODUCTION

The International Kitchen comprises a collection of representative appetizers, soups, meat, fish and fowl entrées, and desserts from many countries around the world. The series is designed to provide students of the culinary arts, professional and amateur, with a handy reference to a number of interesting culinary specialities from diverse cultures. It is hoped that it will also afford them an opportunity to further their skills and knowledge, add variety to their menus, and bring joy to their friends and patrons.

Obviously, the number of recipes embraced by any single national or regional cuisine is enormous. And, if one multiplies this wealth of material by the number of countries represented in these volumes, the total number of potential recipes becomes staggering. To deal effectively with this abundant source of culinary ingenuity and invention, the recipes selected for inclusion had to meet four objectives:

1. have a strong association with a specific national cuisine;
2. use basic, raw ingredients that are readily available in the United States market;
3. be within the culinary realm of a broad spectrum of diners and therefore marketable;

4. reinforce basic culinary skills through the processes involved in their production.

The recipes are formulated in portions that are appropriate to the particular preparation. Items that should be produced in volume are designed, for the most part, for 10 to 12 portions that can then be expanded or reduced, if desired. Other dishes, primarily sauté items, which are best treated in individually prepared servings, are scaled for the single portion. If any components of these single-portion recipes can be prepared in advance (sauces, for example), directions are given to yield quantities sufficient for 10 to 12 servings.

The recipes are formatted in three columns. The first column is the ingredients, the second is the quantity, and the third is the method. This format was used because it presents each stage of the preparation in proper sequence. Furthermore, it relates the raw product to the operation necessary to process that phase of the recipe. This format eliminates going back and forth between a list of ingredients and the method of preparation. To assemble all ingredients prior to preparation, simply read down columns one and two. The following is an example.

CORNISH HENS WITH CALVADOS   *Northern France*

Yield: 10 servings

Cornish hens	5, halved	Brown Cornish hen halves in butter and oil. Remove from pan and keep in warm place.
Butter	2 oz.	
Olive oil	2 oz.	
Carrots, diced	1 lb.	Remove excess fat from pan and sauté vegetables until they begin to brown.
Shallots, whole, peeled	10 small	
Calvados	8 oz.	Add calvados, cover, and cook over medium heat for 3–4 minutes.
Apple cider	24 oz.	Add cider, herbs, salt, pepper, and nutmeg and bring to a boil. Lower heat to a simmer and return hens to pan. Cook for 20 minutes, or until hens are tender.
Parsley	4 sprigs	
Bay leaf	3 large	
Salt and black pepper	to taste	
Nutmeg	to taste	

Heavy cream	4 oz.
Lemon juice, fresh	to taste

Remove hens to a warm place. Reduce pan liquids by half. Remove bay leaf and add heavy cream and return hens to sauce and heat through. Do not boil. Prior to serving, add a small squeeze of lemon juice.

Serve with buttered green beans and small potato pancakes or with small potatoes that have been sautéed in clarified butter and roasted in the oven.

THE COUNTRIES' CULINARY BACKGROUNDS

Every nation boasts of food preparations that it calls its very own and that its people believe have made distinctive contributions to the world of gastronomy. Many times this is true. The national origins of many dishes, however, are clouded by the passage of time. One may find exactly the same dish, with perhaps some small variation, in a number of neighboring countries, each claiming the dish to be an integral part of that particular country's national heritage. Long before many contemporary nations existed as cohesive political entities, however, the inhabitants of those regions were busy creating, experimenting, and refining culinary practices that in later times would come to be identified with a particular "national" cuisine. In terms of culinary practice these geographically defined zones, which did not necessarily occupy the same exact area later to be known as a particular country, were and are today to some extent governed primarily by their soil's fertility, their proximity to the sea or mountains, their relationship to trade routes, and, above all, the restraints imposed by their climates.

Ingenious cooks, working within the constraints of their surroundings, created a body of indigenous cuisine of astonishing variety. Using locally available ingredients, they fashioned the character of what would later become the "national cuisine." Their preparations reflected the possibilities inherent in nature's often

1

unpredictable bounty, creating new delights for the palate through trial and error. These cooks found ways to combine ingredients to create variety, in what must have been a limited choice of food products. Their preparations give testimony to our desire and ability to alter nature's diet to suit our own tastes. Discovering the processes necessary to preserve foods from natural decay, through air-drying, salting, and smoking, lessened their dependency on nature's capricious cycles and enabled them to sustain themselves in times when food was not plentiful. From these experiments, created out of necessity, many of the delicacies that we enjoy today were born.

In our times, this process continues. Modern food technology has brought us the possibility of having an incredible number of choices in our daily diets and in greater variety than could have been imagined just a short while ago. We eagerly embrace new foods and innovative food combinations from many other lands, and, when appropriate, incorporate them into our daily diets. But, as in many aspects of our modern world, the mechanisms and systems that have enabled us to choose at will from the products of the world have also internationalized our tastes and made the distinct national and regional differences that defined the culinary world of yesterday less and less clear. This global menu, reflecting culinary concepts from even Earth's remote areas, has become an integral part of a world grown closer, more knowledgeable, and more demanding. It has also created a discriminating consumer with expanded tastes and preferences.

In choosing recipes for this book, I acknowledged the invisible geographical boundaries drawn by the laws of nature and governed by the good taste and skills of the various areas' native cooks. The articles on the nations from which the recipes in this book were chosen focus on those countries whose historical significance, present commercial influence, or contribution to the culinary arts was deemed to be representative not only of a distinctive national cuisine, but of a broader regional cuisine.

THE INFLUENCE OF
THE AUSTRO-HUNGARIAN EMPIRE

This vast political entity, which reached from the borders of Imperial Russia to the Adriatic Sea, lasted for more than six hundred years. It consisted of over a dozen nationalities embracing today's Austria, Hungary, Yugoslavia, and Czechoslovakia, as well as parts of other neighboring nations. At the height of its power during the 1800s, the empire was populated by more than fifty million people speaking sixteen different languages and occupied much of what we call Central Europe today. Contained within this empire were a number of distinct smaller nations such as Bohemia, Bosnia, Slovakia, Serbia, Montenegro, among others, each with its own customs, language or dialect, culinary traditions, and specialities.

Despite the multinational character of the Empire, the influence of its capital —Vienna—with its powerful court, could be felt throughout the domain and even beyond its specified borders. Similarities in customs, dress, and gastronomic traditions are still apparent today in many of the regions that formerly came under the domain of the Austro-Hungarian rulers. The redrawing of the map of this area of Europe after the end of the First World War changed many boundaries and allegiances. If one examines the culinary customs of the countries that were part of this great empire, however, many common culinary practices are still to be found that transcend the national borders of the now independent countries of Central Europe. The names of many dishes such as *Kaisertorte* (Emperor's Cake), *Kaisersemmein* (Emperor's Roll), or *Schnitzel Holstein* (a veal cutlet topped with an egg, caviar, and anchovies) are vestiges of earlier imperial times and still indicate a kind of homage to the once powerful nobility.

An indication of the multinational roots of this part of the world's cuisine is the recurring culinary themes found throughout the former Empire: the roasts and sausages emanating from southern Germany; the *gulasch* or *gulyas* with its paprika sauce from Hungary; the schnitzel, which probably came from northern Italy; and the luxurious pastries of Bohemia. The world-famous *apfel strüdel*, strongly associated with the Viennese school of baking, was most likely inspired by the flaky pastries brought to that part of the world by the Turks when they lay siege to Vienna. These dishes, all popular throughout Central Europe, express the complex mix of ethnic and nationalistic elements. Combined with a large and influential aristocracy with cosmopolitan tastes and a general populace with peasant traditions, these influences have resulted in one of the world's most interesting cuisines—a unique blending of different flavors and perspectives from almost all of Europe's regions.

An important trading center by the tenth century, Vienna, the empire's capital, was introduced to the spices of the East by the returning Crusaders. In the late 1600s, coffee arrived with the invading Turks who, according to legend, also became the inspiration for the croissant, the crescent-shaped roll that Viennese bakers created to show their disdain for the national symbol of the invaders. The arrival of coffee as a new and popular beverage created a new institution, the coffee house, which became an integral part of the social life in Vienna and most of the cities throughout the Empire. And to accompany the coffee, the bakers of Vienna developed, in the form of pastries and cakes, an elevated art form imitated today throughout Europe and the world.

Today, the Empire no longer exists as a political entity and Austria is a small landlocked country in Central Europe, bordered by the now independent countries of Czechoslovakia and Germany on the north, Hungary on the east, Yugoslavia and Italy on the south, and Switzerland and Liechtenstein to the west.

Austria's present population is only 7.6 million people. Its chief products are grains, potatoes, beets, grapes, and livestock. Ninety percent of its agricultural needs are raised or grown in the country and approximately eighteen percent of the labor force is engaged in agriculture. Its neighbor to the east, Hungary, shares a common culinary tradition. Regional differences in this also landlocked country, a nation of more than ten million people, are marked primarily by flavor intensity and the use of spices. The primary cooking fat is lard, and its most renowned spice, paprika, is generously used in a variety of dishes and is exported throughout the world. At the present time, twenty-one percent of Hungary's labor force is involved in agriculture. The principal crops are corn, wheat, potatoes, sugar beets, vegetables, fruits, and grapes for the manufacture of wines, the best known of which are Tokay and Egri Bikaver.

EGYPT

Egypt, located in the northeastern corner of Africa, has served as a link between Africa and the Middle East for thousands of years. It is bordered by Sudan to the south, Libya to the west, the Mediterranean Sea to the north, Israel to the northeast, and the Red Sea to the east. The climate is mild and extremely dry most of the year, with intensely hot periods during the summer. Surrounded by deserts, yet easily approachable, the Egyptians have faced invasions by numerous conquerors over the millennia. The Egyptian civilization during the times of the various kingdoms and reigns of the pharaohs was renowned for its advanced sciences and building arts. First conquered by Alexander the Great and later by the Romans, Egypt was part of the Graeco-Roman world for almost a thousand years. In the seventh century, the country was conquered by the Arabs, whose religion, Islam, remains the predominant religion to this day.

Although Egypt has an extremely limited agricultural area (sand dunes and stony, sandy soil make up almost ninety percent of the land), the arable areas along the Nile River are capable of producing abundant crops due to the soil's unusual richness. For countless centuries, the Nile's annual flooding brought nutrient-laden silt from upriver, fertilizing the soil of the Nile Delta. A mixed blessing, the flooding also at times caused total crop devastation. In an attempt to control this flooding and to create more arable land to feed Egypt's burgeoning population, the Aswan Dam was constructed in 1971. With a more predictable water supply, complex irrigation techniques have now created more arable land farther away from the river. Although crops are not lost as frequently to flooding and food production has increased, the natural fertilization process that for so many centuries enriched the soil no longer occurs. As a result, there has been an increased dependence on chemical fertilizers; unfortunately, this use has had an irreversible, negative impact on the environment. Over ninety percent of Egyptians live in the Nile basin and depend on agriculture as a source of livelihood.

Common crops today include bananas, figs, mangoes, dates, squash, corn, and sugar cane. Archeological studies have indicated that onions, garlic, radishes, leeks, and lentils have been cultivated in Egypt for thousands of years. Another agricultural product, raw cotton, has been a major export crop since the early nineteenth century and today makes up about forty percent of the value of the country's agricultural exports.

Egyptian culinary history can be traced as far back as 2345 B.C. Funerary texts that have been unearthed tell us that the common people ate three meals a day and the royalty ate five. Today, Egyptian cuisine is an amalgam of Turkish, Palestinian, Greek, Syrian, and Lebanese food with strong overtones from Europe. Cairo's major hotels, catering to the local population as well as to numerous international visitors, maintain separate European and Arabic kitchen facilities and staffs. The Arabic kitchens offer menus listing wide regional representations of Middle Eastern cuisine. These foods are presented in restaurant settings that are distinctive in atmosphere and representative of the local traditions. Bread is consumed in quantity and the Egyptians make a number of different varieties. The most common, however, is *balady* bread—round, small, slightly leavened loaves that open up for filling or are used to spoon up various pureed *mezze*. *Mezze*, which are assorted hors d'oeuvre composed of vegetables, meats, and grains, are usually presented as a first course. They can be very simple or highly elaborate presentations and include standard dishes such as *tehina*, *babaganouj*, eggplant salad, stuffed vine leaves, cheese, olives, nuts, fried brains, liver, etc.

Following the *mezze* are a wide variety of entrées, which include simple grilled meats, fish, and fowl, sometimes marinated and cooked on skewers. Other popular entrées include *kushari*—a pasta, rice, and lentil dish in a tomato sauce —and small chickens, pigeons, or Cornish hens, stuffed with rice and pine nuts and roasted on the spit.

Spices and herbs are very important in Egyptian cuisine, especially the combination of garlic and crushed coriander. Other commonly used spices include cumin, turmeric, ginger, dill, cinnamon, and allspice. Egyptian pastries, very sweet and rich, are typical of Middle Eastern desserts. A few of the most popular sweets are *baklawa*—a flaky pastry dough filled with honey and nuts; *om ali*— which consists of puff pastry, nuts, and raisins, soaked in milk and baked in the oven; and *mahallabia*—a pudding made with milk and flavored with orange flower water.

FRANCE

None of the national cuisines of Europe has captured the attention of the international public as has that of France. The French have elevated their cuisine and the making of wine to internationally appreciated art forms. Their approach to cooking is scientific, exact in its formulation, and, therefore, readily exportable. The standardized *haute cuisine* that emerges from major hotel kitchens and restaurants throughout the world gives eloquent testimony to the popularity and acceptance of the French school of food preparation.

Not as familiar, perhaps, is the *cuisine bourgeoisie,* or the cooking found in homes and smaller, bistro-type restaurants throughout the country, which closely mirrors the availability of local products and the creative culinary skills of the local practitioners. Less pretentious, this cuisine is distinguished by simpler presentations and an inclination toward honest, straightforward, and hearty dishes. Locally produced fish and meats, and fresh, readily available produce are the hallmarks of these preparations. The numerous and sometimes subtle recipe variations reflect both the spirit of the cook and the seasonal availability of products.

As one might expect, agriculture plays a large role in the economy of this industrialized country of fifty-six million inhabitants. Favorable climate, and varied soils and growing conditions, enable the extensive farmlands to produce an abundant variety of agricultural products and livestock. France also produces some of the world's finest cheeses and wines. Nearly forty percent of the country is under cultivation, with twenty percent devoted to the traditional crops of wheat and grapes. Areas less suitable for farming support major cattle and dairy production and, in the southeastern sections, major olive and citrus groves. France's extensive Atlantic coastline is home to an important fishing industry, with cod, herring, sardine, tuna, and mackerel the principal catches. In the south, along its Mediterranean coast, a smaller, locally oriented, commercial fleet provides many of the fish needed for the culinary specialities of the region.

In France, as in most countries, there is a long-standing relationship between the traditional cuisine of the region and the local products. Although modern food distribution systems have tempered distinct regional differences to a large degree by increasing the availability of many products over a wide geographic area, certain strong influences still dominate regional cooking. In the northern and central regions, butter is used extensively and has become widely thought of as a basis for all French cuisine. Cooks of other areas of the country, however, prefer other cooking fats. To the east, in Alsace-Lorraine, with its proximity to Germany, and also in the southwestern region, lard and duck and goose fat are preferred. In the southeastern regions like Provençe, with its Mediterranean climate, the use of olive oil is common.

The food specialities, like the wines of France, are closely associated with particular geographic areas, and as such, are internationally recognized. Provençal cooking, for instance, is closely linked to the olive, tomato, and garlic, as well as to the indigenous fish from the Mediterranean Sea. Bouillabaisse, probably the world's most celebrated fish soup, is closely associated with the coastal city of Marseilles. In the north, the important fishing industry in the coastal area of Brittany is reflected in the numerous fish dishes from that area. Normandy, with its extensive dairy production and large apple orchards, gives us many preparations that use butter as the principal cooking fat and a combination of apples cooked with meats and fowl. In this area, apple cider is a popular table beverage. It is also used as a braising liquid and many dishes are flavored and flambéed with Calvados, the region's excellent apple brandy. Alsace-Lorraine is noted for its outstanding sausage and sauerkraut dishes, suckling pig, and, of course, the ever-present luncheon staple with its numerous variations—quiche Lorraine. From the southwest of the country comes the prized *foie gras d'oie*— the fattened livers of force-fed geese.

Although not the largest wine producer in Europe, France remains the continent's most important producer and exporter of high-quality wines. Derived from a number of specific localities where viticulture has been intensively practiced for generations, these wines continue to set the world's industry standards for quality.

GERMANY

Compared to the cuisine of other European countries, cooking in Germany remained rather unrefined until recent times. The traditional fare appears to have been influenced by early contact with the culinary customs of Bohemia and Hungary. Although this linkage is not perfectly clear, some fifteenth-century cookbooks from these areas give instructions for cooking meat, poultry, game, offal, soups, cheese dishes, fish, baked goods, vegetables, and the still-cherished sauerkraut. These influences first shaped German cuisine.

Historically, the foods eaten by the common man tended toward heavy, ample dishes and were based on meat preparations with little refinement. Even in the houses of the rich and in public eating houses, the food was weighty and uninspired. Thick soups and heavy sauces (many of which were made from sweet, boiled vegetables, noodles, or dumplings) and an occasional fish dish on Fridays characterized these preparations. If one is searching for "traditional" German cooking today, many of these characteristics would still be in evidence.

As in other countries containing significant land area, the varied terrain of Germany, from the northern province of Schleswig-Holstein with its fishing ports on the Baltic Sea to the southern region of Swabia with its orchards and vineyards, produces a wide variety of products. The local specialities, which one finds from region to region, reflect the creative efforts of local culinarians. Another influence on the development of these distinctive regional preparations stems from Germany's absorption of culinary traditions and customs from neighboring countries. Germany is a land of many borders. Austria and Switzerland are to the south; France, Luxembourg, Belgium, and The Netherlands are to the west; Denmark and the North and Baltic seas border the north; and on the eastern borders are Poland and Czechoslovakia. The incorporation of many of the culinary practices of these bordering nations is apparent in the regional cooking of Germany.

Dumplings, sauerkraut, smoked and fresh pork roasts, and the world-famous wursts come to mind when one thinks of German food. These dishes, characteristic of Germany's largest province, Bavaria, have been the most popular representations of German cooking exported to other lands. Other lesser-known, but deserving regional specialities feature the use of caraway, paprika, and sour cream in their sauces. Noodle and cheese dishes, distinctive game entrées flavored with juniper berries and wild mushrooms, hearty, flavorful soups (including ones made with beer), and one of Europe's richest assortments of breads, pastries, and cakes are outstanding representatives of the cuisine of contemporary Germany.

But these traditional, "too solid" preparations are not the only gastronomic offerings one finds today. German chefs, responding to the nutritional and dietary demands of the public, have taken a leading role in the international culinary area by creating dishes that are responsive to these new needs. They are becoming known in culinary circles for their original and colorful preparations that use fresh herbs and unprocessed, whole food ingredients and that are based on sound nutritional concepts.

GREECE

Greece is a small country on the Balkan peninsula with a population approaching ten million people. It is bordered by the Ionian sea to the west, the Mediterranean to the south, the Aegean Sea and Turkey to the east, and Albania, Yugoslavia, and Bulgaria to the north. With one of the longest coastlines in Europe and almost two thousand islands under its jurisdiction, Greece has a very mountainous terrain, much of which is dotted with olive trees. It is not surprising, therefore, that these two geographical factors should play a major role in the economy. Greece is the third largest grower of olive trees in the world and maintains one of the world's largest merchant fleets. Today, Greece exports olives and different grades of olive oils, as well as figs, currants, tobacco, and wine. Many succulent fruits are grown, but on a small scale, because only twenty-nine percent of the land is arable. Wheat, vegetables, and cotton are also harvested.

Because of its location, Greece has been a major link between the East and West. Cultural influences from Europe and Asia have had a strong impact on local traditions. It is said that Athens, the capital, is the first Eastern city one finds when traveling from the West, and the first Western city when traveling from the East.

Greece's turbulent history embraces a number of culturally significant civilizations such as the Minoan, Mycenaean, Hellenistic, Roman, and Byzantine. In more recent times, the Greeks were subjected to four hundred years of Turkish rule. To this day, there is debate over the origins of Greek cuisine—whether it is an outgrowth of the Turkish kitchen or merely the result of Greek adoption of Turkish names for many indigenous and perhaps even ancient Greek dishes during the Turkish occupation. Wherever its roots lie, Greek cuisine is indisputably very similar to Turkish. As in all Mediterranean countries, olive oil and lemons are used frequently, along with oregano and thyme, which grow wild in great profusion.

Most Greek meals begin with *mezethes*, which are hors d'oeuvre and form a major part of many Greek meals. *Taramasalata*—made from salted carp roe; *tzatziki*—a yogurt-based, cucumber, dill, and garlic dip; *dolmadakia*—stuffed grape leaves with an *avgolemono* (egg and lemon) sauce; and *melintzanosalata*—an eggplant salad—are a few of the most commonly found *mezethes*. Many times, *mezethes* are accompanied by ouzo, an anise-flavored liquor that is the national aperitif. Fish are very plentiful in Grecian waters and are usually eaten grilled or baked and flavored with a combination of olive oil, lemon juice, and oregano. Other popular and traditional seafood dishes include *marides*—a tiny fish similar to white bait, which is lightly breaded and deep-fried; *barbounia*—small red mullet, usually sautéed or grilled, and squid and octopus, deep-fried or stewed.

Lamb is the favorite meat, usually grilled on a spit or done *souvlaki* style: small pieces of marinated meat are put on a skewer and are served with tomatoes, peppers, and onions. *Moussaka*—ground meat, eggplant, potatoes, and béchamel sauce baked in the oven, and *lamb fricasee*—served with lettuce and egg and lemon sauce, are both common dishes in the Greek home and in local *tavernas* or restaurants. Greeks also enjoy making *pites*, which are usually phyllo dough pies filled with meat, cheese, spinach, or various other green, leafy vegetables. The desserts are quite rich and show the influence of Middle Eastern cultures. The best known are *baklava*, made with phyllo dough, honey, and nuts, and *kadaifi,* which is made with a light dough that appears to be shredded but contains ingredients similar to *baklava*. These sweets are usually eaten as an afternoon snack and accompanied by coffee. Fresh fruits, especially melons, are for the most part the favorite choice for dessert after dinner.

ITALY

The Italian peninsula has long been a crossroad for successive waves of invaders. Some stayed and incorporated their own customs and practices with those of the indigenous population. Others visited and then departed, leaving behind vestiges of their own cultures. Italian cuisine is, therefore, indelibly linked with many diverse foreign influences and its own ancient history. The *puls* or *pulmentum,* for example, a porridge that nourished the Roman legions thousands of years ago, is a staple of today's diet throughout northern Italy. Known now as polenta and undoubtedly a much refined product, this very basic starch product in its many guises remains a popular first course in regions throughout the north of Italy. The fine, flaky pastry that is enjoyed in any number of sweet and savory preparations and the introduction of rice can be directly attributed to the Saracen invasions of the eighth century. Grappa, the famous liquor of Italy, is derived from an earlier version distilled from figs whose beginnings may be traced to the early Greek colonizers.

The influence of imported foodstuffs continues into more modern times. After the discovery of the New World, products from the American continent were ingeniously incorporated into the daily fare: tomatoes from Mexico, peppers from Peru, and other staple products such as corn, potatoes, peanuts, turkey, string beans, vanilla, and chocolate. Over the centuries, these products were instrumental in the formation of one of the most creative, varied, and distinctive cuisines found in Europe today and appreciated around the world. Although not indigenous to the country, it is difficult to conceive of the cuisine of modern Italy without these products.

A country of over 57 million inhabitants, Italy has a higher percentage of arable land than any of its neighbors. The Italians have reclaimed swamp lands, terraced many of the hilly slopes in the country's numerous mountainous areas, and improved infertile lands. The regional distribution of crops shows an increase of garden vegetables, cereals, citrus, and legumes as one travels from the northern parts toward the south. Major olive groves are found in the south, which has less-fertile land. A large percentage of the olive crop is converted into oil for export. Tomato crops are also cultivated extensively in this region and are canned whole or converted into concentrate. The north supports the cultivation of apples, pears, peaches, and cherries, while the central region of the northern plain supports a large cattle and dairy industry. Italy is also the largest European producer and exporter of rice.

The mountainous terrain of the Italian peninsula encouraged the isolation of groups of inhabitants and led to the inevitable development of distinct culinary practices. This fragmentation resulted in a wide variety of regional culinary practices and preferences still apparent today. In addition to the specialities of these numerous pocket-sized regions, a well-defined north/south culinary division is unmistakably clear, with Bologna in the north and Naples in the south generally viewed as the gastronomic centers of each area. Today, this division is still evident if one follows the ancient Roman road called the Via Saleria, or "Salt Road," which begins a few hundred miles southeast of Rome and wanders northward toward the Adriatic Sea. With origins as a route for salt traders living at the mouth of the Tiber, this artery developed into one of the major trading routes bisecting the Italian peninsula. In the more prosperous area north of this route, the use of meat, coffee, butter, and freshly made, egg-enriched, flat pasta is prevalent. Menus in the north of Italy reflect a preference for soups, rice, and polenta as first courses rather than pasta, and the frequent use of cream and other dairy products in preparations. Cured hams from Parma and hard cheeses for grating are among this area's most sought-after export products. Menus also feature an excellent supply of fresh vegetable and meat products and a variety of seafood.

South of the Via Saleria, other products begin to dominate the menus. Tomatoes, garlic, more heavily spiced sauces, and tubular pasta are preferred, along with such popular cheeses as ricotta, provolone, and mozzarella. The poorer quality of the soil lends itself more to the cultivation of the olive tree and the use of numerous delicacies found, uncultivated, in the environment. Pine nuts, dandelion greens, porcini mushrooms, and white truffles are skillfully incorporated into the culinary specialities of the region. The diet in the south tends to feature less meat and fewer dairy products and to revolve more around vegetables, fish, and dried, commercially prepared pastas.

Italy is a major producer and exporter of red and white wines and viticulture is found throughout the country. Grapes are grown with other field crops and all but seven percent of the grape harvest is converted into wine. The best-known districts for production of exported wines are the Monti del Chianti in Tuscany, Asti in the Piedmont region, Orvieto in Umbria, and Marsala in Sicily.

MOROCCO

Morocco, located on the northwest coast of Africa, is bordered to the west by the Atlantic Ocean, to the north by the Mediterranean, and to the south and east by Algeria and the Sahara Desert. It lies only a few miles across the Strait of Gibraltar from Europe. This unique geographical location, with its proximity to so many diverse cultures, has given Morocco a colorful, rich, and turbulent history.

Many current culinary traditions and practices can be traced to the numerous conquering forces from the Arabian peninsula. In the seventh century, Arab invaders conquered the indigenous Berber tribespeople and settled in Morocco, planting the roots of today's culinary traditions. During the seven-hundred-year period in which the Moors occupied Spain, many cultural and economic exchanges were made between the Moroccans and the Spanish. This interchange strongly influenced each society, creating many similarities in customs and practices that are still evident today.

In more recent times, Morocco was governed as a protectorate under the rule of Spain and later of France. In 1956, its 20.4 million people received their independence. As one might expect, these diverse and compelling cultures, each in its own turn, left a strong imprint on the culinary characteristics of the Moroccan kitchen. The influence of these important European cultures, combined with the already deeply rooted Arabic heritage, has created one of the region's most interesting national cuisines.

Morocco is fortunate in having some very fertile areas that produce an abundance of wheat, barley, and corn. Mint, olives, quince, figs, nuts, oranges, and lemons are also grown. Although there are some regional differences in the way that foods are prepared, by and large, preparations tend to be consistent throughout the country. Moroccan meals begin with a ceremonial washing of the hands, a custom with great practical importance, because Moroccans who eat their food in the traditional way use the three middle fingers of their right hand. Many dishes have been created that allow the diner to use bits of bread to carry the food from the serving platter to the mouth. It is said that Moroccan food truly tastes better this way.

Moroccan cuisine is distinct in its use of individual spices, as well as of combinations of spices to create flavoring agents; exotic flavored waters, such as rose water and orange blossom water; and a blending of fruits and meats in cooked dishes. Probably the most notable Moroccan preparation is *couscous*, a dish that almost eludes formulation. A complex and highly individualized preparation, *couscous* consists of a grain-like pasta, made from semolina, which must undergo several steaming and drying steps, combined with a variety of meats and fowl (or seafood). It is then steamed with dried fruits, vegetables, and beans over broth. Another national specialty is *bastya*, which consists of flaky layers of pastry dough filled with pigeon (or chicken/Cornish hen), cooked with cilantro, onions, sweet almonds, cinnamon, sugar, and orange blossom water.

Two other dishes commonly enjoyed throughout Morocco are *harira*—a chicken- or lamb-based soup that contains chickpeas, lemons, and eggs; and *tajine*, which is a meat, vegetable, and fruit stew, cooked in special earthen pots and prepared in a number of ways depending on the availability of product and preference of the individual cook. Other popular entrées include meats and fowl prepared on the spit or over coals, and stewed dishes. Grilled foods are, in many instances, flavored prior to cooking in strongly flavored marinades containing garlic, cumin, coriander, cayenne, and chili pepper.

The national beverage is mint tea, which was introduced to Morocco by British traders. Desserts usually consist of sweet honey pastries or of a variety of fresh fruits served simply or flavored with orange flower water and spices.

PORTUGAL

Portugal, with a population of 9.9 million, is located on the western side of the Iberian Peninsula and includes the Azores and the island of Madeira. Portugal has a rich cultural heritage, very similar in many aspects to that of Spain. Like Spain, Portugal fell to the Roman Empire and was conquered in later centuries by the Moors. Both the Romans and the Moors brought many foods from their native lands and the Portuguese integrated these foods into their cuisine. At the turn of the sixteenth century, Vasco de Gama's ships brought curry, cinnamon, cloves, pepper, and nutmeg to Portugal. Portuguese colonies in Africa, the New World, and the Far East generated tea, coffee, rice, beans, nuts, pineapples, tomatoes, peppers, and potatoes for home consumption, and these foods became very important in Portuguese culinary traditions.

Today, olive oil and wine are among Portugal's leading export items, with vineyards occupying more than ten percent of the farm land. Portugal produces many of the world's leading wines, especially red wines, including the world renowned ports and Madeiras. The largest and most common crops, cereals, and fruits such as apples, pears, and oranges are widely cultivated and exported. Unfortunately, much of the Portuguese soil is unsuitable for farming because of erosion over the centuries. With only one-third of the land arable, the country does not yield a large amount of produce. Portugal does have a large fishing industry. Its waters yield fish in abundance and in numerous varieties. Throughout the country, one can find a huge variety of fish and shellfish cooked in many delicious ways.

Portuguese cuisine is quite similar to that of Spain. It has, however, more noticeable traces of Italian and French influence than that of its neighbor. Many Portuguese dishes include tomatoes, onions, and olive oil as a base. Two common types of restaurants in Portugal are the *marisquerias*, which specialize in seafood, and the *churrasquerias*, which specialize in broiled chicken and meat. Popular dishes in Portugal include *bacalhau*—dried salt codfish that is served a number of ways, depending on the region, *piexe espada grelhado*—grilled swordfish, *caldeirada*—a stew made with vegetables and assorted fish, *carne de porco a alentejana*—pork with clams in coriander sauce, and, from the north, *caldo verde* —a green cabbage soup made with potatoes, olive oil, and sausages. There are also some distinctive cheeses, such as *Cabreiro* (goat cheese) and, from the area south of Lisbon, *azeitao*, which is made of ewe's milk. Although they are not plentiful, fresh fruits such as apricots, green plums, pineapples, cherries, peaches, figs, oranges, quinces, grapes, melons, and pears are excellent and are all-time favorites for dessert.

SOVIET UNION

Soviet cuisine mirrors the more than one hundred national strains that make up the population of its fifteen republics, including its largest, Russia. Straddling two continents, Europe and Asia, the Soviet Union has a cuisine that expresses a unique combination of Eastern and Western influences. Occupying approximately one-sixth of the inhabited areas on the globe, this vast country embraces many diverse climates and terrains of every description. Its countless lakes, rivers, streams, and forests in the north produce a rich variety of game animals and more than a hundred varieties of edible fish. The regions close to central Europe—the fertile steppes of the Ukraine and the farms of the Baltic states—

are prime suppliers of grains and other agricultural products, while citrus fruits and teas are grown in the almost subtropical areas of Transcaucasia.

Prior to the founding of St. Petersburg (now known as Leningrad) in 1703, there was little difference between the food of the common people and that eaten by the ruling classes. Everyone ate the same food cooked in the same way; the only difference was in the quality and quantity of the ingredients. With the building of this elegant city and the large-scale construction of palaces, public and government buildings, came an influx of foreign artisans from Holland, Germany, Italy, and France. These western Europeans brought with them the prevailing tastes and skills of their native countries. They created a new era in art and architecture and were instrumental in developing what became known as a "Master's Cuisine," a luxurious culinary repertoire, usually served in huge quantities, in which the rich native products were subjected to the sophisticated culinary skills of chefs imported primarily from France and Germany. And, until the advent of the Russian revolutionary period, cooks and chefs were regularly imported from Europe to serve in the household kitchens of the aristocracy and the wealthy. Regrettably, this distinctive fusion of classical foreign influences and the indigenous food products and native preparations known as "Master's Cuisine" has all but disappeared from contemporary menus, a victim of the political and economic forces of our times.

Copious portions of foods, however, are still served and the presentation of a well-stocked table is still a matter of pride throughout the Soviet Union. Appetizers known as *zakuski* are a popular tradition and feature an expansive array of hors d'oeuvre made of fish, meats, stuffed eggs, marinated and pickled fruits and vegetables, excellent breads, a wide variety of condiments, and, if affordable, the world-renowned caviar. Ice-cold vodka, either plain or flavored, is the beverage of choice. Other conspicuous characteristics of Soviet cuisine are stuffed dough preparations called *piroghi* or *piroshki*, numerous hearty soups (the most well-known of which is borscht), and the use of grains and pickled vegetables.

DENMARK

The southernmost Scandinavian country, Denmark is comprised of the Jutland Peninsula and five hundred islands, one hundred of which are inhabited. It borders Germany to the south and divides the North and Baltic seas. The country is primarily flat and low-lying, with seventy percent of its land arable. Denmark has for many years been a leading exporter of agricultural products, notwithstanding the poor quality of its soil. Farming cooperatives have developed extremely efficient farming methods, enabling the Danes to maximize productivity. Approximately six percent of the population is engaged in agriculture. The major crops are root vegetables, potatoes, and grains such as barley, oats, and wheat. Pork, beef cattle, dairy products, and poultry are also produced. Due to the limited season for growing crops and the needs of the local population, meat and dairy products are the primary foods produced for export.

Despite its northern location, the climate is unusually mild, due to the warm ocean currents. The large fishing industry makes a considerable contribution to the local food supplies, and, in addition, produces considerable tonnage of both fresh and processed fish for export.

As in Norway and Sweden, the Danes enjoy the *smorrebrod*, a table consisting of a wide variety of cold, open sandwiches that may be had in restaurants throughout the day. Cold meats, sausages, shellfish, herring prepared in numerous ways, salads, and specialty hot dishes such as roast beef and pork are some of the foods most commonly found. Dairy products are excellent, as are the breads and pastries.

NORWAY

Norway occupies the western part of the Scandinavian peninsula, bordered on the east by Sweden and on the west by the North Sea and the Atlantic Ocean, where it forms a rugged, mountainous strip. Half of the country lies within the Arctic Circle. The Soviet Union and Finland border the country to the north. Norway's coastline is dotted with tens of thousands of islands and indented with many fjords. From the coast, the land rises sharply to high plateaus and mountains. Although it has fertile valleys and abundant rivers, only thirty percent of the land is inhabitable. The four million citizens of Norway live primarily in the south.

Like Denmark, warm ocean currents create a mild climate for this most northern country. Despite this, less than four percent of the land is under cultivation. Agriculture contributes less than four percent of the gross national product and employs about seven percent of the labor force. Norway's principal products are grains, potatoes, and livestock and dairy products. In addition, fish products, such as cod, herring, and mackerel, are major export products.

The cuisine of Norway is very hearty and is noted for seasonal specialties such as elk and reindeer. The abundant supply of fresh fish and shellfish, however, makes Norway one of the world's primary fishing nations and this is apparent in the numerous products of the sea that are served in restaurants and homes. Especially renowned are the shrimp, cured salmon, various cod preparations, and the herring that can be found in countless variations—fresh and cured.

SWEDEN

Swedish cuisine prides itself on being natural in at least three ways: it is based on indigenous ingredients; it is prepared in ways that are quick and simple; and it has not been highly influenced by other cultures.

Located between Norway and Finland on the Scandinavian Peninsula, Sweden has a coastline of 4,700 miles along the Baltic Sea and the Gulf of Bothnia. This country of 8.3 million inhabitants has twenty-five regions, each with its own typical specialties resulting from differences both in taste and ingredient availability. In the southern areas, the cuisine is characterized by a great variety of fish, vegetables, and grains. On the coasts, as one might expect, ocean-going fish and shellfish are dominant. The cooking of the interior of Sweden is rich in fresh-water fish from the many lakes and rivers that mark Sweden's central regions, as well as game, mushrooms, and berries of all kinds. In Lapland, the home of many of the country's oldest culinary traditions, there are many reindeer products: roasts, chops, and stews. And on the islands of Sweden are found, in addition to vegetables and fish, a fondness for lamb and rabbit.

There are, nevertheless, a number of Swedish dishes that are enjoyed throughout the country. There is, needless to say, the ubiquitous smorgasbord, a concept synonymous with Sweden, which is as delightful as it is varied. Very popular are such preparations as boiled crayfish, pickled herring, and meatballs.

Swedes share the enjoyment of some special, traditional foods. A special Christmas buffet based on lutfisk, a cured salmon, and *surstrommin*, which are fresh Baltic herring, is common. There is also a traditional Thursday lunch consisting of yellow splitpea soup made with ham and served with pancakes and lingonberries. Beside the well-known gravlax—a fillet of salmon cured with sugar, salt, and dill—there is the less familiar *Jansson's frestelse*, or Jansson's temptation, a classic Swedish baked dish made from potatoes, onions, salted or cured fish such as sprats or anchovies, and cream.

The people of the various regions have favorite foods as well. These include *kroppkaka*—dishes prepared from Baltic herring and eels—and a boiled lamb served in a dill sauce *(dillkott pa lamm)*. There are special meat sausages from farm land in the west-central region along the Norwegian border and *reibekuchen* served with the ever-present lingonberries or cranberries. And, when available, there is *bleak roe*, an orange, mildly salted, fine-grained and inexpensive caviar, as well as whitefish caviar.

Some common flavors in Swedish cooking arise from the liberal use of paprika, juniper, and dill. And many foods are marinated in either a salt/sugar cure, or a sweet/sour cure. If a Swedish chef were to pack a cupboard for cooking abroad, he or she would no doubt include the following items: herring; such mushrooms as the morel, cepes, and chanterelles; and berries of all sorts, including cloudberries, lingonberries, raspberries, and brambleberries. The chef would also want adequate supplies of salted fish; reindeer; game birds such as pheasant, hazel hen, black grouse, snow partridge, and ptarmigan.

Modern cooking techniques have influenced Swedish cuisine in that foods are generally prepared in a more sanitary and healthful way. But the food remains extremely traditional, a combination of unusually wholesome and exotic cuisines. Swedish food is a wonderful blend of ocean, lake, and river fish, berries from the vast meadows, mushrooms that grow in the great forest regions, and game of all sorts.

SPAIN

Spain occupies more than three-fourths of Europe's second largest peninsula—the Iberian, seven-eighths of which is surrounded by water. It is a country of approximately thirty-nine million people and has a wide variety of climate, topography, and ethnic traditions. It is bordered by Portugal to the west, France to the northeast, the Mediterranean Sea to the east and southeast, and the Atlantic Ocean to the south and north. Spain has abundant fresh produce, nuts, and grains and is the largest olive oil producer in the world and the third largest wine producer. Fruits are heavily exported as well. In terms of acreage planted, however, Spain's main crop is wheat. Cotton and tobacco are also very widely cultivated. Because the mountainous areas are very rugged and unsuitable for cattle, smaller animals (principally pigs and sheep) are more widely raised.

Spanish cuisine is very diverse; as in Italy, there is no "national" cuisine due to the rich mix of cultural influences and regional differences. The original foundations of Spanish cuisine date back to the Roman Empire, when the occupying Roman troops introduced olive oil and garlic. Later, during the nearly eight centuries of Moorish occupation (dating from 711 A.D. to 1492 A.D.), saffron, cumin, nutmeg, black pepper, peppermint, oranges, and lemons were introduced, creating a cuisine highly distinctive from that of other European countries. With the Moors' influence well-established, the staples of modern Spanish cuisine—the tomato, sweet pepper, and potato—were integrated in the eighteenth century. Although Spaniards had known of these three vegetables since the discovery of the New World, they were not incorporated into the cuisine until that time. Today, it is hard to imagine Spanish cuisine without these three important ingredients.

Spanish culinary traditions are sharply divided by region. The most notable regional cuisines are the Basque (in the northwest), which is known for its fish dishes prepared in mild sauces and the Catalonian (in the northeast), known for its progression of new foods following the change of seasons. Overall, Spanish recipes are simple and easy to prepare. Dishes are often boiled or broiled, with the addition of a simple sauce. The Spanish enjoy many bean, rice, and egg dishes, and meat and vegetable pies. It is also very common to find meat and seafood mixed together in a number of dishes, the most popular of which is *paella*, a mix of saffron rice, chicken stock, and an assortment of seafood and fowl.

Although there is no set "national cuisine," there are a few traditional dishes that are popular throughout Spain, varying only slightly from region to region. One of the most popular features of Spanish cuisine are *tapas*, a variety of tasty hors d'oeuvre. Special restaurants in Spain serve only tapas and are in many places the focal point of the community. *Angulas*—baby eels, usually prepared with olive oil and garlic; *bacalao*—salted cod fish; *calamares*—squid; and *sardinas* —grilled or broiled sardines, are among the most popular seafoods. *Gazpacho*, which is a soup served hot or cold and consisting basically of tomatoes, bread, vinegar, garlic, green pepper, and cucumber, can be found in a number of variations from region to region. Garlic soup, flan, and sponge cake are also commonly found throughout the country.

Perhaps the diversity of Spanish cuisine can also be attributed to the extended daily eating schedule. The Spanish prefer to dine late in the evening and enjoy many snacks to fill in the large gaps between meals. The day begins with *desayuno*, which usually consists of coffee and a roll, followed by a midmorning snack called *almuerzo*, which can be as simple as an omelette or as involved as a whole hot meal. Around 2 p.m. or 3 p.m., *comida*, the main meal of the day, is served; at about 6 p.m., a coffee and light snack meal called the *merienda* refreshes everyone after the afternoon siesta. Finally, the day comes to a close with *cena*, dinner, which is eaten between 8:30 p.m. and midnight.

The influence of Spanish cuisine can be found throughout the world, especially in South and Central America. As these lands were affected by the culture of their Spanish rulers, they in turn provided the new food products that have become the staples of modern Spanish cuisine.

TURKEY

Turkey's forty-nine million people and approximately 296 thousand square miles span two continents, Europe and Asia. Turkey is bordered to the east by the Soviet Union and Iran, to the south by Iraq, Syria, and the Mediterranean, to the west by Greece, Bulgaria, and the Aegean Sea, and to the north by the Black Sea. The Bosphorus, Sea of Marmara, and Dardanelles Strait separate the three percent of Turkish land that lies in Europe from its Asiatic counterpart.

Little is known about Turkish cuisine before the days of the Ottoman Empire. As the empire expanded in territory and population, so did the range of Turkish cooking. Until the advent of a stable empire, the production of crops was difficult, due to constant raids by the Mongols and other tribes. Once the Ottoman Empire had expanded and solidified, new fruits and vegetables indigenous to newly conquered territories were discovered and brought back to enrich the Turkish larder.

As one might expect, the sultans and their court followers were instrumental to the development of Turkish cuisine. Early sultans, with access to an expanded variety of food products, maintained large kitchen staffs with many specialized cooks. The palaces boasted elaborate kitchen facilities with enough settings of fine china to serve thousands of diners at a single meal. By the end of the sixteenth century, the formalities and demands of the court necessitated kitchen staffs of several hundred people. By the mid-seventeenth century, the sultan's staff had expanded to more than a thousand cooks, bakers, and other culinary specialists. The practices of this ruling elite influenced the eating habits of the general population, who enjoyed some of the fruits of conquest, although not to such an elegant and elaborate degree.

Cereals are the main crop in present-day Turkey, with much cotton and tobacco being grown as well. Turkey also produces a number of excellent wines. A large producer of meat and livestock, Turkey exports these products throughout Europe. Common preparation ingredients include olive oil, lamb, rice, and a large variety of vegetables. As in other countries from this part of the world, the Turks are very fond of hors d'oeuvre, which are called *mezeler*. Some of the more commonly found *mezeler* are beans in spicy oil; *bastirma*—a spicy, cured meat; eggplant salad; cheeses; *tahini*—sesame paste with lemon juice; smoked sausages; and caviar. Special restaurants are devoted only to serving *mezeler* and some offer a variety of more than one hundred different dishes. The accompanying drink is the national apperatif *raki*, an anise-flavored liqueur.

One of the main foundations of Turkish cooking is rice. The Turks enjoy making a number of *pilafs*, baked rice dishes enriched with different meats and vegetables. Bulgur is sometimes used in place of rice. Common Turkish dishes include *sis kebab*—small pieces of lamb marinated in vinegar, oil, onions, cloves, and parsley, and then grilled on skewers; cold yogurt soup with dill; *kilic*—swordfish roasted on a spit with bay leaves; *dolmas*—grape leaves stuffed with meat or rice and herbs; and vegetables such as tomatoes, zucchini, and small eggplant stuffed with rice or meat. *Borek*, savory phyllo dough pastries filled with cheese or meat, are eaten frequently as a snack.

The popular beverage, *ayran*, is a cold yogurt drink, and other refreshing beverages are made from a large variety of freshly squeezed fruits. Turkish coffee is famous throughout the world and it was the Turks who, through their conquests, brought coffee to Europe. Hot tea served in small, thin glasses is also very popular. Turkish desserts are similar to those found throughout the Middle East. They are, for the most part, sweet, nut-filled pastries saturated with honey. Other popular desserts are milk-based custard products redolent with rose water, orange blossom water, and crushed pistachios.

CONDIMENTS

AIOLI   *France*   Yield: approx. 1 lb.

A garlic-flavored mayonnaise, Aioli is served with Bourride and can be used as an accompaniment with crudités or as a base for other hors d'oeuvre.

Egg yolks	2	Place the egg yolks and salt into the bowl of a food processor. Pulse a few times until blended.
Salt	½ tsp.	

Olive oil	16 oz.	With the motor of the food processor running, add the oil slowly in a thin stream.

Garlic, pureed	1 tbsp.	When done, add the garlic puree and a squeeze of lemon juice and blend thoroughly.
Lemon juice	to taste	

ANCHOVY BUTTER   Yield: 1¼–1½ lbs.

Salt-cured anchovy fillets	8 oz.	Soak anchovies in salt water for several hours. Drain and rinse in cold water. Scrape off loose bits of skin and then remove all fins and bones. Reserve fillets. (If you wish to prepare larger amounts for other uses, place fillets in olive oil and store in the refrigerator.)

Butter, sweet	16 oz.	Whip butter together with the lemon juice and white pepper. Mix thoroughly, then add the mashed anchovy fillets and place in a food processor or blender until all ingredients have been thoroughly combined.
Lemon juice	3 oz.	
White pepper	to taste	
Reserved anchovy fillets		

CHERMOULA   *Morocco*   Yield: approx. 1 lb.

Used for fish and poultry, this aromatic mixture is rubbed on the product and allowed to marinate for several hours.

Coriander leaves, chopped	10 tbsp.	Combine all ingredients in a food processor. Pulse until they are thoroughly blended.
Parsley leaves, chopped	10 tbsp.	
Garlic, pureed	8–10 cloves	
Paprika, sweet	2 tbsp.	
Cumin, ground	4 tsp.	
Cayenne	½ tsp.	
Lemon juice	4 oz.	
Olive oil	16 oz.	
Salt	1 tbsp.	

HARISSA— VERSION I   *Morocco*   Yield: approx. 1 lb.

Harissa, a fiery and potent condiment, is used sparingly.

Olive oil	16 oz.	Mix all ingredients well. Store in a sealed jar.
Garlic, pureed	10 cloves	
Cumin, ground	10 tbsp.	
Coriander seeds, ground	10 tbsp.	
Cayenne pepper	4 tbsp.	
Lemon juice (optional)	4 oz.	

HARISSA—VERSION II

Yield: approx. 1 lb.

Chili peppers, red, hot, and dried	4 oz.
Cumin seeds	4 oz.
Paprika	1 tsp.

Place the chili peppers, cumin seeds, and paprika in a small pan. Over low heat, stirring constantly, toast them for about 10 minutes. Cool the mixture and transfer it to a mortar. Using a pestle, pulverize to a fine consistency.

Onion, chopped fine	8 oz.
Parsley leaves, flat, chopped	4–5 tbsp.
Olive oil	8 oz.

Add these ingredients and blend well.

Lemon juice	to taste
Salt	to taste

Season with lemon juice and salt.

PROVENÇAL HERB MIXTURE   *France*

This is a dried herb mixture that is used on grilled meats and fish or as a flavor enhancer for stews.

Savory	6 parts
Thyme	3 parts
Fennel seed	2 parts
Marjoram	1 part
Corinder, ground	1 part
Lavender buds	1 part

Place all ingredients in the bowl of a food processor and mix, using the steel blade, until thoroughly blended and of a uniform consistency. Store in a tightly sealed container.

LATHOLEMONO *Greece*   Yield: approx. 12–14 oz.

This is used as a marinade, basting sauce, and table sauce for meats and fish.

Olive oil	8 oz.	In a mixing bowl, combine all ingredients, using a wire whisk. There should be a good flavor balance. The oil or the lemon should not be too pronounced. Adjust to taste.
Lemon juice, fresh-squeezed	4–6 oz.	
Oregano	1 tbsp.	
Salt and black pepper	to taste	

PRESERVED LEMONS *Morocco*   Yield: 10 servings

Lemons	10–20	Wash the lemons and soak them for several days to soften the peel. Change the water daily. Cut the lemons into quarters, stopping an inch from the stem end.
Salt	as needed	Generously sprinkle the exposed portions with salt. Close the quarters so that the lemon nearly assumes its original shape. Place 1 tbsp. of salt in a sterilized mason jar. Pack the jar with the lemons, sprinkling each with a little more salt. Repeat, using as many jars as necessary.
Lemon juice, fresh squeezed	as needed	Fill the jars with enough lemon juice to cover the lemons, leaving a small space at the top. Let the lemons ripen for 3–4 weeks before using.

Rinse the lemons. Cut away the pulp and discard. Use the quartered strips of peel as a flavoring agent for fish, poultry, or lamb stews. Cut the peel in a fine julienne and add to salads. Before using the lemons, rinse off any white film that may have appeared. The pickling liquid can also be used as a flavoring agent.

ROUILLE   *France*   Yield: approx. 12 oz.

Rouille is used to flavor fish dishes and soups. If served with fish, a small amount of fish stock should be added to the rouille.

Bread crumbs or fresh bread	4 oz.	Soak the bread crumbs in water, then squeeze dry.

Red pepper flakes	1 tbsp.	With a mortar and pestle, grind the peppers and garlic to a paste. Add the soaked bread crumbs and continue to mix.
Garlic, minced	2 tbsp.	

Olive oil	8 oz.	Add the olive oil and blend all ingredients well.

SKORTHALIA   *Greece*   Yield: approx. 2½ lbs.

Skorthalia is used as an accompaniment for boiled vegetables and for fried foods, especially fish.

Garlic, pureed	6 cloves	Place all ingredients in the bowl of a food processor and pulse until very smooth. The sauce should be very thick. For a thinner consistency, add a little water.
Potatoes, peeled, boiled, and mashed	2½ lbs.	
White vinegar	3 oz.	
Olive oil	6–8 oz.	
Salt	1 tsp.	
Water	if needed	

APPETIZERS AND LIGHT DISHES

BAKED EGGS IN RATATOUILLE *Southern France*

Yield: one serving

Olive oil	1 tsp.

In an individual-portion, enameled, oven-proof dish, heat the olive oil over medium heat.

Ratatouille (see recipe on p. 261)	as needed

Add a layer of ratatouille to cover the bottom of the dish. Heat for several minutes, then make two indentations—each large enough to hold one egg.

Eggs	2
Salt and black pepper	to taste
Gruyère cheese, grated	as needed

Add the eggs and salt and pepper to taste. Then sprinkle a light layer of Gruyère cheese on the top and cook on top of the stove for a few minutes until the eggs begin to set. Transfer the dish to a 400 degree F oven and bake until the whites are firm.

This recipe can be served on a late-night menu or as a luncheon entrée. Accompany it with crisp, fried shoestring potatoes.

MOZZARELLA IN CARROZZA *Southern Italy*

Yield: 10 sandwiches

This is a light sandwich.

White bread, crusts removed	20 slices
Mozzarella cheese, fresh	1½ lbs. approx.

Prepare 10, ¼-inch-thick slices of mozzarella cut ½ inch smaller than the slices of bread. Place 1 slice of cheese between 2 slices of bread. Reserve until needed.

Eggs, beaten	as needed
Milk	as needed

To prepare an individual serving, mix the eggs and milk together: use 1 egg for every 6 oz. of milk. The amount needed will vary, depending on the type, size, freshness of the bread and the number of sandwiches you wish to prepare at 1 time. Dip the sandwiches in the egg and milk mixture. Press the edges together to form a seal.

(Continued)

Bread crumbs	as needed	Dredge each sandwich lightly in bread crumbs.
Olive oil	as needed	Sauté in hot olive oil ½ inch in depth until they are lightly browned.

To serve as an appetizer, slice each sandwich diagonally twice to create four triangular quarters. Reheat in a 400 degree F oven just prior to serving and serve very hot. Garnish each piece with a dollop of anchovy paste that has been mixed with softened butter or anchovy butter. If served whole, a complete sandwich, garnished with a lemon twist and/or the anchovy paste, accompanied by a salad would be sufficient for a luncheon offering. For an interesting variation, add a thin slice of prosciutto to the cheese filling.

TARAMASALATA   *Greece*   Yield: 15 servings

A caviar appetizer, Taramasalata is usually eaten as a dip with bread, such as pita bread.

White bread	10 slices	Use a fairly dense, textured bread. Trim and discard the crusts. Then soak the bread in cold water. When they are saturated, remove from water and squeeze dry. Place in the bowl of a food processor.
Tarama (salted carp roe)	6 tbsp.	Add the tarama and onion to the bread. Using the pulse action, blend thoroughly.
Onion, diced	2 tbsp.	
Olive oil	8 oz.	Then gradually add the oil with the processor on constant speed. The mixture should have the consistency of a thick mayonnaise.
Lemon juice	to taste	Add the lemon juice and pulse a few times to thoroughly blend. If the mixture is too salty, add more bread and olive oil.

Serve as part of an array of appetizers.

BRANDADE   *Southern France*

Yield: 10–12 entrée servings, 15–20 appetizer servings

Salt cod, dried	2 lbs.
Milk	as needed
Water	as needed

Soak the salt cod for 24 hours, changing the water several times. When ready to cook, place the fish in a sauce pan and cover with a 50/50 mixture of water and milk. Bring to the boil, then lower the heat and simmer for 5 minutes. Remove the fish and discard any skin or bones. (Use only the white portions of the fish.) Place the fish in the bowl of a food processor. Discard the cooking liquid.

Potatoes, peeled and quartered	1 lb.

Place the potatoes in boiling water and cook until tender. Remove them from the water and add to the fish.

Garlic, minced	2 tbsp.
Nutmeg, ground	⅛ tsp.
White pepper	½ tsp.

Season with the garlic, nutmeg, and pepper.

Olive oil, extra-virgin	8 oz.
Heavy cream	12 oz.
Salt and white pepper	to taste

In separate saucepans, heat the oil to just below the smoking point; bring the cream to the boil. With the processor on, add the oil and cream alternately. Mixture should be light and smooth. Add the salt and pepper to taste.

Serve as a luncheon dish, garnished with fresh tomatoes and cucumbers. If used as an appetizer, serve with triangles of buttered toast or thinly sliced French bread.

MARINATED HERRING WITH AQUAVIT   *Scandinavia*

Yield: 3 lbs., or 20–25 appetizer servings

Herring fillets, fresh	3 lbs.

Remove all bones. Cut the fish into ½-inch pieces. Keep pieces in order so that the original shape of the fillet is retained. Place them in a shallow, flat-bottomed glass or enameled container in a single layer.

(Continued)

Wine vinegar	12 oz.
Sugar	12 oz.
Water	24 oz.
Black peppercorns	1 tsp.
Allspice, whole	1 tsp.
Caraway seed	1 tsp.
Cloves	½ tsp.

Bring vinegar, water, and sugar to a boil. Add the remaining ingredients and simmer, covered, for 5 minutes. Let cool.

Lemon, sliced	1

Pour the cold marinade over fish fillets, distribute lemon slices, and cover well. Let marinate in refrigerator for 2 days. Baste after first day.

Carrot, julienne	as needed
Onion rings	as needed
Dill, fresh, chopped	as needed
Apples, small dice, tossed in lemon juice	as needed
Aquavit	8 oz.

Blanch the carrots and onion rings. Let cool. On a display platter, arrange the fish fillets, carrots, and onion rings. Distribute the diced apples and chopped dill on top of the fish and the vegetables. Sprinkle the aquavit over the entire platter.

Serve as part of a cold fish presentation in a buffet or as a luncheon entrée.

ROLLMOPS   *Germany*

Yield: 10 servings

Herring fillets, pickled	10

If overly salty, soak the fillets in cold water overnight.

Marinade:

Cider vinegar	16 oz.
Pickling spices	1 oz.
Water	8 oz.
Bay leaf	4

Combine the marinade ingredients and bring to a boil. Lower the heat and simmer for 5 minutes. Cool to room temperature.

Spanish onion	as needed	Slice the onion and separate into rings.

To Assemble

Mustard	3 oz.	Dry the herring fillets and spread the skin side with mustard. On each fillet, place 1 piece of pickle crosswise, 2 pieces of onion, and a sprinkling of capers. Roll up the fillet, starting with the narrow end. Tie once around the middle of each fillet with butcher's twine.
Dill pickle	10 pieces cut 2 inches long × ¼-inch square	
Capers	as needed	

Onion rings	as needed	Pack the rollmops tightly and place in a glass or enameled container over a bed of onion rings. If recipe is extended, add more onions between the layers of rollmops. Add marinade and keep covered in refrigerator four to five days before serving.

Pickled beets, sliced	as needed	Garnish with pickled beets and whipped cream.
Cream, unsweetened, whipped	as needed	

Serve on bed of strongly flavored greens such as chicory or curly endive.

MONKFISH IN ANCHOVY SAUCE   *Spain*

Yield: one serving

Monkfish	3 oz.	Cut the cleaned and skinned monkfish into bite-sized cubes. Dust lightly with flour.
Flour	as needed	

Olive oil	2 tbsp.	Heat the oil and sauté the fish over medium heat, turning frequently, until slightly underdone.

(Continued)

Anchovy paste	½ tsp.
Stock, fish	2 oz.
Pepper, black	to taste

Add the anchovy paste, fish stock, and a generous amount of black pepper and blend well with the oil. Continue to cook for another ½ minute. Arrange the monkfish cubes on a warm plate, taste the sauce, and add pepper, if necessary (the sauce should have a strong peppery taste). Pour the pan liquids on top.

| Lemon wedges | as needed |

Garnish with lemon wedges.

BAKED OYSTERS   *Germany*

Yield: one serving

| Oysters | 6 |
| Butter, clarified | as needed |

Open oysters, rinse in cold water, and let drain. Wash the shells to remove any sand or other debris. Oysters will be served on the half shell. Reserve six of the most uniform half shells.

Bread crumbs	as needed
Parmesan cheese, grated	as needed
Butter	as needed

Dip the oysters in clarified butter, then roll in mixture of half bread crumbs and half Parmesan cheese. Place an oyster on each half shell with a small piece of whole butter. Place the shells on a bed of rock salt and place in 450 degree F oven for 5–7 minutes.

| Lemon juice, fresh squeezed | as needed |

Add a few drops of fresh lemon juice to each oyster prior to serving.

MUSSELS WITH GAZPACHO   *Spain*

Yield: 10 servings

| Mussels | 40–50, depending on size |
| Stock, fish | as needed |

Scrub and debeard the mussels. In a stockpot, bring 2 inches of fish stock to the boil. Add the mussels, cover, and cook until they are opened. Remove from the heat and let cool.

Gazpacho (see recipe on pp. 119–21)	2½ pts.

Pour the fish stock through a double layer of cheesecloth to remove all sand and debris from the liquid. Mix the stock with the gazpacho and pour over the mussels. Refrigerate until needed. Serve 4–5 mussels in a bowl with the gazpacho/fish stock mixture.

Lemon juice	to taste
Parsley, fresh, chopped	as needed

Add a squeeze of fresh lemon juice just before serving and a sprinkling of parsley.

Accompany with a crusty French or Italian bread for dipping.

PICKLED MUSSELS   *Scandinavia*

Yield: 10–15 servings, depending on use

Mussels	8–9 lbs.
White wine	16 oz.

Wash mussels and remove beards. Place them in a soup pot, add wine, cover and steam until mussels open. Allow to cool, discard top shell and refrigerate mussels on the half shell. Let cooking liquid settle and then decant, leaving sand in the pot bottom.

Olive oil	4 oz.
Lemon juice	2 tbsp.
Sugar	2 tbsp.
Salt	1 tbsp.
Pepper, white	1 tsp.

Add the rest of the ingredients to the decanted mussel broth. Check the taste for good flavor balance. Adjust, if necessary. Pour over mussels and let marinate covered, in refrigerator for 1–2 hours before serving.

Drain marinade and arrange mussels on the half shell on a round serving plate. Pipe onto each mussel a small rosette of mayonnaise mixed with a small amount of fresh lemon juice and white pepper.

(Continued)

| Dill, fresh, chopped | 6 large sprigs and as needed for garnish | Garnish with dill. |

Serve as part of a smorgasbord or buffet.

STUFFED MUSSELS AND CLAMS   *France*

Yield: 10 servings

| Mussels | 30 | Scrub clams and scrub and debeard mussels. |
| Cherrystone clams | 30 | |

Vermouth	8 oz.	Bring these ingredients to a boil, cover, and reduce heat to low. Simmer for 10 minutes.
Parsley	4 sprigs	
Onion, diced	1 lb.	Add mussels and clams, raise the heat to high, and steam until they open. When cool enough to handle, remove mussels and clams from the shells. Reserve half the shells.
Thyme	1 tsp.	
Bay leaf	3 large	

Butter, softened	½ lb.	Combine these ingredients, except for the bread crumbs. Return the mussels and clams to their appropriate shells and cover with the butter mixture. Smooth the tops and sprinkle with bread crumbs. Place an individual serving, consisting of 3 clams and 3 mussels under the broiler for 1–2 minutes just before serving. Shells may be broiled on bed of kosher salt to keep them stable.
Shallots, minced	10 tsp.	
Garlic, minced	5 tsp.	
Parsley, chopped	8 oz.	
White pepper	to taste	
Bread crumbs	as needed	

| Lemon wedges | as needed | Serve with lemon wedges. |

SALMON CURED WITH DILL   *Norway*

Yield: 3 lbs.

Any firm-fleshed, very fresh fish can be treated in this manner. For variations in flavor, use other fresh herbs or cracked black pepper.

Salmon fillet	2, 1½ lb. pieces

Fish must be very fresh. Remove all bones, including the pin bones (use heavy tweezers or pliers).

White pepper, coarse ground	2 tbsp.
Sugar	8 oz.
Salt, kosher	8 oz.
Dill, fresh, chopped	8 oz.
Olive oil	1 oz.

Mix all ingredients thoroughly. Rub generous amounts on all sides of fish.

Put fillets together, placing the thick end of 1 fillet against the thin end of the other, skin-side out. Place in glass or enameled container just large enough to hold the fillets. Cover the container with plastic wrap. Place another pan on top, containing weights (several full #10 cans) so that uniform pressure is exerted on the fillets.

Refrigerate for 24 hours, then baste with liquid that has accumulated. Cover, replace the weights, and refrigerate for another 24 hours. Rinse well before serving.

Serve as part of a cold fish presentation for a buffet or as a first course. Slice fish on an angle. Make slices as thin as possible. Slices should have a translucent appearance. Serve with dill sauce and fresh lemon or other garnishes such as capers, mayonnaise, chopped onions, and so forth.

SHRIMP IN GARLIC   *Spain*

Yield: 10 servings

Shrimp, medium	3 lbs.
Lemon juice	as needed
Olive oil	as needed

Peel and devein the shrimp, leaving the tail section of the shell on. Toss the shrimp in a little lemon juice and olive oil and refrigerate until needed.

Olive oil	4 oz.
Onion, small	1 lb.
Garlic, minced	2 tbsp.
Parsley, chopped	3 tbsp.

Heat the oil and sauté the onions over medium heat until soft. Add the garlic and the chopped parsley, lower the heat, continue to sauté for another minute. Reserve.

(Continued)

Olive oil	1 tsp.
White wine, dry	as needed

To prepare individual portions, in a small skillet, sauté 3–4 oz. of the shrimp for 15 to 20 seconds over high heat. Lower heat to medium and add 2 tbsp. of the onion/garlic mixture and splash of white wine. Cook, stirring, for 2–3 minutes.

Parsley, fresh, chopped	as needed

Serve with a sprinkling of parsley.

Serve as an appetizer or in larger portions as an entrée over a bed of rice.

CALAMARI SALAD   Yield: 10–12 servings
Southern Italy

This dish may be used as an appetizer or in larger portions as a luncheon entrée.

The Marinade:

Olive oil	6 oz.	Combine all these ingredients and reserve.
Lemon juice, fresh	4 oz.	
Onion, thin sliced	8 oz.	
Green and red peppers, cored, peeled, and sliced very thin	12 oz.	
Garlic, minced	1 tsp.	
Parsley leaves, fresh, chopped	2 tbsp.	
Basil leaves, fresh, chopped	2 tbsp.	
Red pepper flakes	½ tsp.	
Salt and black pepper	to taste	

Squid, head, viscera, ink gill removed	3 lbs.

Pull out the head and tentacles. Cut off the tentacles just above the eyes and reserve. Squeeze out the beak at the base and discard. Remove the transparent backbone and any other material from inside the body. Wash under running water, peeling off the purple skin. Cut into thin rings.

Olive oil	as needed
Garlic, sliced	2 cloves
Olives, black, pitted	as needed
Lemon wedges	as needed

Over medium heat, sauté the garlic in the olive oil until lightly browned, then mash with a fork, remove from oil, and discard. Dry the squid with a towel and sauté in the garlic-flavored oil for just a few minutes. Overcooking will toughen the squid. Add the squid to the marinade and refrigerate overnight. When serving, garnish with olives and lemon wedges.

Serve the squid along with the vegetables in the marinade on a bed of mixed greens.

FRIED SQUID WITH GARLIC SAUCE   *Spain*

Yield: 10–12 servings

Squid, head, viscera, ink gill removed	5–6 lbs.
Salt	as needed

Pull out the squid's head and tentacles. Cut off the tentacles just above the eyes and reserve. Squeeze out the beak at the base of the tentacles and discard. Remove the transparent backbone and any other material from inside the body. Wash under running water, peeling off the purple skin. If the squid are very small, leave them whole. If not, cut into rings ½-inch wide. Sprinkle lightly with salt, place in a colander to drain, and refrigerate until needed.

Batter:

Flour	1 lb.
Olive oil	1 oz.
Water	1 qt.
Salt	2 tsp.

Make a well in the center of the flour. Gradually add the oil and water and mix into a smooth, but not too thick, batter. Adjust water to obtain a consistency that pours easily.

(Continued)

Garlic Sauce:

Bread, white	1 lb.
Garlic, pureed	1 small head
Olive oil	8 oz.
Vinegar, white	4 oz.
Water	2 oz.
Salt and white pepper	to taste

Soak the bread in water, then squeeze dry. Place in a food processor along with the other ingredients and puree to a very smooth consistency. Season with salt and pepper.

Prepare individual portions just prior to service. Coat 5–6 oz. of squid with batter.* Deep-fry in oil at 400 degrees F for about 1 minute. Squid should be very lightly browned. Overcooking will make the squid tough.

Lemons, halved or cut in wedges	as needed

Serve with the garlic sauce on the side. Garnish the plate with lemons cut in half or in wedges.

---

* A simple dusting of flour may be used instead of the batter.

TABBOULEH   *Lebanon*   Yield: 10–12 servings

This salad is mainly composed of a grain called bulgur, which is cracked wheat.

Bulgur	1 lb.

Soak the bulgur in cold water to cover to a depth of 3–4 inches for 30 minutes, or until the wheat is soft. Drain and place in a colander that has been lined with a double layer of cheesecloth. Let drain for 10 minutes, then squeeze dry.

Tomatoes, peeled, seeded, and chopped	3 lbs.
Onion minced	8 oz.
Scallions, minced, green parts included	6
Mint leaves, fresh, chopped	6 tbsp.
Parsley leaves, flat, chopped	6 tbsp.
Salt and black pepper	to taste
Olive oil	8–10 oz.
Lemon juice, fresh	6 oz.

Mix all of these ingredients with the bulgur. Adjust the seasonings, if necessary. Cover and refrigerate for several hours before serving.

Use as a salad garnished with olives and fresh vegetables or as part of an appetizer plate containing other Middle Eastern appetizers.

FAVA BEAN SALAD   *Egypt*

Yield: 10–12 servings

Fava beans, fresh, shelled	2 lbs.
Onion, peeled, cut in half	1 medium
Salt	1 tsp.

Place the beans in water to cover to a depth of 2 inches. Add the onion and salt and bring to the boil. Lower the heat and simmer for 20–25 minutes. The beans should be very tender but not mushy. Drain and discard the onion.

Olive oil	4 oz.
Coriander leaves, fresh, chopped	6 tbsp.
Parsley leaves, flat, chopped	6 tbsp.
Lemon juice, fresh-squeezed	3–4 oz.
Cumin, ground	1½ tsp.
Garlic, minced	1 tsp.
Salt and white pepper	to taste

While the beans are still warm, add these ingredients and blend well.

(Continued)

Scallions, sliced	as needed	Garnish with scallions, black olives, and radishes.
Olives, black, pitted	as needed	
Radishes, sliced	as needed	

FOOL MIDAMESS   *Egypt*   Yield: 10–12 servings

This fava bean purée can be varied by the addition of different optional ingredients.

Fava beans, dried	1½ lbs.	Soak the beans and lentils overnight in a generous amount of water. Drain and rinse. Place the beans in a small stockpot with 2–3 inches of water to cover and bring to the boil. Lower heat to simmer.
Lentils	½ lb.	

Tomato, peeled, seeded, and chopped	1 lb.	Add all these ingredients. Cover the pot and place in a 275 degree F oven for 6–8 hours, or overnight. Add more boiling water from time to time if beans appear to be drying out.
Onion diced	1 lb.	
Carrot, small dice	½ lb.	

Olive oil	4 oz.	Put the beans through a food mill. Discard any skins that remain. Add the olive oil, lemon juice, and salt to taste.
Lemon juice, fresh-squeezed	4 oz.	

Garlic, crushed	to taste	Add any of the following optional ingredients to taste.
Onion, grated	to taste	
Tomatoes, chopped	to taste	
Cumin, ground	to taste	

Eggs, hard-boiled, sliced	as needed	Garnish with eggs, onions, and pickles.
Onions, pickled	as needed	
Pickles, mixed	as needed	

BASTIRMA *Egypt*   Yield: approx. 2 lbs.

Bastirma, which is air-cured beef, is usually eaten as is with or without the rind.

Beef tenderloin	2–2½ lbs.
Salt	as needed

Trim the meat of all fat and, using the sharp tip of a knife, score the meat in several places on all sides. Roll the meat in salt so that the entire surface has a generous coating. Place the meat on a wire rack over a roasting pan. Cover with foil and place a cutting board with about 5 lbs. of weight on top to help express the moisture from the meat. Refrigerate for 4 days.

Garlic, crushed	3 heads
Fenugreek seed	4 oz.
Pepper flakes, hot red	2 tbsp.
Salt	6 oz.
Paprika	3–4 tbsp.

Peel and crush the garlic. Puree it with the fenugreek, hot pepper, salt, and paprika. The mixture should be soft and pastelike. Thread a string through the smaller end of the meat. Coat the meat with the garlic mixture (⅛ inch thick) and suspend it from the string in the refrigerator for another 3–4 days. The meat should be dried and have a fairly dense texture.

When serving bastirma, make slices as thin as possible, almost transparent. Three to 4 slices will be adequate as a single-serving appetizer. Bastirma can also be cut into small pieces and scrambled with eggs.

PEL'MENI *Russia*   Yield: approx. 40–80 depending on shape

These Siberian dumplings may be made well in advance and frozen, uncooked, for future use.

Flour	1 lb.
Eggs yolks, beaten	3
Salt	½ tsp.
Water	8–12 tbsp.
Egg whites	reserved

Sift the flour. Make a well in the center. Add salt and water to the beaten yolks and pour into the well. With a fork, begin to incorporate flour from the well's sides into the egg mixture until all the flour has been worked in. (It may be necessary to add a bit more water.) Knead the dough until smooth and let it rest for 1 hour. This can be done more quickly in the food processor. (Mix the dry ingredients first by pulsing 3–4 times. Add the beaten eggs and water. Process until the dough masses. Let rest for 1 hour.)

(Continued)

Butter	4 oz.
Onion, finely minced	6 oz.
Beef, ground twice	8–10 oz.
Salt and black pepper	to taste
Ice water	2 oz.

Sauté the onion in butter over low heat. Mix with the raw meat and season with salt and pepper. Add ice water and mix until the texture is light. (An electric mixer works well for this step.)

Reserved egg	

On a well-floured board, roll out the dough to a thickness of $\frac{1}{16}$ of an inch. Using a 2½-inch round cookie cutter to cut out rounds. Roll out the trimmings and cut more rounds. Put a small spoonful of the meat filling on half the rounds. Brush the edges with the reserved egg whites or water and cover the meat with another round. Pinch the edges together to seal. An alternate method: use a smaller amount of meat, then fold the rounds in half. Seal the edges in the same manner to create a half-moon shape.

Drop pel'meni into salted, boiling water. When they float, cook for 5 minutes longer.

Serve 3 or 4 pel'meni as a garnish for consommé or for clear meat or chicken broth. They may also be served topped with a little melted butter as an appetizer or main course. If used for the latter, sprinkle them with vinegar and fresh-ground black pepper or serve with side dishes of yogurt or sour cream. Adjust portions as needed. For alternate fillings, use other ground meats, singularly or in combination. Traditional vegetarian versions include potatoes and onion, cabbage and onion, or mushrooms and onion. Boil or sauté vegetables, puree, then season them before filling the pastry rounds.

SWEDISH MEATBALLS   *Sweden*

Yield: 10–20 servings, depending on size and usage

Onion, minced	8 oz.
Butter	2 oz.

Sauté the onion in butter over low heat until it is soft.

Beef, ground	1 lb.
Veal, ground	1 lb.
Pork, ground	8 oz.
Bread crumbs	4 oz.
Light cream	8 oz.
Eggs, beaten	2 lg.
Cloves, ground	½ tsp.
Salt and white pepper	to taste
Water	2 oz.

Mix the meats together and grind twice to assure a very fine texture. Add onions, bread crumbs, cream, and beaten eggs. Add salt, pepper, and water and mix thoroughly to create a very smooth consistency. Test a small sample by sautéing a spoonful in butter. Adjust the seasonings, if necessary.

Butter, clarified	as needed

Shape the mixture into balls about 1½ inches in diameter (smaller if using for an appetizer). Sauté in the clarified butter until brown all over. Remove the meatballs and reserve in a warm place. Discard fat and wipe out pan.

Butter, whole	5 oz.
Flour	4 oz.

Using the same pan, melt the butter, then add flour. Cook, stirring, for 5 minutes to ensure a smooth, textured roux.

Stock, beef	32 oz.

Reduce the stock by half. Add to the roux and mix well.

Light cream	16 oz.
Salt and white pepper	to taste

Add the cream and bring to a boil. Adjust the seasonings. Return meatballs to the pan and simmer for 30 minutes. If sauce is too thick, adjust to desired consistency with additional beef stock.

Swedish meatballs may be served in a variety of ways: hot, with the sauce, or cold, without the sauce. If served as an entrée, accompany with a puree of potatoes and cranberry sauce. If served as part of a buffet, make the meatballs about the size of walnuts.

RABBIT PÂTÉ   *Germany*

Yield: thirty 2–3 oz. servings

Rabbit	3, 2–3 lbs. each

Bone the rabbits. Remove the saddles in 1 piece and reserve.

Slab bacon, diced	1 lb.
Chicken livers	1 lb.
Onions, minced	1 lb.
Garlic, chopped fine	4 cloves

Sauté the bacon until fat begins to run. Add the onions, chicken livers, and garlic and sauté until livers lose their red color. They should remain pink inside.

Veal	1 lb.
Pork	1 lb.

Combine the rabbit meat (excluding the saddles), pork, veal, and liver-onion mixture and put through a meat grinder twice, using a fine blade.

Beef stock	16 oz.
Brandy	12 oz.
Eggs, beaten	4
Allspice	1 tsp.
Thyme	1 tsp.
Salt	2 tbsp.
Peppercorns, crushed	2 tbsp.
Pistachios, shelled	6 oz.

Reduce the stock by half. Cool and add the rest of these ingredients. Mix well and add to the meat mixture. Blend all ingredients thoroughly. Sauté a spoonful and taste for seasonings. Adjust, if necessary. Refrigerate for 2 hours.

Rabbit saddles	
Prunes, pitted	20
Brandy	6 oz.
Salt	2 tsp.
Thyme	½ tsp.
Allspice	½ tsp.

Combine these ingredients and marinate for 2 hours. Remove the saddles and prunes. Add marinade to the meat mixture.

Bacon, sliced, or caul fat	as needed

Line a 4- by 4- by 20-inch pâté pan with the bacon slices. Add half the meat mixture. Arrange the rabbit saddles and the prunes in straight columns down the length of the pan. (This inlay arrangement can be varied.) Add the remaining meat. Fold bacon slices over the top so that the pâté is completely encased in bacon. Cover tightly with aluminum foil and place the pâté pan in a roasting pan. Add boiling water to the roasting pan to reach halfway up the sides of the pâté pan. Place in a 350 degree F oven for 2 hours. Add boiling water from time to time to maintain the water level. Let cool, place weights on top (clean bricks wrapped in foil work well), and refrigerate overnight. Place in warm water for 2 or 3 minutes to unmold prior to serving.

Garnish with any combination of the following: cornichons, pickled beet slices, mustards, capers, chopped radish, watercress, or freshly minced onions.

LIVER PÂTÉ WITH ANCHOVIES *Scandinavia*

Yield: 10–12 servings

Pork liver	3 lbs.

Remove any fat or membrane from the liver and soak in 1 part white vinegar and 3 parts water for several hours. Change water/vinegar once.

Anchovies	4 oz.
Onion, diced	1 lb.
Pork fat, diced	1 lb.

In a food processor, place the liver, anchovies, onion, and pork fat and process to a smooth consistency, using the pulse action.

(Continued)

Eggs, large	5
Black pepper, coarse-ground	1 tsp.
Pistachios (optional)	2 oz.
Salt	to taste

Add the beaten eggs and pepper. Add pistachios, if desired. Test a small amount by cooking in simmering water. Adjust salt if needed. Keep in mind that anchovies are salty.

Place mixture in a pâté or loaf pan with a size such that, after cooking, you will be able to cut square slices. Set this pan in one that is a little larger and pour boiling water in the larger pan so that the water reaches halfway up the smaller pan's sides. Cover with foil and bake for 45 minutes in a 325 degree F oven for 45 minutes or until firm. Place on a rack and let cool.

Serve as part of a buffet presentation. May also be served as an appetizer. Garnishes include capers, minced onions, cornichons or other pickled vegetables, and a variety of mustards.

FRITO MISTO   *Southern Italy*   Yield: one serving

This dish can be simple or elaborate, depending on the variety and types of items used.

Vegetables:

Zucchini	4–6 oz. per
Asparagus	serving of
Cauliflower	mixed
Broccoli	vegetables
Eggplant	
Mushrooms	
Sweet pepper	
Green beans	
Potato croquettes	
Other seasonal vegetables	

Wash and trim the vegetables. Cut them in bite-sized pieces. Green beans, if small and tender, may be left whole. Large mushrooms may be cut in half. Prepare a balanced mixture. In briskly boiling water, blanch each vegetable separately, then plunge them immediately in cold water. Vegetables should remain crisp. Reserve. (The resulting stock should be reserved for other uses.)

Vegetable Batter:

Flour	½ lb.
Water	20 oz.
Salt	1 tsp.
White pepper	½ tsp.
Olive oil	1 oz.

Combine all ingredients. This batter should be somewhat thinner than the batter for the meats. The amount of water needed may vary.

Meats:

Sweetbreads	5–6 oz. per
Calf's liver	serving of
Veal brains	mixed meats
Veal or lamb kidneys	
Veal scallops	
Lamb chops	

Meats should be trimmed of all fat and cut into bite-sized pieces or thin strips. If brains are used, they should be blanched first. Baby lamb chops should be lightly pounded and left whole.

Meat Batter:

Flour	8 oz.
Water	16 oz.
Eggs, beaten	4 large
Salt	1 tsp.
White pepper	½ tsp.
Olive oil	1 oz.

Combine these ingredients.

Dip 10–12 oz. per serving of meats and vegetables in the appropriate batter. Deep-fry at 350 degrees F until crisp and golden. Drain briefly on a clean towel. If only one deep-fryer is available, do the meats first and keep them warm in a 300 degree F oven until the vegetables are prepared.

Lemons, sliced	as needed

Garnish with lemon slices when serving.

(Continued)

Any combination of meats and vegetables may be used. Meats may be substituted with a variety of fish and/or shellfish. The oil temperature is very important to ensure a light, crisp crust. It is recommended that a few pieces be test-fried in advance of service.

Serve on a napkin-lined plate.

CHICKEN LIVER PÂTÉ   *Northern France*

Yield: 10–12 servings

Chicken livers	1½ lbs.

Remove all excess membranes or fat. Puree in a food processor.

Eggs	7 large
Heavy cream	12 oz.
Ginger, fresh, finely minced	½ tsp.
Thyme	¼ tsp.
Nutmeg, ground	¼ tsp.
Garlic, paste	2 cloves
Apple brandy	2 oz.
Butter	4 oz.
Salt and black pepper	to taste
Flour	6 oz.

Add other ingredients and puree until very smooth. In a small pan of simmering water, place 1 tsp. of the mixture and cook for several minutes. Taste this test batch and adjust the seasonings.

Pour the mixture into 10–12 individual, buttered ramekins. Cover with foil. Place in a pan containing enough boiling water to reach halfway up the ramekins' sides.

Bake in 300 degree F oven for 1 hour. If a toothpick emerges clean when placed in the center of the ramekin, the pâté is done. If not, return it to the oven for an additional 10 minutes.

Let cool and refrigerate. Remove from refrigeration ½ hour before service.

Unmold by placing ramekin in warm water for a minute or two before serving. Serve on a bed of greens garnished with cornichons, capers, minced onions, and mustard. This recipe may also be done in a single, large mold for buffet service.

BABAGANOUJ   *Egypt*   Yield: 10–12 servings

An eggplant salad, Babaganouj is usually eaten with pita bread.

Eggplant, washed	3 lbs.
Lemon juice	4 oz.
Water	as needed

Pierce the eggplants' skins in several places with a sharp-tined fork. Place on a baking sheet and bake in a 400 degree F oven for 1–1½ hours, or until they become very soft and the skins begin to char. When done, immerse immediately in cold water and lemon juice to cover. When the eggplant is cool, peel and place in a colander to drain. When the bitter juices have been expressed, place the eggplant pulp in the bowl of a food processor and reserve.

Yogurt, unsweetened	16 oz.
Garlic, puree	1 tbsp.
Mint leaves, fresh, chopped	2 tbsp.
Olive oil	1 tbsp.
Salt and black pepper	to taste

Add these ingredients to the eggplant and puree until very smooth.

Olive oil	as needed
Parsley, fresh, chopped	as needed

When serving, garnish with a sprinkle of olive oil and parsley.

Serve as part of an array of appetizers. Place a portion on a small plate and garnish.

CAPONATA   *Southern Italy*   Yield: approx. 5 lbs.

This eggplant relish frequently is part of an antipasto plate or an accompaniment for lamb, pork, chicken, or poached fish.

(Continued)

Eggplant, peeled, in ½-inch cubes	3 lbs.
Salt	as needed

Place eggplant in a colander and lightly salt. Cover with a heavy plate placed directly on the eggplant. Let stand for ½ hour.

Olive oil	as needed
Onions, diced	2 lbs.
Plum tomatoes	2 lbs.
Raisins, white	3 tbsp.
Kalamata olives, pitted and chopped	3 oz.
Green Sicilian olives, pitted and chopped	3 oz.
Capers	3 tbsp.
Pine nuts	3 tbsp.
Salt and black pepper	to taste

Sauté the onions in olive oil over low heat until they are lightly colored. Do not brown. Put the tomatoes through a food mill. Discard the seeds and tomato skins. Add the pureed tomatoes, raisins, olives, capers, and pine nuts to the onions and simmer for 30 minutes. Season with salt and pepper.

Olive oil	4 oz.
Celery, peeled and diced	6 stalks

Rinse the eggplant cubes to remove the salt, then pat dry with a towel. In another pan, heat olive oil over medium heat and sauté the cubes to a rich brown color. When done, add to the tomato mixture. In the same pan, adding more oil if necessary, sauté the celery briefly so that it still remains a bit crunchy. Add to the tomatoes and eggplant.

Red wine vinegar	4 oz.
Salt and pepper	to taste

Pour wine into the same sauté pan and, over high heat, deglaze the pan and reduce liquid by half. Add this to the other ingredients and mix well. Season with salt and pepper.

Cool before serving. It can also be used as a filling for stuffed tomatoes or artichokes. It may be served as an appetizer alone on a bed of flavorful greens accompanied by a good, crusty bread.

EGGPLANT CAVIAR   *Russia*

Yield: approx. 5 lbs.

Eggplant, washed	5 lbs.

Prick the eggplants skins 8–10 times each with a sharp-tined fork. Bake in a 400 degree F oven until they are very soft and the skins begin to char. When the eggplants are cool enough to handle, squeeze gently to express the juices. Slit the eggplants, remove all pulp, and discard the skins.

Lemon juice, fresh	3 oz.
Garlic, chopped	2 lg. cloves
Scallions, chopped	2 tbsp.
Dill, fresh, chopped	2 tbsp.
Tomato, chopped	2 medium
Green pepper, seeded, chopped	1 medium
Black olives, pitted, chopped (Kalamata or similar olive preferred)	15–20
Olive oil	2 oz.
Salt and black pepper	to taste

Combine these ingredients and add to eggplant pulp. Place in food processor and, using pulse action, process until blended. Do not overprocess. The mixture should be slightly grainy. Season with salt and pepper.

Use as a buffet dip, canapé spread, canapé base for sliced, hard-boiled egg, or other topping or as part of mixed hors d'oeuvre plate.

STUFFED MUSHROOMS   *Northern Italy*

Yield: 10 servings

Mushrooms, 2–3 inches in diameter	20
Olive oil	as needed

Wipe the mushrooms with a slightly damp towel. Trim the stem ends and discard. Detach the stems and chop them fine. Place the chopped stems in a clean towel and squeeze out the liquid. Lightly oil the mushrooms caps.

(Continued)

Olive oil	2 tbsp.
Onion, minced	8 oz.
Marsala	6 oz.

Heat oil and sauté the onion over low heat until soft. Add wine and continue cooking until wine is reduced by half.

Swiss cheese, grated	8 oz.
Bread crumbs	4 oz.
Parmesan, grated	4 oz.
Salt and white pepper	to taste
Nutmeg	to taste
Heavy cream	as needed
Parsley, chopped	2 tbsp.

Combine these ingredients with the onion mixture and the minced mushroom stems. Add enough heavy cream to bind the mixture together. Adjust seasonings. Stuff the mushroom caps, creating a small mound on each cap. Cover and refrigerate until needed.

Swiss cheese, grated	as needed
Butter	as needed
Lemon wedges	as needed

Sprinkle tops with grated cheese and a small piece of butter. Bake in a 400 degree F oven for 10–15 minutes. Caps should be tender and stuffing should be lightly browned. Garnish with lemon wedges.

Serve as an appetizer on a bed of green, leafy lettuce. Use 2 mushroom caps per serving.

STUFFED GRAPE LEAVES   *Greece*

Yield: varies according to usage

Olive oil	2 oz.
Onion, minced	1 lb.
Rice, short-grain	6 oz.
Mint leaves, fresh, chopped	6 tbsp.
Parsley leaves, flat, chopped	2 tbsp.
Stock (beef, veal, lamb, or chicken)	8 oz.
Salt and black pepper	to taste

Heat the oil in a heavy skillet. Sauté the onions until they are soft. Add the rice, herbs, and stock. Mix well and cook over low heat, uncovered, until the liquid has been absorbed. Season with salt and pepper. Cook for several more minutes. Remove from heat.

Lamb, ground twice	2 lbs.
Olive oil	2 oz.

Add the ground meat and olive oil to the onion/rice mixture and mix thoroughly. Reserve.

Grape leaves*	as needed

Because the size of the leaves may vary, the amount of filling will also vary, from a teaspoon to a tablespoon per leaf. If leaves are small or you wish to make a larger portion, use 2, placed side by side and overlapping slightly. Prepare a heavy-bottomed saucepot by placing a layer of unfilled grape leaves on the bottom.

Fill the leaves as follows: Place a leaf on a flat surface, dull side up and stem end toward you. Place a teaspoon to a tablespoon of the filling in the leaf's center. Fold over the sides to the center, then roll up toward the point of the leaf. Place the stuffed grape leaves around the outer edge of pot, working inward until you have a tightly packed layer on the bottom. Place a few torn leaves or a piece of unglazed, lightly pricked paper on top. Continue in this way, making other layers, until all of the filling has been used.

Stock (beef, veal, lamb, or chicken)	as needed

Place a heavy plate on top of the grape leaves. Pour enough stock into the pot to just cover the top layer. Place a lid on the pot and simmer for 30–40 minutes. Let cool in pot for 15–20 minutes before serving. Drain, reserve stock, reheat if necessary.

Eggs, beaten	4
Lemon juice, fresh-squeezed	2–3 oz.
Stock	8 oz.

To make a sauce, combine the eggs and the lemon juice and whisk until foamy. Add the hot, reserved stock, a little at a time, whisking continuously.

(Continued)

---

* If fresh grape leaves are used, remove the stems and blanch the leaves in boiling water for several minutes. Place immediately in cool water when done, then drain well before filling. Grape leaves packed in brine are also available year-round. If using brine-packed leaves, be sure to rinse them well in cold water first. If brine-packed leaves appear to be very tough, blanch in boiling water for a minute or two, then proceed as for fresh leaves.

This may be used either as an appetizer or entrée. It may be served warm with the egg/lemon sauce or cold with an unflavored yogurt sauce, or garnished with black olives and fresh lemon juice.

PEPPERS WITH FETA CHEESE   *Greece*

Yield: 10 servings

Olive oil	3 oz.
Onion, very fine dice	8 oz.
Oregano	½ oz.
Dill, fresh, chopped	2 tbsp.

In a small skillet, heat the olive oil and sauté the onions over low heat until they are very soft. Do not brown. Add the oregano and dill, mix well, and sauté for another minute. Remove from heat and let cool.

Feta cheese	1¼ lbs., approximately
Olive oil	as needed

In a mixing bowl, crumble the feta and add the onion mixture. If the cheese is very dry, add a small amount of olive oil.

Peppers, green and/or red, washed and with cores, seeds, and membranes removed	5 large
Olives, Kalamata	as needed
Tomatoes, sliced	as needed
Cucumbers, sliced	as needed

Fill each pepper firmly. The amount of cheese needed will depend on the size of the peppers. Refrigerate for 3–4 hours. To serve, slice peppers into rings, about ¼-inch thick, and use 2 to 3 slices per serving.

Garnish with olives, tomato, and cucumber slices that have been sprinkled lightly with oregano and few drops of virgin olive oil.

PEPERONATA *Southern Italy* Yield: approx. 5 lbs.

Peppers, green, bell	2 lbs.
Peppers, red, bell	2 lbs.
Olive oil	as needed

Slice the peppers in half, lengthwise, and remove the core and seeds. Wash them under running water to remove all seeds. Place on a baking sheet, cut side down. Brush with olive oil and place in a 450 degree F oven until the skins start to blister. Remove from oven and cover for about 10 minutes. When cool enough to handle, remove the skins and cut into ¼-inch strips. Reserve.

Tomatoes, plum	3 lbs.
Olive oil	2 oz.
Onions, sliced	1 lb.
Basil leaves, fresh, chopped	20
White wine, dry	4 oz.
Salt and black pepper	to taste

Plunge the tomatoes into boiling water for a minute or until the skins begin to split. When cool enough to handle, remove the skins and seeds. Over moderate heat, sauté the onions until they are soft. Add the tomatoes, white wine, basil, and the reserved pepper strips. Season with salt and pepper. Simmer until most of the liquid has evaporated. Remove from heat and chill before serving.

May be used as part of an antipasto, as an accompaniment for cold meats, or as a cold buffet item.

PASTA, RICE, POLENTA, AND PIZZA

EGG PASTA—BASIC RECIPE

Yield: 3 lbs.

Flour, unbleached, all-purpose	2 lbs.

Sift flour onto a cutting board. Create a mound of flour in as small an area as possible. Make a well in the center of the mound large enough to receive the following ingredients.

Olive oil	1 oz.
Salt	1 tsp.
Eggs, beaten, with two tbsp. of water	8 large

Mix oil, salt, and eggs. Pour this mixture into the well and, using a fork and a rotary motion, incorporate the flour from the well's inside wall. Continue until all of the flour has been absorbed. Knead the dough by hand for at least 10 minutes.

Divide dough into 5 or 6 equal parts and roll out on a floured surface to desired thickness. The use of a pasta machine at this point can accomplish the same task with much less labor. The pasta may be cut in a variety of ways or left in sheets, depending on recipe requirements.

To make a dough in a food processor, place the flour in the processor bowl and start the machine. Add the equivalent of 6–7 beaten eggs and mix. If the dough mixture still feels too dry, add the additional egg and process until the dough forms a ball. The dough should have a stiff consistency. Let rest for 1 hour, unrefrigerated, then roll out by hand or with a pasta machine.

The following are several variations: *Green pasta:* Use 5–6 eggs. Add 4 tbsp. blanched, chopped, and thoroughly drained spinach. Place the spinach in a clean cloth and squeeze dry before adding to pasta dough. *Red pasta:* Use the same proportions as for the green pasta. Eliminate the spinach and substitute 2 tbsp. pureed boiled beets or 2 tbsp. tomato paste.

FETTUCINE WITH GORGONZOLA   *Northern Italy*

Yield: one serving

| Fettucine | 4 oz. | In 1 qt. of boiling, salted water, cook the pasta until just barely done. The sauce can be prepared while the pasta is cooking. If fresh pasta is used (preferred), begin preparation of sauce first, because the pasta's cooking time will be much shorter. |

Half and half	4 oz.	In a 10-inch sauté pan, heat the half and half and butter to the boiling point. (Cream can be substituted for the half and half to make a richer sauce.) Add the Gorgonzola, lower the heat, and thoroughly blend all the ingredients, using a wire whisk.
Butter	1 oz.	
Gorgonzola	2 oz.	

| Egg, beaten | 1 | Add the egg and incorporate it quickly into the other ingredients. Do this as fast as possible to avoid cooking the egg and forming lumps. Use a whisk for the best results. |

| Parmesan cheese, grated | 1 tbsp. | Drain the pasta and add to the sauce in the sauté pan. Toss to mix and turn out onto a warm plate. Sprinkle grated Parmesan on top. |

| Parsley, fresh, chopped | as needed | Garnish with parsley. |

Serve immediately. If the pasta is done prior to the sauce's completion or has been done in quantity earlier and is cool, it may be reheated in sauce just prior to serving.

SPAGHETTI ALLA PUTANESCA   *Southern Italy*

Yield: 10 servings

Olive oil	4 oz.
Garlic, coarsely chopped	1 tbsp.
Anchovies	3–4 oz.
Tomatoes, plum, peeled and chopped	4–5 lbs.
Tomato paste	3 tbsp.
Red pepper	1 tsp.
Olives, pitted and sliced in quarters	1 lb.
Salt and black pepper	to taste

Heat the oil in a heavy saucepan and sauté the garlic over low heat until soft. Do not brown. Add the anchovies and cook for another minute. Add the tomatoes, tomato paste, and red pepper flakes. Simmer for 20 minutes. Add the olives and simmer for another 10 minutes. Season with salt and pepper.

Spaghetti	3–4 oz. per serving

To prepare an individual serving, cook the spaghetti in boiling water, as desired. Heat 4–5 oz. sauce. Add the hot spaghetti to the sauce and toss well before serving. Transfer to a warm plate.

This is usually served without grated cheese.

STUFFED PASTA SHELLS IN TOMATO SAUCE   *Southern Italy*

Yield: 10–12 servings

Pasta shells, large	1¼ lbs.

Cook the shells in boiling water until just tender. Drain and reserve in cold water.

(Continued)

Filling:

Ricotta cheese	3 lbs.
Romano cheese	2 oz.
Egg yolks	3
Italian parsley leaves, chopped fine	15 sprigs
Salt and black pepper	to taste
Nutmeg, grated	to taste

Combine these ingredients and mix well by hand or use an electric mixer on medium speed for about a minute. Mixture should be thoroughly blended and smooth.

Drain the shells completely and stuff with the cheese mixture. Refrigerate until needed.

Tomato Sauce:

Olive oil	2 oz.
Onions, diced	1 lb.
Garlic, minced	1 tbsp.
Tomatoes, plum, peeled and seeded	4 lbs.
Tomato paste	4 oz.
Oregano	1 tbsp.
Basil, dried	1 tsp.
Salt and black pepper	to taste

Sauté the onions over medium heat until soft. Add the garlic and continue to cook for another minute. Add the rest of the ingredients. Bring to the boil. Lower heat and simmer, partially covered, for 1 hour. Adjust seasonings. If sauce is too thick, add a small amount of water; if too thin, reduce to desired consistency.

Cover the bottom of an individual-portion, oven-proof baking dish with a layer of tomato sauce. Arrange the pasta shells (4–6 per serving) on top. (Shells will require less time to prepare if they are at room temperature at this point.) Add enough tomato sauce to just cover the shells. Place in a 400 degree F oven until the sauce begins to bubble.

Parmesan cheese	as needed
Parsley, freshly chopped	as needed

Garnish with a sprinkling of grated cheese and parsley.

Serve in the baking dish.

PASTA WITH LOBSTER SAUCE   *Southern Italy*

Yield: 10–12 servings

Scallops, shrimp, or other shellfish may be substituted, singly or in combination, for the lobster.

Marinade:

Lobster meat, fresh, cooked, bite-sized pieces	1½ lbs.	Combine these ingredients, mix well, and refrigerate for 6 hours. Toss 2 or 3 times.
Olive oil, virgin	16 oz.	Bring the lobster pieces (2 oz. per serving) and the marinade (2 oz. per serving) to room temperature. Remove the garlic. Place the marinade in a very warm bowl and pour drained, hot pasta (3–4 oz. per serving) on top. Toss well so that pasta is well-coated with the oil. Arrange the lobster meat on top.
Italian parsley leaves, chopped fine	10 sprigs	
Garlic, cut in half	6 cloves	
Lemon juice, fresh	4 oz.	
Salt and black pepper	to taste	
Black pepper	as needed	Garnish with a few grindings of black pepper and the red peppers.
Red peppers, roasted, julienned	2 oz. or as needed	

PASTA WITH FRESH SARDINES   *Southern Italy*

Yield: 10 servings

Sauce:

Raisins	4 oz.	Soak the raisins in water, to cover, for 30–45 minutes or until the raisins are soft and plump. Reserve.
Water, warm	as needed	
Sardines, fresh, heads and tails removed	20	Make a slit down the length of the sardines' bellies. Eviscerate and fillet the sardines, keeping the 2 halves of the fish joined. Close the halves and reserve, in a little lemon juice, in the refrigerator.
Lemon juice	as needed	

(Continued)

| Pine nuts | 4 oz. |
| Olive oil | as needed |

Toss the pine nuts in a little oil and toast them in a hot oven until lightly browned. Coarsely chop and reserve.

Olive oil	4 oz.
Onion, diced	1 lb.
Anchovy fillets, mashed	5
Tomatoes, peeled, seeded, and chopped fine	4 lbs.

Heat the oil and sauté the onions over low heat until they are very soft and lightly browned. Add the anchovies and mix well. Add the tomatoes and reserved raisins and pine nuts. Simmer for 10 minutes. Add salt and pepper. Reserve.

To prepare an individual serving, reheat the sauce, as needed, with 2 sardines per serving for 3–4 minutes, or until the fish is cooked through. Do not overcook the fish.

| Pasta of choice | 3–4 oz. (per serving) |

Cook pasta as desired. Remove the cooked sardine fillets carefully so they remain whole and reserve them on a warm plate. Toss the drained pasta with the sauce and place in a warm bowl or plate. Arrange the sardine fillets on top.

PASTA WITH SHRIMP AND PEAS   *Southern Italy*

Yield: one serving

| Butter, whole | 1 tbsp. |
| Shrimp, medium, peeled, deveined, and butterflied | 2–3 oz. |

Heat the butter over medium heat and sauté the shrimp briefly until they begin to turn pink. Remove from pan and reserve.

Onion, minced	1 tbsp.
Garlic, minced	½ tsp.
Flour	as needed

Add the onion and garlic and sauté for a minute or so, then sprinkle lightly with flour. Continue cooking for another minute, stirring, until the flour has been completely incorporated.

Heavy cream	5 oz.
Tomato paste	1 tsp.
Peas, fresh	2 tbsp.
Salt and white pepper	to taste

Add the cream and stir well. Cook over medium heat until the cream begins to thicken. Add the tomato paste and blend thoroughly. Add the peas and cook for a half minute or so. Return the shrimp to the sauce to heat through. Season with salt and pepper.

Fettuccine, fresh	3 oz.
Pecorino cheese, grated	as needed

Cooking time for fresh pasta is very brief, so the pasta can be prepared simultaneously. When pasta is done, drain, add to the sauce, and mix thoroughly. Serve with grated cheese on the side.

PASTA WITH TUNA AND ANCHOVIES   *Northern Italy*

Yield: 10 servings

Onion	8 oz.
Tomatoes, crushed, finely diced	2 lbs.
Black pepper	½ tsp.
Oregano	1 tsp.

Heat the oil and sauté the onions until soft. Add the tomato, pepper, and oregano. Simmer for 20 minutes.

Anchovies	6 oz.
Butter	12 oz.

Mash anchovies together with softened butter. Set aside.

Olive oil	as needed
Tuna	3 oz. per order
Pasta, fresh, cooked	4 oz. per serving

To prepare an individual order, sauté the tuna in olive oil over high heat until it flakes easily with a fork. Break into bite-sized pieces. Add 3–4 oz. of the tomato sauce and 2 tsp. of the anchovy butter (amount of anchovy butter may vary, according to taste). Heat through but do not let boil. Pour over the pasta and toss.

(Continued)

Parsley, chopped	as needed	Garnish with parsley and chopped black olives.
Olives, black, Kalamata or Alphonso	as needed	

BAKED PASTA   *Southern Italy*   Yield: 10–12 servings

This dish is excellent for lunch when served with a salad and can also be used in buffets.

Sauce:

Olive oil	1 oz.	Heat the oil in a large skillet. Add the sausage, beef, and prosciutto. Sauté until lightly browned. Remove with a slotted spoon and reserve.
Sausage, sweet Italian, casing removed	8 oz.	
Beef, top round, ground	1 lb.	
Prosciutto, thick, sliced, diced	4 oz.	

Carrot, small dice	4 oz.	Pour excess fat from skillet and sauté the vegetables until they are soft.
Onion, small dice	8 oz.	
Celery, small dice	4 oz.	
Italian parsley leaves, chopped	5 tbsp.	

Red wine, dry	12 oz.	Add the wine and deglaze the pan. Reduce wine by half. Add tomatoes and reserved meats. Mix well and simmer for 1 hour. If sauce gets too thick, add a small amount of beef stock. Season with salt and pepper. Remove from heat, let cool, and reserve.
Tomatoes, crushed	2 lbs.	
Stock, beef	as needed	
Salt and black pepper	to taste	

Spaghetti	2 lbs.	Partially cook the spaghetti. Because it will be baked, it should still be very firm. Drain and cool under running water.

Eggs, beaten	4	Beat the eggs and cheese together, then add to the meat sauce. Add sauce to the spaghetti and mix thoroughly.
Parmesan cheese, grated	4 oz.	

Butter	as needed	Butter a 12-inch springform or other similar sized baking dish. Sprinkle bread crumbs uniformly over surface. Fill baking dish with the pasta. Dot the top with butter and bake in a 350 degree F oven for 45 minutes to 1 hour. Top should be nicely browned. Let pasta rest in a warm place for 10 minutes before slicing.
Bread crumbs	as needed	

To serve, slice in pie-shaped wedges.

PASTA WITH LAMB SAUCE   *Southern Italy*

Yield: 10–12 servings

This dish traditionally uses macaroni cut on a chitarra, or guitar, a pasta-cutting device that creates a flat cut approximately $\frac{1}{16}$ of an inch by $\frac{1}{8}$ of an inch wide. Fettuccine may be substituted for the macaroni.

Lamb shoulder	2 lbs.	Trim fat from meat and cut into very small, irregular pieces. Salt and pepper the meat and sauté in olive oil over medium to high heat. When lamb begins to brown, add the garlic, lower the heat, and continue to cook for 1–2 minutes longer.
Salt and pepper	as needed	
Olive oil	1 oz.	
Garlic, minced	2 tsp.	

(Continued)

White wine, dry	8 oz.	Add wine and deglaze the pan over high heat. Reduce the liquid by half. Add the tomatoes, green peppers, and bay leaves. Simmer for 45 minutes. If sauce becomes too thick, add a little stock. Season with salt and pepper, let cool, and reserve.
Tomatoes, crushed	2 lbs.	
Green peppers, julienned	8 oz.	
Bay leaves	3	
Salt and black pepper	to taste	
Stock, lamb or veal	if needed	
Fettuccine	3–4 oz. per serving	Reheat sauce, as needed. Cook fettuccine to desired doneness.

FUSILLI ALLA NAPOLITANO   *Southern Italy*

Yield: 10 servings

Bacon, slab, or pancetta	8 oz.	Sauté the bacon or pancetta until the fat is rendered. Remove the bits and reserve. Discard most of the fat and sauté the vegetables until they begin to color.
Onion, diced	1 lb.	
Carrots, diced	8 oz.	
Celery, diced	8 oz.	
Tomatoes, crushed	2 lbs.	Add the tomatoes and garlic, and simmer for 1 hour, partially covered. Return bacon or pancetta bits to the sauce and simmer for 15 minutes. Season with salt and pepper.
Garlic, minced	3 tsp.	
Salt and black pepper	to taste	
Fusilli	3–4 oz. per serving	Heat the sauce, as needed. Toss with freshly cooked fusilli or pasta of choice.
Mozzarella, tiny cubes	1 heaping tbsp. per serving	Garnish with tiny cubes of fresh mozzarella, fresh parsley, and a sprinkling of Parmesan.
Parsley, fresh, chopped	as needed	
Parmesan cheese, grated	as needed	

MACARONI WITH PANCETTA, TOMATO, AND HOT PEPPERS   *Southern Italy*

Yield: one serving

Pancetta or slab bacon, rind removed, blanched	2 oz.
Onion, diced	2 tbsp.
Tomato, plum, peeled, seeded, and chopped	4 oz.
Red pepper flakes	⅛ tsp. or to taste

Cut the pancetta or bacon into small dice, then sauté until the fat is rendered. Remove from the pan and reserve in a warm place on an absorbent towel. Discard the excess fat in the pan and sauté the onion until soft. Add the tomato and hot pepper flakes and cook over low heat for 5 minutes.

Macaroni or pasta of choice	3–4 oz.
Parsley, fresh, chopped	as needed

Cook pasta until tender but still firm. Drain well, then add to the sauce in the pan and mix well. Place the pasta on a warm plate and sprinkle with the reserved pancetta or bacon bits and parsley.

VERMICELLI WITH PANCETTA AND PEAS   *Southern Italy*

Yield: one serving

Pancetta, in ½-inch dice	3 oz.

Sauté the pancetta until all of the fat has been rendered. Remove from pan and drain on an absorbent towel. Reserve in a warm place.

Onion, small dice	3 tbsp.
Red wine, dry	2 oz.
Stock, beef	6 oz.
Peas, fresh or frozen	2 tbsp.
Sugar	¼ tsp.
Salt and black pepper	to taste

Discard excess fat and sauté the onion in the small pan until very soft but not browned. Add the wine and bring to a boil. Deglaze the pan and reduce the wine by half. Add the beef stock, peas, and sugar. Return the sautéed pancetta to the pan and reduce the liquids by half. Season with salt and pepper.

(Continued)

Vermicelli	3–4 oz.	Cook vermicelli until tender but still firm. Add to the sauce and mix well. Place in a heated bowl, add the Parmesan cheese, and toss briefly.
Parmesan cheese, grated	1 tbsp.	

CANNELLONI WITH RICOTTA AND PROSCIUTTO   *Italy*

Yield: 10 servings

Pasta:

Egg pasta (see recipe at beginning of this section)	1–1¼ lbs.	Roll the pasta into sheets. If using a pasta machine, begin with the widest setting and roll the pasta gradually until reaching the thinnest setting. If you prefer a thicker pasta, stop before the last setting. Sheets should be about 5 inches wide. Using a pastry cutter, cut in sections 6 inches in length. Let the pieces dry for about 15 minutes on a floured board.

Boiling water	6 qts.	Bring water to a rolling boil. Add the pasta pieces, 1 at a time. When water returns to the boil, stir, and cook for 30 seconds. Remove the pasta from the pot and place immediately in a bowl of cold water. Reserve.
Salt	to taste	

Filling:

Ricotta cheese	20 oz.	Combine these ingredients and blend thoroughly. Reserve.
Eggs, beaten	2	Drain the pasta and place on a clean kitchen towel. Place approximately 2–3 tbsp. of the filling lengthwise, down the center of the pasta. Roll up the pasta. Leave the ends of the rolls open or fold under, if preferred. If ends are folded under, use a smaller amount of filling. Reserve.
Prosciutto, fat trimmed	6 oz.	
Parsley leaves, flat, chopped	3 tbsp.	
Parmesan cheese, grated	4 oz.	
Black pepper, coarsely ground	½ tsp.	

Tomato sauce	as needed
Parmesan cheese, grated	as needed

To prepare an individual serving, place 2 cannelloni in a buttered, single-serving, oven-proof dish. Spoon a generous amount of tomato sauce over the cannelloni and top with a sprinkling of grated cheese. Place in a 375 degree F oven for 15–20 minutes, or until sauce has reached the boiling point.

The size of the cannelloni and the amount of filling and sauce can be varied. Serve as a first course or as a luncheon offering accompanied by a salad.

PAGLIA E FIENO

Yield: one serving

This dish is known as straw and hay on many menus.

Butter	1 tsp.
Prosciutto or smoked ham, finely chopped	3 tbsp.
Heavy cream	4 oz.
Salt and white pepper	to taste
Nutmeg, grated	to taste

In a 10-inch skillet, heat the butter and sauté the prosciutto or ham for several minutes over medium heat. Add the heavy cream and bring to the boil. Lower heat and simmer until the cream begins to thicken. Season with salt, white pepper, and nutmeg.

Tagliatelle, white	2 oz.
Tagliatelle, green	2 oz.
Parmesan cheese, grated	as needed

Cook pasta until desired doneness is reached, then drain well and add to the sauce. Stir well, place on a heated plate, and sprinkle generously with grated cheese.

LASAGNA WITH VEAL AND FRESH TOMATOES

Yield: 12 servings

Sauce:

Olive oil	2 oz.
Butter	2 oz.
Onion, fine dice	1 lb.
Veal, ground twice	2½ lbs.

In a large skillet, heat the oil and butter and sauté the onions until they become soft. Add the veal and continue to sauté, stirring, until the meat is lightly browned.

(Continued)

White wine	8 oz.
Tomatoes, plum, peeled, seeded, and chopped	5 lbs.
Tomato paste	3 oz.
Eggs, beaten	2
Parmesan cheese, grated	2 oz.
Salt and black pepper	to taste

Add the wine and cook until the wine has been reduced by half. Add the tomatoes and the tomato paste and mix thoroughly. Beat the eggs together with the Parmesan cheese and add to the sauce. Bring the sauce to the boil, lower the heat, and simmer for 45 minutes, stirring occasionally. Season with salt and pepper.

Eggs	10

Boil the eggs until they are hard-boiled. Plunge into cold water when done. Peel, chop coarsely, and reserve.

Mozzarella, fresh	2 lbs., or as needed

Dice the cheese and reserve.

Lasagna, fresh	2 lbs.

Cook pasta in a generous amount of water until barely tender. Drain and rinse in cold water. Place on clean, damp towels and reserve.

Olive oil	as needed

To assemble the lasagna, oil a 12- by 18- by 3-inch pan. Cover the bottom with a single layer of pasta. Spread a thin layer of sauce, a layer of chopped, hard-boiled egg, then a layer of diced mozzarella. Top with another layer of pasta and repeat this process until all ingredients have been used. Reserve the largest and most uniform pieces of pasta for the top.

Butter, melted	as needed
Parmesan cheese, grated	as needed

Brush the top pasta layer generously with melted butter and sprinkle lightly with grated cheese. Bake in a 350 degree F oven for 30–40 minutes, or until the top is golden. Reheat individual servings, covered, for 10–15 minutes. Uncover and continue to bake for a few minutes, just prior to serving.

PASTA WITH BROCCOLI   *Southern Italy*

Yield: 10–12 servings

Broccoli	2½ lbs.

Wash the broccoli and cut away the tough stem ends. Using a vegetable peeler, peel remainder of stems. Cut off the florets about 1½ inches from the top. Cut the peeled stems crosswise into ¼-inch-thick disks. In boiling water, blanch stems until just tender, then plunge into iced water. Repeat this process with the florets. Reserve.

Olive oil, virgin	16 oz.
Anchovies	20–25 fillets
Red pepper flakes	½ tsp.

Heat oil over low heat. Add anchovies and mash in the oil. Add red pepper flakes and cook over very-low heat for 5 minutes. Remove from heat and reserve.

Pasta of choice	3–4 oz. per serving

To prepare an individual serving, cook pasta until just done. Just prior to draining, add 3 oz. of the broccoli stems and florets to the pasta and heat through for 15–20 seconds. Drain and toss with approximately 2 oz. of anchovy sauce.

Italian or Greek black olives, pitted, chopped	as needed

Garnish with the olives.

PASTA WITH EGGPLANT, OLIVES, AND ANCHOVIES   *Northern Italy*

Yield: 10 servings

The robust sauce of this dish is best when used with heavier tubular- or spiral-shaped pastas (3–4 oz. per serving).

Eggplant, ½-inch dice	1 lb.

Wash and dice the eggplant, leaving the skin on. Lightly salt, place in colander with heavy plate on top, and let stand for 30 minutes to express liquid.

(Continued)

Olive oil	4 oz.	Over moderate heat, sauté garlic until light brown and remove from pan. Dry eggplant cubes with towel and sauté over high heat until browned. Add more olive oil, if necessary.
Garlic, medium cloves cut in half	4	

Onion, small dice	1 lb.	Add onions and sauté for 2–3 minutes. Add tomatoes and seasonings and simmer for 30 minutes.
Tomato, peeled, seeded, and chopped	2 lbs.	
Oregano, ground	2 tsp.	
Black pepper	1 tsp.	
Red pepper, crushed	½ tsp.	

Anchovies, mashed	4 oz.	Add anchovies, parsley, and olives. Simmer for 15 minutes. Adjust for salt and pepper.
Parsley, finely chopped	10–12 sprigs	
Black olives, pitted, chopped, Kalamata or Alphonso	20	

PASTA WITH GARLIC AND OLIVE OIL   *Southern Italy*

Yield: one serving

Pasta of choice	3–4 oz.	Cook pasta in lightly salted water until tender but still firm.

Olive oil	2 oz.	Over medium heat, sauté the garlic until it is soft. Do not brown. Add red pepper flakes and a few grindings of black pepper. Continue to sauté until the garlic becomes pale gold. The entire procedure should take no more than a few minutes.
Garlic, chopped	1 tsp.	
Red pepper flakes	¼ tsp.	
Black pepper	to taste	

Parsley, chopped	as needed	Pour sauce over pasta, sprinkle with the parsley, and toss.

As a variation, increase oil to 3 oz. Sauté garlic until lightly colored. Do not brown. Discard garlic and add chopped parsley and any fresh herbs, such as basil or rosemary, along with the red pepper flakes. Sauté briefly. Add a scant tablespoon of coarse bread crumbs to the oil and sauté until lightly browned. Toss with cooked pasta of choice.

To facilitate cooking individual portions in a number of single portion recipes, place the pasta in a heavy strainer that can be immersed into a pot of boiling water. Keep an empty pot nearby. Place the strainer in this pot to drain.

SPAGHETTI WITH LEMON SAUCE *Southern Italy*

Yield: one serving

Pasta:

Spaghetti, fresh	3–4 oz.

Because the sauce will take just a few minutes to make, it and the pasta should be done at exactly the same time. Cook the pasta in a strainer immersed in a pot of boiling water. When pasta is done, raise the strainer to drain the pasta, then add the pasta directly to the skillet in which you have prepared the sauce.

Sauce:

Heavy cream	6 oz.
Butter, whole	2 oz.
Lemon peel, grated	1 tsp.
Egg	1
Parmesan cheese, grated	1 tbsp.
Salt and white pepper	to taste

In a 12-inch skillet, bring the cream to a boil. Add butter and lower heat to medium. Add the lemon peel and grated cheese. Reduce cream by ⅓. Add egg, using a rapid motion with a wire whisk (if this is not done very quickly, the egg will coagulate). Season with salt and pepper.

Parsley, fresh, chopped	as needed

Add cooked, hot pasta to the sauce. Stir and toss to mix well. Turn out on a very warm plate. Garnish with a sprinkling of fresh, chopped parsley.

PASTA WITH PORCINI MUSHROOMS   *Southern Italy*

Yield: 10 servings

Mushrooms,* porcini, dried	5 oz.
Water, warm	20 oz.

Soak the mushrooms in warm water for 1 hour. Using a slotted spoon or small strainer, lift the mushrooms from the water, taking care not to disturb the sediment. Rinse them under running water then chop fine. Carefully decant the soaking water and reserve. Discard the sediment.

Olive oil	5 oz.
Onion, diced	1 lb.
Garlic, chopped	1 tbsp.
Tomato paste	4 oz.

Heat the oil and sauté the onion and garlic until soft. Add the tomato paste and continue to cook for several minutes.

Marsala wine	12 oz.

Add wine, stir well, and bring to a boil. Reduce by half, then add reserved mushroom liquid and chopped mushrooms. Lower heat and simmer, partially covered, for 45 minutes. Cool and reserve.

Pasta of choice	3–4 oz. per serving
Butter, whole	1 tsp.
Parsley, fresh, chopped	as needed

To prepare an individual serving, cook the pasta so that it is tender but firm. In a separate pan, heat the butter and 3–4 oz. of the sauce. Drain pasta, pour sauce on top, and toss to mix. Garnish with the parsley.

---

* If fresh porcini mushrooms are available, use 1½–2 lbs. Slice them thin and sauté with the onions and garlic. Use chicken or veal stock as a substitute for the water used to soak the dried porcini.

PASTA WITH RED AND YELLOW PEPPERS

Yield: 10 servings

Peppers, red	2 lbs.
Peppers, yellow	2 lbs.

Broil the peppers under a broiler or grill on top of a charcoal grill until the skins are charred. Peel the skins, remove the core and seeds, and cut into thin strips. Reserve.

Olive oil	3 oz.
Peppers, red, dried	2
Garlic, sliced	1 tbsp.
Tomatoes, peeled, seeded, and chopped	4 lbs.
Salt and black pepper	to taste

Heat the oil and sauté the peppers and garlic over low heat until the garlic is very soft but not browned. Discard the dried peppers and add the reserved red and yellow peppers and tomatoes. Cook over medium to low heat until the peppers are soft and most of the tomatoes' juice has evaporated. Season with salt and pepper. Let cool and reserve.

Penne or pasta of choice	3–4 oz. per serving
Parsley leaves, fresh, chopped	as needed
Parmesan cheese, grated	as needed

To prepare an individual serving, cook the pasta in boiling water until it reaches the desired doneness. In a separate pan, reheat the pepper/tomato sauce. Pour the sauce over the hot pasta and add a generous sprinkling of the parsley and cheese. Mix well and serve with additional Parmesan on the side.

FETTUCINE WITH FRESH SPINACH AND GARLIC

Yield: one serving

Olive oil	2 tbsp.
Butter	1 tsp.
Garlic, chopped	1 tsp.

Heat butter and oil, then sauté the garlic over moderate heat until it begins to soften.

Spinach, washed, chopped	8 oz.
Parmesan cheese	2 tbsp.
Salt and black pepper	to taste
Fettucine	3–4 oz.

Add spinach to the pan. Turn the spinach so that the leaves are well-coated with the oil and butter. Sauté, stirring, until the spinach is wilted. Add the cheese, salt, and pepper and mix well. Arrange the spinach on top of a bed of hot fettucine.

If using fresh pasta, start cooking the pasta at the same time as the sauce. If using dried pasta, start the pasta first. The sauce should take no longer than 3–4 minutes to prepare. Sauce and pasta should be done at the same time. Serve with additional cheese on the side.

PASTA STUFFED WITH SPINACH AND SERVED WITH TWO SAUCES   *Northern Italy*

Yield: 10 servings

It is best to use fresh pasta in this dish so the size of the sheet can be controlled. The end product will resemble a jelly roll slice approximately 2–3 inches in diameter.

Pasta, rectangular sheets 8 by 12 inches	1½ lbs.	If using dried pasta sheets, cook them al dente. The pasta should be very flexible but not too soft.
Spinach	3 lbs.	Clean the spinach thoroughly and blanch until just wilted. In a clean towel, squeeze dry and chop. Set aside.
Butter, clarified	4 oz.	Sauté the onion until soft. Add prosciutto and cook for another minute. Add spinach and continue to cook for a few minutes or until no liquid appears in the pan. Reserve.
Onion, small dice	8 oz.	
Prosciutto, thin-sliced, then diced	4 oz.	
Ricotta cheese	12 oz.	Mix ricotta, eggs, and Parmesan. Add spinach mixture. Add nutmeg, salt, and pepper and blend thoroughly. Adjust seasonings, if necessary.
Eggs, beaten	2	
Parmesan cheese, grated	2 oz.	On pasta rectangles, spread spinach/cheese mixture in a thin layer, leaving a 1-inch border around the edges. Roll up like a jelly roll, beginning with the rectangle's long side. Wrap the roll in cheesecloth and tie the ends with butcher's twine. Cook in lightly salted, simmering water for 10 minutes. Remove and let cool. Unwrap, oil lightly, and set aside.
Nutmeg	½ tsp.	
Salt and white pepper	to taste	

Béchamel sauce	as needed
Tomato sauce	as needed
Parmesan cheese, grated	as needed
Butter	as needed

In a 6-inch, oven-proof dish, cover half with a small ladle of Béchamel; the other half with tomato sauce. Slice the stuffed pasta into ¾-inch slices (two slices per serving). Sprinkle top with Parmesan and a few small pieces of butter. Place in a 400–450 degree F oven for 5 minutes, or until heated through. Serve in the baking dish.

This dish can be served as a first pasta course or as a luncheon dish. Increase the portions if served as an entrée and accompany with a mixed greens and radicchio salad.

LINGUINE WITH TOMATO SAUCE AND CAPERS   *Southern Italy*

Yield: 10 servings

Olive oil	2 oz.
Garlic, minced	2 tsp.
Plum tomatoes, peeled and seeded	4 lbs.
Capers (if packed in salt, wash thoroughly)	2 tbsp.
Basil leaves	10–15

Heat the oil over medium heat. Add garlic and sauté briefly until garlic softens. Add the tomatoes, capers, and basil. Simmer for 45 minutes. Place in a food processor and puree.

Butter	4 tbsp.
Flour	3 tbsp.

Melt butter in a small saucepan. When it foams, add the flour and mix well. Cook over low heat for 5 minutes, stirring occasionally.

Salt and black pepper	to taste
Lemon juice, fresh	to taste
Linguine	3–4 oz. per serving

Add the roux to the sauce and mix well. Over medium heat, bring to a simmer. Season with salt, pepper, and lemon juice. Simmer for 15–20 minutes. Serve over linguine.

Capers, whole	as needed
Parsley, fresh, chopped	as needed

Garnish each serving with a sprinkling of capers and parsley.

PIZZA: A VARIED CREATION

Pizzas are made in many shapes and sizes: round, square, rectangular, small, medium, large, individual serving, for two or more, thin-crusted, thick-crusted, crust on the bottom, crust on the bottom and top, stuffed pockets, cocktail size, and probably a number of other versions. They appear in many degrees of complexity, from the very elaborate and abundant using numerous ingredients, to simple preparations, consisting of little more than a flat piece of dough flavored with olive oil. They are served as first courses, entrées, snacks, and as hors d'oeuvre. In many instances, pizzas with readily identifiable names and ingredients are still subject to the inspiration of the chef, the locality, or the necessity of the moment. The results are interesting variations on old themes. Very few food preparations offer such a wide variety of possibilities and variations and are used in so many ways.

Recognizing this, the following are some suggestions for combinations of ingredients. Exact proportions, quantities, shapes, and sizes are left to the judgment of the individual and may be varied to suit the occasion. A basic recipe for bread dough, which most pizzas have in common, can be found in this section. Roll or stretch dough to desired thickness and shape, taking care to leave a raised edge around the perimeter. Bake pizzas on the lowest shelf or on tiles in a 450–500 degree F oven until the edge of the crust is browned or the garnish is bubbling. Place toppings on the dough just prior to baking.

BASIC BREAD DOUGH

Yield: 3 lbs.

Water, lukewarm	16 oz.
Yeast, active dry	½ oz.

In the bowl of an electric mixer, combine the water and the yeast and let rest for 5 minutes.

Salt	2 tsp.
Olive oil	6 tbsp.

Add the salt and olive oil and mix well.

Flour, unbleached, all-purpose	1¾ lbs.

Using the dough hook on the mixer, add the flour, 1 cup at a time, and beat at medium speed. Mix for about 5 minutes or until the dough has pulled away from the bowl's sides and has a uniform, elastic consistency. Place the dough in an oiled bowl. Cover with a towel and let rest in a warm place until the dough has doubled in size. Punch down and allow the dough to rise once again before using.

PIZZA WITH ANCHOVIES AND CHEESE   *Southern Italy*

Mozzarella, fresh

Anchovies

Basil, fresh

Grate the cheese, using the large holes of a grater. Mash the anchovies, chop the basil, and add them to the cheese. Mix well and reserve.

Bread dough

Parmesan cheese, grated

Olive oil

Roll out dough to desired thickness and place on an oiled pan. Cover the dough with a layer of the mozzarella mixture. Sprinkle with grated cheese and a little olive oil.

PIZZA WITH CLAMS OR MUSSELS

Olive oil

Garlic, sliced

Tomatoes, crushed

Oregano

Red pepper flakes

Salt and black pepper

Heat the oil in a skillet and sauté the garlic over low heat until soft but not browned. Add the tomatoes and sauté for a few minutes. Season with the oregano, red pepper flakes, salt, and pepper and simmer for 15 minutes. Reserve.

Clams, small, or mussels

Olive oil

Scrub the clams or mussels and place in a pot with a small amount of water. Over high heat, steam them open. Remove from heat and rinse them to remove any sand. Reserve the broth for other purposes. Toss the clams in a little olive oil and reserve.

(Continued)

Bread dough	Roll out the dough to desired thickness and place on an oiled pan. Cover the dough with the tomato sauce. Sprinkle a little olive oil on top and bake. A few minutes before the pizza is done, remove it and quickly add the clams. Return to oven for 1–2 minutes to heat through.
Olive oil	

PIZZA QUATTRO STAGIONI

Bread dough	Roll out the dough into a rough circle. Divide the circle into four parts by placing a 1 to 1½-inch-strip of grated mozzarella from the top of the circle to the bottom. Give the dough a quarter turn and place another strip of grated mozzarella from top to bottom, creating four equal quadrants. Place a thin layer of chopped tomato in each of the quadrants.
Mozzarella, fresh, grated	
Tomato, plum, peeled, seeded, and chopped	

Mushrooms, sliced, sautéed in butter	Place any four of these ingredients, one in each of the four quadrants of the pizza and bake in a hot oven. Other ingredients may be substituted. Try to achieve a good variety of flavors and colors.
Ham or pancetta, diced, sautéed	
Artichoke hearts, quartered	
Olives, green and/or black, chopped or sliced	
Basil, fresh, chopped	
Anchovies, chopped	
Capers, chopped	
Peppers, green and/or red sweet, roasted, peeled	
Egg, hard-boiled, sliced	

PIZZA STUFFED WITH MEAT AND TOMATOES

Olive oil	Heat the olive oil and sauté the onions until soft. Add the ground beef and continue to cook until the beef is browned and the pan juices have evaporated. Remove the meat and onions and reserve.
Onion, sliced	
Beef, ground	

Tomatoes, crushed	In the same pan, cook the tomatoes and parsley until most of the liquid has evaporated. Season with salt, pepper, and fennel seed and cook for a few minutes. Reserve.
Parsley, fresh, chopped	
Salt and pepper to taste	
Fennel seed to taste	

Bread dough	Roll out dough in a thin layer and place in an oiled pan with a 1-inch lip, pressing the dough up over the pan's edges. Cover the dough with the ground meat, then cover the meat with the tomato mixture. Prepare another layer of rolled dough and cover the top. Press the edges together to create a sealed pie.

Egg yolk, beaten	Brush the pie's surface with beaten egg yolk and bake in a 400 degree F oven for 20–25 minutes, or until browned.

PIZZA STUFFED WITH BROCCOLI AND RICOTTA

Broccoli, tough ends removed	Peel the stalks and blanch the broccoli until slightly tender. Plunge immediately in iced water. When cool, drain and chop into bite-sized pieces. Reserve.

Bread dough	Roll out dough in a thin layer and place in an oiled pan with a 1-inch lip. Press the dough up over the pan's edges. Reserve.

(Continued)

Olive oil	Heat the oil and sauté the garlic over medium heat. When the garlic begins to soften, add the broccoli and heat through quickly.
Garlic, sliced	

Ricotta cheese	Cover the dough with a layer of Ricotta cheese. Add the garlic and broccoli to create another layer. Sprinkle with salt and pepper. Prepare another layer of rolled dough and cover the top. Pinch the edges together.
Salt and pepper to taste	

Egg yolk, beaten	Brush the pie's surface with beaten egg yolk and bake in a 400 degree F oven for 20–25 minutes, or until browned.

PIZZA WITH SWISS CHARD

Swiss Chard	Cut the chard into ¼-inch slices, cutting across the stem. Place in a saucepan with an inch of water. Cover the pan and cook until the stems are tender. Drain and let cool. Place the chard in a clean kitchen towel and squeeze dry. Reserve.

Olive oil	Heat the oil and sauté the onion until soft but not brown. Add the garlic and parsley and sauté for another minute. Add the reserved chard and blend ingredients thoroughly. (Can be prepared in quantity up to this point and reserved. Escarole or chicory may be used instead of the chard.)
Onion, sliced thin	
Garlic, sliced thin	
Parsley, fresh, coarsely chopped	

Bread dough	Roll out the dough to desired thickness and place on an oiled pan.

Tomatoes, ripe, sliced	Cover the dough with the chard mixture. Top with a few slices of fresh tomato. Sprinkle with salt and a little olive oil.
Salt	
Olive oil	

PIZZA MARGHERITA

Bread dough	Roll out the dough to desired thickness and place on an oiled pan.
Tomatoes,* ripe	Remove the core and slice the tomatoes ⅛- to ¼-inch thick. Put tomatoes in slightly overlapping rows over the surface of the dough, about ½ inch from the pan's sides.
Mozzarella, fresh, sliced thin	Place the cheese on top of the tomatoes.
Basil leaves, fresh Salt and black pepper Olive oil Parmesan cheese, grated	Chop the leaves and scatter them over the cheese. Sprinkle with salt, pepper, a little olive oil, and Parmesan cheese.

* If ripe tomatoes are not available, use canned Italian tomatoes. Be sure to drain the canned tomatoes before using.

BAKED MAMALIGA WITH CHEESE   *Rumania*

Yield: 10 servings

Polenta (see p. 91)	1 recipe	Prepare the polenta according to the recipe.
Bacon, sliced	1 lb.	Sauté the bacon until crisp. Reserve. Mix the cheese with the sour cream and season lightly with white pepper.
Farmers or cottage cheese	2 lbs.	
Sour cream	½ lb.	Oil a loafpan large enough to hold three or four polenta layers. Cut the polenta to size and place one layer on the bottom of the pan. Place a layer of bacon and the cheese mixture on top. Continue layering these ingredients, ending with a layer of polenta. Top with pieces of butter and bake at 400 degrees F for 15–20 minutes.
White pepper	to taste	

(Continued)

Serve as a light luncheon dish accompanied by a mixed salad. Also may be served with stuffed cabbage rolls.

PISSALADIÈRE   *Southern France*   Yield: one 12- by 17- by 1-inch pan

This item is an onion, black olive, and anchovy tart.

Olive oil	2 tbsp.	Heat oil and sauté the onion over low heat, stirring frequently, until they are very soft. Add the tomatoes and cool until all of the moisture has evaporated. Reserve.
Onion, diced	1½ lbs.	
Tomato, peeled, seeded, and chopped (optional)	1½ lbs.	

Bread dough	1 lb.	Roll out the dough to fit an oiled, 12- by 17- by 1-inch jelly-roll pan. Push and stretch the dough until it touches all the pan's sides.

Anchovy fillets	as needed	To assemble, spread a layer of the onion/tomato mixture over the dough. Arrange the anchovy fillets in an attractive pattern over the top, then sprinkle liberally with olives. Bake in a 450 degree F oven for 20–25 minutes on the lower shelf of the oven. The crust should be well-browned.
Black olives, cured, pitted, and chopped	as needed	

Accompany with a green salad for luncheon or cut into finger-length pieces and serve as an hors d'oeuvre.

POLENTA   *Northern Italy*

Yield: 10 servings as entrée accompaniment or appetizer

Water	2 qts.
Salt	1½ tsp.

Bring water to a boil.

Corn meal, stone-ground, medium ground	1 lb.

Gradually add the cornmeal to the boiling water, stirring continuously with a wooden spoon. Crush any lumps that may form. When well-mixed, lower to a simmer and cook for 30 minutes. Stir occasionally, making sure the mixture is smooth. When done, the polenta should begin to pull away from the pot's sides. When this occurs, turn the heat up to medium-high for a minute or so without stirring.

Pour polenta into an oiled pan large enough to spread it to a thickness of ½ inch. Let cool, then refrigerate for future use.

An alternate method: Mix all ingredients together in the upper portion of a double boiler and cook, covered, over simmering water. Stir occasionally until the polenta is thick and has a very smooth consistency. Cornmeal may be obtained in finer or coarser grinds. Amount of water used may vary somewhat, depending on the grind.

RISOTTO MILANESE
Northern Italy

Yield: two servings

Risotto should be prepared just prior to service so that the characteristic creamy, firm texture is retained. The number of flavorings and garnishes are limited only by the imagination of the individual chef. Variations reflect local product availability and regional preferences. The basic preparation, however, remains consistent.

(Continued)

Saffron threads	1 pinch	Soak the threads in warm stock for 30 minutes. Reserve.
Stock, chicken	4 oz.	

Stock, chicken	as needed	Bring to a slow boil. Reserve.

Olive oil	2 tbsp.	In a 2-qt. saucepan, heat the oil over moderate heat and sauté the onions until they are soft. Do not allow them to brown.
Onion, finely minced	as needed	

Arborio rice	¾ cup	Add the rice and continue to sauté for a minute or so until the rice is well-coated with the oil, and the oil is absorbed.

Butter, sweet	1 oz.	Add 1 cup of boiling stock and stir. Continue to cook over moderate heat, uncovered, stirring occasionally, until the stock is almost absorbed. Add the saffron/stock and continue to cook over moderate heat, stirring occasionally. Continue to add stock, until the rice is done. The texture should be soft but not mushy. Remove from heat and vigorously stir ¼ cup of stock into the rice, along with the sweet butter and grated cheese. Serve immediately as is or garnished.
Parmesan cheese, fresh, grated	1 tbsp.	

Risotto Milanese can be varied by adding a wide variety of garnishes. The possibilities are many. They mostly involve the use of vegetables sautéed in oil that may or may not be flavored with garlic or other seasonings and fresh herbs. Vegetables may be used individually, in combinations, or mixed with small bits of beef, veal, lamb, poultry, fish, or smoked and cured meats. Such garnishes are usually prepared separately and added to the risotto just prior to serving. Various cheeses, either singly or in combination, may also be used. Risotto is usually presented as a first course as an alternative to pasta or soup. It may also be served as a luncheon entrée accompanied by salad.

SOUPS

BEER SOUP   *Germany*

Yield: 10–12 servings

Dark beer	2 qts.	Pour the beer into a container and let stand until it reaches room temperature. When the bubbles have disappeared, bring it to a simmer over medium heat.
Butter	4 oz.	In a 3½ qt. heavy-bottomed saucepan, melt butter over low heat. Mix flour and sugar together and add. Cook over low heat, stirring constantly, until the sugar begins to caramelize. Add the beer and mix well, using a wire whisk.
Sugar	8 oz.	
Flour	4 oz.	
Cinnamon stick	1 small	Add cinnamon stick and simmer for 5 minutes.
Egg yolks	6	Beat yolks well. Remove beer from heat. Remove cinnamon stick and beat in eggs yolk until mixture is foamy.
Cinnamon, ground	as needed	Serve in warm mugs with a light sprinkling of cinnamon.

WINE SOUP   *Germany*

Yield: 10 servings

Moselle, dry	2 qts.	Bring wine and seasonings to a boil. Lower heat and simmer for 10–15 minutes. Remove from heat.
Cinnamon stick	1 medium	
Clove, powdered	½ tsp.	
Sugar	to taste	
Eggs, beaten	4	Using a wire whisk, quickly beat a small amount of the hot wine into beaten eggs. Repeat this once again to temper the eggs. Pour this mixture into the remaining wine.

(Continued)

Cinnamon, ground	as needed

Serve in very hot mugs with a sprinkle of cinnamon on top.

YOGURT SOUP   *Turkey*

Yield: 10–12 servings

Stock, chicken	2½ qts.
Rice, long grain	6 oz.
Salt and white pepper	to taste

Bring the stock to a boil. Lower heat and add the rice; simmer until the rice is tender. Season with salt and pepper.

Yogurt, unflavored	1 lb.
Cornstarch	2 tbsp.
Egg yolks	3

In a mixing bowl, whisk a small amount of yogurt with the cornstarch. Add the egg yolks and the rest of the yogurt and mix well. Add a ladle of the hot chicken stock and blend. Repeat this 2 more times to temper the eggs, then add this mixture to the stock. Cook for 3–4 minutes, stirring. Do not allow the soup to boil.

Mint leaves, fresh, chopped	

Garnish with mint leaves.

LITTLENECK CLAM SOUP   *Northern Italy*

Yield: 10–12 servings

Olive oil	4 oz.	Heat the oil. Over low heat, sweat peppers and garlic in a covered soup pot until garlic becomes soft. Do not allow to brown.
Garlic, chopped	6 medium cloves	
Peppers, hot red	3 whole	

| Onion, small dice | 1 lb. | Add onion and celery and cook, covered, for 2–3 minutes over low heat. |
| Celery, small dice | 4 oz. | |

White wine	8 oz.	Add these ingredients and bring to a boil. Lower to simmer for 30 minutes. Remove red peppers and season with salt and pepper. (If you wish to prepare this recipe "to order" let broth cool, then refrigerate. Before serving, reheat appropriate amount of broth and add 4–6 well-scrubbed clams per serving.)
Tomatoes, peeled, seeded, and chopped	5 lbs.	
Parsley, chopped	10 sprigs	
Salt and black pepper	to taste	

| Littleneck clams or mussels | 5 doz. | Scrub clams and add. Cover and cook 3–5 minutes, or until the clams open. Do not overcook or the clams will toughen. If the clams are sandy, steam them in a small amount of water in another pot until they just open. Decant the clam broth and add enough to the tomato mixture to achieve the desired consistency. |
| Salt and black pepper | to taste | |

| Croutons, sautéed | as needed | Place 4–6 clams with shells in each heated bowl. Add broth and serve with croutons and a sprinkling of parsley. |
| Parsley, fresh, chopped | as needed | |

BOURRIDE   *Southern France*   Yield: 10–12 servings

This fish soup is served with a side dish of aioli and/or rouille.

Sauce:

Stock, fish	3 qts.
White wine	8 oz.
Leek, white part only, sliced	2 medium
Onion, sliced	8 oz.
Carrot, sliced	4 oz.
Fennel bulb, sliced	1
Thyme, fresh	1 sprig
Orange peel, strips	½ orange
Salt and pepper	to taste

Combine these ingredients in a soup pot. Simmer for 15 minutes. Strain stock and reserve. Discard the thyme and orange peel and reserve the vegetables.

Any firm fleshed white fish such as monkfish, swordfish, seabass, halibut, or turbot	6–7 oz.

To prepare an individual portion, bring 8–9 oz. of stock to the boil in a small pot. Lower heat to simmer and gently poach the fish until it loses its transparency. Transfer fish to a large, warm soup bowl and hold in a warm place. Take pot containing the fish stock off the heat.

Aioli (see the recipe in the "Condiments" section)	2 tbsp.
Egg yolk	1
Heavy cream	1 tbsp.

In a mixing bowl, whisk the aioli and the egg yolk together with the cream. Pour very slowly into the fish stock. Return to very low heat, stirring with a wooden spoon, until the stock thickens enough to coat the spoon. Do not allow to boil.

Croutons	as needed

Pour the thickened soup over croutons placed in a warm bowl. Serve fish on a separate plate with a little of the soup poured on top and garnished with some of the reserved vegetables. Serve with a side dish of aioli and/or rouille (see recipe in the "Condiments" section). An alternate way of service would be to combine the soup, vegetables, and fish.

MONKFISH SOUP WITH RED PEPPERS   *Spain*

Yield: 10–12 servings

Peppers, sweet red, halved, seeds and stems removed	2½ lbs.

Place the peppers on an oiled baking pan, cut side down. Roast in a 450 degree F oven until the skins begin to char. Remove from oven and cover for 10 minutes. Remove skins and discard the skin. Slice the peppers into thin strips. Reserve.

Potatoes, all-purpose, peeled, sliced	2 lbs.
Stock, fish	2 qts.
Saffron threads	½ tsp.
Tomato, peeled, seeded	3 lbs.
Garlic, minced	2 tsp.
Paprika	2 tsp.
Cumin, ground	½ tsp.
Salt and white pepper	to taste

Cook the potatoes in simmering fish stock for 5 minutes. Add the saffron, tomato, garlic, paprika, and cumin and cook until the potatoes are very soft. Strain the liquid, season with salt and pepper, and reserve.

(Continued)

Olive oil	2 oz.	In a food processor, puree the vegetables. Return the vegetables to the stock, add the olive oil, mix well and reserve.

Monkfish, cubed	2 oz. per serving	To serve, reheat the fish stock containing the pureed vegetables. Add the monkfish and cook over low heat until the fish is done. Do not overcook. Just prior to serving, add approximately 1 tbsp. per serving of the roasted, sliced red pepper. Heat through and serve in large, heated bowls.

To serve as an entrée, increase the fish portion to 4–5 ounces.

MUSSEL SOUP   *Southern Italy*   Yield: 10 servings

Olive oil	2 oz.	Heat oil and sauté onions over medium heat until soft. Do not allow to brown. Add rice and sauté for a few minutes until the rice is well coated. Add garlic and ham and continue to sauté for a few minutes.
Onion, small dice	1 lb.	
Rice	8 oz.	
Garlic, minced	2 tsp.	
Ham, smoked, small dice	8 oz.	

Tomatoes, plum, peeled, seeded*	1 lb.	Add tomatoes and stir well. Add fish stock, sherry, paprika, salt, and pepper. Simmer for 15 minutes and reserve.
Stock, fish	2 qts.	
Sherry, dry	8 oz.	
Salt and black pepper	to taste	

---

* Canned, crushed tomatoes may be substituted.

Mussels, washed, de-bearded	4–6 per serving

To serve, heat soup as needed. Add the mussels, cover the pot, and heat until the mussels have opened. Pour the soup into large, warmed soup bowls and arrange the opened mussels around the perimeter.

Serve with a thick-crusted, warmed bread. Accompany with a hearty green salad and serve as a luncheon entrée.

GOLDEN FISH SOUP *Russia* Yield: 10 servings

Stock:

Fish bones	5 lbs.
Water	1 gal.
Butter	4 oz.
Onion, diced	1 lb.
Carrot, sliced	1 lb.
Parsnip, sliced	8 oz.
Celery, sliced	2 stalks
Bay leaf	3
White peppercorns	1 tbsp.
Saffron threads	⅓ tsp.

Wash and chop the bones. Place them in the water in a soup pot. Bring to a boil. Lower heat, skim liquid, and continue to simmer, skimming as necessary.

Heat butter and sauté the vegetables until soft. Add to fish bones and water and continue to simmer.

Add bay leaf and peppercorns. Crush saffron threads and add. Simmer for 30–40 minutes.

Salt	to taste

Strain through a double layer of cheesecloth and discard vegetables and bones. Reduce stock to 2 quarts and season with salt. If necessary, when done, strain again through cheesecloth to obtain a very clear broth. Refrigerate until needed.

(Continued)

Potatoes, ½-inch dice, precooked	10 pieces per serving
Salmon, fresh, boned, in 1-inch chunks	2 oz. per serving

To prepare an individual serving, bring 5–6 oz. of stock to a boil in a small saucepan. Add potatoes and salmon. Simmer, uncovered, for 3–5 minutes, or until fish is done. Do not overcook. Fish should flake easily.

Lemon, peeled, thinly sliced	as needed
Parsley, fresh, chopped	as needed
Salmon caviar	1 tbsp. per serving

Garnish with lemon slices dipped in parsley. Float 3 slices in the center of the plate and place salmon caviar on top of the slices.

CREAMED SHRIMP SOUP   *Portugal*

Yield: 10–12 servings

Butter	2 oz.
Olive oil	2 oz.
Onions, sliced thin	2 lbs.
Garlic, mashed	1 tbsp.
Tomato paste	4 oz.

In a soup pot, heat butter and oil over low to medium heat. Add onions and garlic, and cook until soft. Do not allow to brown. Add tomato paste and continue to cook over low heat for 5 minutes.

Tomatoes, peeled, seeded, and chopped	2 lbs.
White wine	8 oz.
Stock, fish	1½ qts.
Hot pepper flakes	½ tsp.
Salt and white pepper	to taste

Add the tomatoes to pot along with white wine and fish stock. Add hot pepper flakes and bring to the boil. Lower heat and simmer for 30 minutes. Add the salt and pepper.

Let cool and strain the liquid. Using a food processor, puree the onions and tomatoes. Return vegetables to stock and reserve. (Seasonings may be made relatively strong. They will lessen in intensity when the heavy cream is added.)

Shrimp, medium	4
Heavy cream	as needed

To prepare an individual serving, peel, devein, and butterfly the shrimp. Bring reserved soup to the boil. Lower heat and add the shrimp. Let simmer until shrimp are no longer transparent, about 1 minute. Pour into heated bowl(s) and float a tablespoon, more or less, of heavy cream on top.

CHILLED APPLE SOUP   *Northern France*

Yield: 10–12 servings

Leeks, white part only	12 oz.
Butter	4 oz.

Slice the leeks and *wash thoroughly*. Drain and sauté over low to medium heat until soft. Do not allow to brown.

Granny Smith apples, peeled, cored, and sliced	3 lbs.

Add and cook until apples are soft.

Potatoes, diced	1 lb.
Stock, chicken	1½ qts.

Add the potatoes and stock, bring to a boil, lower heat, and simmer for ½ hour. Let cool, then puree all ingredients.

Heavy cream	12 oz.
Apple brandy	2 oz.
Nutmeg	to taste
Salt and white pepper	to taste

Add cream and brandy, and blend well. Season to taste. Chill well before serving.

Cream, unsweetened, whipped	as needed

Unsweetened heavy cream may be whipped, then folded into the cold base just prior to serving. Garnish with a rosette of unsweetened, whipped cream.

COLD CHERRY SOUP   *Hungary*

Yield: 10 servings

Water	1 qt.
Cinnamon sticks	2
Sugar	10 oz.

Combine ingredients, bring to a boil, then lower heat to simmer for 15 minutes.

Sour cherries, pitted (reserve pits)	2 lbs.

Remove cinnamon sticks; add cherries. Simmer for 15 minutes.

Put the pits in a towel and crush with a heavy mallet. Reserve.

Arrowroot	3 tbsp.
Water, cold	as needed
Sugar	to taste

Dissolve arrowroot in a small amount of water, add to the cherry liquid, and simmer until liquid is clear and lightly coats spoon. Strain, reserve liquid, and puree cooked cherries. Pour reserved liquid through crushed cherry pits. Discard pits. Combine pureed cherries and liquid. Adjust taste with sugar. Taste should be slightly sweet. The sweet flavor will be lessened somewhat with the addition of the cream and wine in the next step. Chill thoroughly.

Heavy cream	8 oz.
Red wine, dry	8 oz.

Mix cream and wine and chill. Add 1 part of this mixture to 3 parts cherry soup just before serving.

Cream, unsweetened, whipped	as needed

Serve in ice-cold bowls. Garnish with a dollop of unsweetened whipped cream.

EGG AND LEMON SOUP   *Greece*

Yield: 10–12 servings

This soup can be made with fish stock as well and garnished with small cubes of blanched carrots and fresh peas.

Stock, chicken	2–2½ qts.	Bring the stock to a boil. Add the rice and simmer until the rice is done.
Rice, long	6 oz.	

Eggs	4 large	Remove stock from the heat. Beat the eggs and the lemon juice together until foamy. Slowly add 2 cups of the hot soup to the egg-lemon mixture, beating constantly with a wire whisk. Return the diluted egg-lemon mixture to the stock. Reserve.
Lemon juice, fresh	3–4 oz. or to taste	

To serve, heat 6–8 oz. of soup per serving to just below the boiling point. Do not allow the soup to boil.

PLUM SOUP   *Russia*

Yield: 10 servings

Plums	4 lbs.	Wash the plums and remove the pits. In a small soup pot, cook over low heat 5–10 minutes, depending on how ripe the fruit is. When the plums are soft, put them through a food mill with the juices. Discard the skins.
Water	4 oz.	

Cloves, crushed	to taste	Add enough red wine to the plums to bring the total volume to 2½ qts. Add the seasonings and simmer for 5 minutes. Adjust seasonings, if necessary.
Cinnamon, ground	to taste	
Sugar	to taste	
Red wine, dry	as needed	

Cream, whipped	as needed	If served hot, garnish with a dollop of whipped cream and a toasted crouton. If served cold, garnish with a dollop of whipped cream or sour cream.

PASTA E FAGIOLI
NEAPOLITAN STYLE   *Italy*

Yield: 10–12 servings

Cannellini beans	1 lb.
Water	3 qts.

Soak the beans overnight in a generous amount of water. Drain, rinse, and place beans in a soup pot with 3 qts. of water. Bring to the boil, then lower heat and simmer uncovered for 40–50 minutes or until the beans are tender but still firm. Remove half the beans and puree them with a small amount of the cooking liquid in a food processor. When smooth, return the pureed beans to the pot. Reserve.

Olive oil	4 oz.
Garlic, chopped	1 tbsp.
Parsley leaves, flat, chopped	8 tbsp.
Oregano, dried	2 tsp.
Celery, diced	2 ribs
Red pepper	3/4 tsp.

In a separate skillet, heat the oil and sauté these ingredients for 2–3 minutes over medium heat.

Tomatoes, plum, peeled, quartered	3 lbs.
Salt and black pepper	to taste

Add the tomatoes and simmer for 30 minutes, stirring occasionally. Add the tomato mixture to the pureed and whole beans. Bring to the boil, then lower heat and simmer for 30 minutes. Season with salt and pepper.

Rigatoni	12 oz.

Cook the rigatoni or any other tubular pasta in boiling water until tender but still firm. Add to the other ingredients and simmer for 10 minutes. Let the soup rest for at least 1 hour or longer before serving. Reheat soup before serving.

LENTIL SOUP   *Germany*   Yield: 10 servings

Slab bacon, small dice	8 oz.	In a small stockpot, sauté the bacon until the fat is rendered. Reserve the bacon bits. Discard excess fat. Retain enough to sauté the following vegetables.
Carrot, small dice	12 oz.	Sauté these vegetables until soft over low heat.
Onion, small dice	1¼ lbs.	
Parsnip, small dice	6 oz.	
Celery, small dice	6 oz.	
Butter	4 oz.	Add butter and flour and cook until flour is thoroughly incorporated.
Flour	4 oz.	
Stock, veal or beef	2 qts.	Add stock and lentils. Bring to a boil. Add seasonings and lower heat to simmer for 45 minutes.
Red lentils	12 oz.	
Marjoram	2 tsp.	
Salt and black pepper	to taste	
Tomato, peeled, seeded, chopped	1 lb.	Add tomatoes to soup. Simmer for 5 minutes.
Wine vinegar	as needed	Serve with a splash of wine vinegar per serving and garnish with reserved bacon bits.

LIVER DUMPLING SOUP   *Austria*

Yield: 10 servings

| Onion | 4 oz. | Sauté onion in a small amount of butter until they are soft. |
| Butter, clarified | as needed | |

| Bread crumbs | 6 oz. | Add these ingredients to onion and sauté lightly. |
| Parsley | 4 oz. | |

| Marjoram | 1 tsp. | Add and stir over heat until mixed. |

White bread	6 oz.	Soak bread in milk and squeeze dry. Add to onion/bread crumb mixture. Season with salt and pepper.
Milk	as needed	
Salt and white pepper	to taste	

| Calf's liver, finely ground | 1 lb. | Add liver and eggs and mix well. Shape 1 dumpling about the size of a walnut and drop into simmering water. If it falls apart, you may have to add more bread crumbs. |
| Eggs, beaten | 3 large | |

| Stock, beef, or beef consommé | as needed, approx. 5–6 oz. per serving | Bring to the simmer. |

| Parsley, fresh, chopped | ½ tsp. per serving | Shape small dumplings about the size of walnuts and drop into simmering broth for 5–6 minutes. Serve 2 or 3 dumplings as a garnish for clear beef broth or consommé. Add parsley. |

LAMB SOUP WITH CHEESE CROUTONS   *Southern Italy*

Yield: 10–12 servings

Lamb Stock:

Lamb bones and trimmings	6 lbs.
Fat	2 oz.
Onion, chopped	1 lb.
Carrots, chopped	8 oz.
Celery, chopped	8 oz.
Salt and pepper	to taste
Water	5 qts.

Place lamb bones and trimmings in a roasting pan with the fat and roast in a 400 degree F oven until they begin to brown.

Add onion, carrots, and celery ingredients to the pan and continue to roast until the vegetables begin to brown. When done, transfer the bones, trimmings, and vegetables to a clean soup pot. Drain fat from the roasting pan and deglaze with 8 oz. of water. Add this liquid to the soup pot along with the water. Bring to the boil and skim. Lower heat and simmer for 3–4 hours. Season with salt and pepper. Strain liquid and discard the bones and vegetables. Strain liquid through a double layer of cheesecloth. Refrigerate over night.

Remove congealed fat. You should have approximately 3 qts. of clear stock. If less, add water; if more, reduce over high heat.

French or Italian bread, toasted	½-inch slices
Pecorino cheese, sliced thin	as needed

Heat 7–8 oz. per serving of the lamb stock to the boiling point. In individual, oven-proof soup bowls place 1 slice of the toasted bread and top with a slice of the cheese. Repeat this process once again. Fill the bowl with the hot lamb stock and place in a 400 degree F oven for 15 minutes.

Fennel, fresh, shredded	as needed

Garnish with the fennel.

PORTUGUESE CHICKEN SOUP WITH MINT   *Portugal*

Yield: 10–12 servings

Stock, chicken	2½ qts.
Chicken breast, boned, skinned	20 oz.
Mint, fresh	7–8 sprigs

Bring chicken stock to a boil. Lower heat to a simmer. Add chicken breast meat and mint sprigs. Poach chicken about 10 minutes, or until done. Cooking time will vary, depending on the meat's thickness. Remove chicken and let cool. Strain stock through a double layer of cheesecloth and return to a clean pot.

Rice, short-grain or Arborio	8–10 oz.
Salt and white pepper	to taste
Lemon juice, fresh	to taste

Add rice to chicken stock and simmer until just tender. Shred chicken breast meat and add to heat through. Season with salt, pepper, and lemon juice.

Mint leaves, fresh, whole	as needed

Garnish with mint leaves.

Amount of rice can be varied. Blanched vegetables, diced small, and fresh peas can be added for additional color.

BORSCHT   *Russia*

Yield: 10–12 servings

Many regional varieties of borscht exist. Additional vegetables, legumes, cubed meats, sausage, and so on, may be added.

Butter	2 oz.
Leeks, thin slice	2 large
Celery root, thin slice	4 oz.
Carrots, thin slice	8 oz.
Onions, diced	1 lb.
Cabbage, thin slice (optional)	1 lb.

Heat butter, add vegetables, and sauté over low heat until soft.

Beef brisket, fresh, small cubes	1 lb.	Add beef and stock to vegetables. Simmer, partially covered, for 1 hour.
Stock, beef	2 qts.	

Beets, peeled, grated	3 lb.	Add beets and simmer for ½ hour or until meat is very tender.

Lemon juice, fresh	3–4 oz.	Add these ingredients, mix well, and taste. Flavor should be a combination of slightly sweet and sour. Adjust seasonings, if necessary.
Sugar	to taste	
Salt and black pepper	to taste	

Several small, boiled new potatoes may be added to the soup at service and a side dish of sour cream topped with chopped, fresh dill may be used as a garnish.

BROCCOLI SOUP WITH WHITE BEANS AND PASTA SHELLS   *Southern Italy*

Yield: 10–12 servings

Navy beans	8 oz.	Wash beans and remove any discolored ones. Soak beans overnight in cold water. Discard the water and rinse the beans. Place beans in a soup pot and add enough cold water to cover, plus several inches. Simmer until tender, but not mushy. Rinse beans in cold water and toss with a small amount of olive oil. Reserve.
Olive oil	as needed	

Broccoli, washed	2 lbs.	Cut off the florets, including 1 inch of the stem. Steam or blanch the florets until barely tender, then plunge immediately into iced water. Reserve. Remove the tough ends of the stalks and discard. Peel the remainder of the stalk and cut into 1-inch pieces.

(Continued)

Butter	4 oz.
Onion, small dice	1 lb.
Broccoli stems	
Flour	4 tbsp.
Stock, chicken	2½ qts.

In a soup pot, heat butter until it begins to foam. Add onion and cook over low heat until soft. Do not allow to brown. Add the broccoli stems and cook for 2 minutes. Add flour, mix well, and cook until the flour has been thoroughly incorporated. Add the chicken stock, stir well, and simmer until the broccoli stalks are very tender.

Salt and white pepper	to taste
Nutmeg	to taste

Strain liquid and reserve. In a food processor, puree the broccoli stalks and onions, then return to stock. Bring to a simmer. Season with salt, pepper, and nutmeg. Let cool and reserve.

Pasta, small shells	6 oz.
Olive oil	as needed

Cook pasta until tender. Plunge in cold water, drain, and toss in a small amount of olive oil. Reserve.

Bring 6 oz. of soup per serving to the boil. Add about ½ oz. of pasta, several tablespoons of beans, and 4–5 steamed broccoli florets per serving and heat through.

Pecorino cheese, grated	as needed

Garnish with a sprinkling of cheese.

FRESH CABBAGE SOUP   *Poland*

Yield: 10–12 servings

Stock, beef	2 qts.
Beef brisket, fresh	2 lbs.

Trim beef brisket and simmer in stock until very tender. Remove and dice or cut into 1½-inch strips. When cool enough to handle, shred strips, pulling apart meat along the grain. Return to stock and reserve.

Butter, whole	2 oz.
Onions, sliced	2 lbs.
Celery root, diced	1 large
Carrot, shredded	4 oz.
Parsnip, shredded	4 oz.
Cabbage, shredded	8 oz.

In a soup pot, melt butter and sauté the onions over medium heat until soft. Add the rest of the vegetables and cook, stirring occasionally, for 20 minutes over low heat.

Potatoes, diced	1½ lbs.
Tomatoes, peeled, chopped	2 lbs.
Salt and black pepper	to taste

Add beef and stock and simmer for 30 minutes. Add potatoes and tomatoes and simmer until potatoes are done, about 10–15 minutes. Season with salt and pepper.

CELERY SOUP   *Germany*

Yield: 10 servings

Celery root, small dice	4 lbs.
Onion, small dice	8 oz.
Butter, whole	4 oz.

Sauté root and onion slowly in whole butter until soft.

Flour	5 oz.

Add flour, mix well, and continue cooking for 10 minutes over low heat, stirring occasionally. Keep pot covered.

Stock, veal or chicken	2 qts.

Add stock and stir well. Bring to boil, lower heat, and simmer for ½ hour, or until celery root is very soft.

   Pour through sieve, reserving liquid. Puree vegetables and return them to the liquid.

(Continued)

Salt and white pepper	to taste	Season and let simmer for 5 minutes.*
Nutmeg	to taste	

Heavy cream	8 oz.	Add, adjust seasoning and simmer for a few minutes before serving.

Celery stalk, blanched, peeled, julienned	as needed	Garnish with celery.

* Soup may be cooled and held in refrigerator after seasonings are added and soup is simmered for 5 minutes. The next step may be done just prior to service. Individual servings may be prepared in this manner, adding heavy cream, appropriately proportioned.

GARLIC SOUP   *Spain*   Yield: 10–12 servings

Olive oil	5 oz.	Heat the oil in a large, heavy skillet. Add the garlic and sauté over low heat until pale gold. Do not brown. Remove garlic and reserve.
Garlic, peeled, sliced in half lengthwise	12–14 cloves	

Bread, French or Italian	10–12 slices, ½-inch thick	Sauté bread in the oil. When golden, remove and reserve. (Instead of whole-slice croutons, bread cubes prepared in the same manner may be used.)

Paprika, sweet	2 tbsp.	Remove pan from heat and stir in the paprika. Add the tomatoes, parsley, and thyme and return to heat. Cook until most of the liquid has evaporated.
Tomatoes, plum, peeled, seeded	1½ lbs.	
Parsley leaves, fresh, chopped	2 tbsp.	
Thyme leaves, fresh	2 tbsp.	

Stock, chicken	2½ qts.
Saffron threads	½ tsp.
Cumin, ground	1 tsp.
Salt and black pepper	to taste

In a soup pot, bring the stock to the boil. Add the saffron, cumin, the reserved tomato mixture and the reserved garlic. Simmer for ½ hour. Season with salt and pepper and simmer for another 10 minutes.

Crouton	one per serving
Egg, poached	one per serving

To serve, place a crouton in a heated bowl. Add an egg. Fill bowl with hot soup.

If you do not wish to poach eggs in advance, the egg may be cooked in the bowl. Place a crouton in a hot soup bowl. Add soup at the boiling point and slip a raw egg into the soup. Hold in a warm oven for a minute or so until the egg sets.

ZUPPA PAVESE *Northern Italy* Yield: 10 servings

Stock, chicken	1 qt.
Stock, beef	1 qt.
Thyme	½ tsp.
Garlic, minced	1 clove
Tomatoes, chopped	4
Leeks, white only, sliced	4
Salt and white pepper	to taste

Remove all traces of fat from stocks. Add other ingredients and bring to boil. Reduce heat and simmer for 1 hour. Strain through double layer of cheesecloth. Reserve broth.

White bread	10 slices
Olive oil	as needed

Cut bread into rounds each 4–5 inches in diameter. Sauté in olive oil until golden on both sides. Drain on towel. Cut each crouton into even quarters and reserve in a warm place.

(Continued)

Eggs	10

Poach eggs until yolks are just set. If this is done in advance, keep eggs in cool water to prevent overcooking. Yolks should be firm in appearance but still liquid inside. Trim any ragged edges.

Heat soup bowls. Bring broth to a fast boil. Place 1 poached egg in each bowl. Gently ladle the boiling broth over the egg. Arrange the croutons, points up, around the edges of the bowls.

Parmesan cheese, grated	1 tsp. per order
Parsley, chopped	as needed

Sprinkle with grated cheese and parsley.

KALE SOUP WITH CHORIZO   *Spain*

Yield: 10–12 servings

Olive oil	2 oz.
Onion, diced	1½ lb.
Stock, chicken	2½ qts.
Potatoes, all-purpose, thin sliced	3 lbs.

Sauté onion over low heat until very soft. Do not brown. Add chicken stock and bring to a boil. Add potatoes and simmer until soft. Strain stock and reserve. In a food processor, puree potatoes and onions and return to stock. Reserve.

Chorizo or other garlic sausage, sliced thin	1 lb.

Sauté sausage slices until lightly browned and most of the fat has been rendered. Add to stock and reserve.

Kale	2 lbs.

Trim tough stem ends. Using a vegetable peeler, peel backs of remaining stems. Cutting across the stems, slice the kale into very thin strips. Reserve.

Bring soup to the boil. Add the kale and cook until the kale is done. Do not overcook. The kale should retain a good green color.

ONION SOUP WITH MADEIRA   *Portugal*

Yield: 10–12 servings

Butter, clarified	as needed
Onions, sliced thin	3 lbs.
Paprika, sweet	1 tbsp.

Sauté the onions over very low heat until they begin to brown slightly. Stir frequently to ensure uniform consistency. Add the paprika, stir well, and sauté for 1–2 minutes.

Stock, chicken	2 qts.
Raisins, golden	4 oz.
Clove, ground	½ tsp.

Add these ingredients and bring to the boil. Lower heat and simmer for 30–40 minutes.

Madeira, dry	8 oz.

Add the Madeira and simmer for another 5 minutes.

Egg yolks, beaten	6
Water	2 tbsp.
Salt and white pepper	to taste

Beat egg yolks with water. Slowly add a ladle of simmering soup to the eggs, beating constantly with a wire whisk. Repeat this again to temper the eggs. Return this tempered egg mixture to the pot and heat just below the simmer for a few minutes. Do not allow to boil.

If soup is reserved and reheated, heat it through but do not allow it to reach the boiling point.

POTATO PUREE SOUP   *Austria*

Yield: 10 servings

Onions, sliced thin	1 lb.

In a covered pan, sweat onions until translucent.

Stock, chicken or vegetable	2 qts.
Potatoes, sliced thin	4 lbs.

Add stock and bring to boil. Add potatoes and cook until soft.
    Strain; reserve liquid; puree potatoes and onions.

(Continued)

Heavy cream or Béchamel	1 pt.	Combine heavy cream with all previous ingredients and bring to a simmer. Season with salt and pepper.
Salt and white pepper	to taste	

Pork loin, smoked, small cubes	as needed	Sauté pork cubes lightly and add as garnish along with chopped chives.
Chives, chopped	as needed	

BUTTERNUT SQUASH SOUP   *Southern Italy*

Yield: 10 servings

Butternut squash (sweet potatoes or yams may be substituted)	3 lbs.	Wash squash and prick each 4 or 5 times with a sharp-tined fork. Place on a baking sheet and bake in a 375 degree F oven until soft. When cool enough to handle, split down the middle. Remove and discard the seeds. Scoop out the pulp and place in the bowl of a food processor.

Butter, whole	4 oz.	Melt the butter over moderate heat. When foam subsides, add the leeks and sauté over low heat, stirring frequently, until very soft. Add to the squash and puree until very smooth. Add the chicken stock and pulse a few times to liquify the mixture. Transfer to a soup pot.
Leeks, white only, sliced	1 lb.	
Stock, chicken	8 oz.	

Stock, chicken	1½ qts.	Add additional stock to the soup pot. Bring to the boil, then lower heat and simmer for 30 minutes.

Salt and white pepper	to taste	Add seasonings and simmer for 10 minutes more. Let cool and reserve.
Sugar	to taste	
Nutmeg, grated	to taste	

Heavy cream	1 tbsp. per serving	To serve, reheat soup as needed. Float heavy cream on top of each serving.

Serve with a side dish of grated Parmesan cheese.

GAZPACHO— VERSION 1   *Spain*

Yield: 10–12 servings

Tomatoes, ripe	6 lbs.	Remove skins by plunging tomatoes into boiling water for a minute or until the skins split. Peel as soon as they are cool enough to handle. Remove the seeds and place pulp and juices in the bowl of a food processor.

Pepper, green, seeded, diced	8 oz.	Add these ingredients to tomato pulp and puree until very smooth.
Onion, diced	1 lb.	
Cucumber, peeled, seeded, diced	3 medium	
Garlic, minced	5–6 tsp.	
Olive oil	2 oz.	

Red wine vinegar	to taste	Season with vinegar, salt, and pepper and chill well before serving. Add tomato juice to reach desired consistency.
Salt and black pepper	to taste	
Tomato juice	if needed	

(Continued)

Croutons	as needed
Tomato, diced	as needed
Cucumber, diced	as needed
Onion, diced	as needed
Green seedless grapes (optional)	as needed

To serve, sauté bread cubes in a little olive oil that has been flavored with garlic.* Serve the croutons, diced vegetables, and grapes in separate dishes as a garnish for the soup. Chill soup and bowls well before serving.

* To prepare garlic croutons: Heat olive oil and sauté sliced cloves of garlic over low heat until the garlic turns golden. Remove garlic and sauté the bread cubes until they are lightly browned. Drain and reserve.

GAZPACHO— VERSION 2   *Spain*

Yield: 10–12 servings

This version of gazpacho is served hot.

Peppers, green, halved, seeded, stems removed	2 lbs.	Place peppers, cut side down, on a baking sheet. Place in a 450 degree F oven until skins begin to char. Remove from oven and cover for 10 minutes. Peel and discard the skins. Place the peppers in the bowl of a food processor.
Tomatoes, ripe	4 lbs.	Remove skins by plunging tomatoes into boiling water for a minute, or until the skin splits. Peel as soon as they are cool enough to handle. Discard the seeds, and then add the tomato pulp and the juices to the peppers.
Garlic, minced	1 tbsp.	Add these ingredients to the tomatoes and peppers and puree until very smooth. Reserve.
Olive oil	2 oz.	
Salt and black pepper	to taste	
Cayenne pepper	1/4 tsp.	

Bread	10–12 slices, one per serving	Sauté whole slices of French or Italian bread in olive oil until golden. Reserve.
Olive oil	as needed	

| Stock, chicken | as needed | To prepare an individual serving, bring stock to the boil. Place a crouton on bottom of a warm soup bowl. In a saucepan, combine the chicken stock with the reserved tomato/pepper mixture. The ratio should be about 2 parts stock to 1 part tomato/pepper mixture. Return to the boil and serve immediately. |

Peppers, green, peeled, roasted, julienned	as needed	Garnish with green peppers and parsley.
Parsley, fresh, chopped	as needed	

FISH

FISH FILLET "CHERMOULA"   *Morocco*

Yield: 10 servings

Fish fillets (sea bass, scrod, flounder)	4–5 lbs., in 6–7 oz. portions	Marinate the fillets in chermoula (see recipe in the "Condiments" section) for at least 4 hours.

Olive oil	as needed	To prepare an individual serving, heat the oil over medium heat. Remove fillet(s) from the chermoula and pat dry. Dredge in flour, shaking off any excess flour. Sauté on both sides, turning once, until golden brown on both sides.
Flour	as needed	

Coriander leaves, fresh, chopped	as needed	Serve with a sprinkling of coriander leaves and lemon wedges.
Lemon wedges	as needed	

FISH RAGOÛT WITH CORIANDER— VERSION 1   *Egypt*

Yield: 10 servings

Olive oil	as needed	Dredge the fish in flour, then sauté in olive oil until lightly browned. Transfer to a casserole and reserve.
Flour	as needed	
Fish fillet (any firm-fleshed white fish)	10 pieces, 7–8 oz. each	

Garlic	15 cloves	Crush the garlic together with the coriander and the salt. Sauté this mixture, using a little more oil if necessary, for 2 minutes over low heat.
Coriander, ground, or cumin	2 tsp.	
Salt	1 tsp.	
Olive oil	as needed	

(Continued)

Tomatoes, peeled, seeded, and chopped	5 lbs.
Salt and black pepper	to taste

Add tomatoes to the garlic mixture and cook for 10–15 minutes over medium heat. Season with salt and pepper. Pour this mixture over the fish and bake in a 350 degree F oven for 15–20 minutes.

Parsley, fresh, chopped, or coriander	as needed

Garnish with parsley or coriander.

FISH RAGOÛT— VERSION 2   *Egypt*

Yield: 10 servings

Olive oil	as needed
Flour	as needed
Fish fillet (cod or halibut)	10 pieces, 7–8 oz. each

Heat the oil over medium heat. Dredge the fish in flour, then sauté in olive oil until lightly browned. Transfer fish to a casserole and reserve.

White raisins	4 tbsp.
Onions, thin slice	3 lbs.
Tomatoes, diced	4 lbs.
Sugar	2 tsp.
Vinegar, wine	2 tsp.
Paprika, sweet	1 tsp.
Nutmeg	½ tsp.
Cinnamon	¼ tsp.
Salt and black pepper	to taste

In the same pan, sauté the raisins until they begin to puff, then remove from the pan and reserve. Add the onions and sauté until soft and lightly browned. Add the tomatoes, sugar, vinegar, and spices. Simmer for 30 minutes then season with salt and pepper.

Almonds, blanched	4 tbsp.

Cut almonds in half and toast them. Add the reserved raisins and the almonds to the tomato sauce and mix well. Pour over the fish and bake in a 350 degree F oven for 15–20 minutes. Serve the fillet surrounded by the tomato sauce.

Parsley, fresh, chopped	as needed	Garnish with parsley.

BAKED COD LISBON   *Portugal*   Yield: 10 servings

Sauce:

Olive oil	2 oz.	Over a moderate heat, sauté the onion, pepper, and garlic in olive oil until soft. Add the tomatoes, wine, bay leaves, and clove, and simmer, partially covered, for 45 minutes. Season with salt and black pepper. Remove bay leaves and reserve sauce.
Onion, diced	1 lb.	
Pepper, green, diced	8 oz.	
Garlic, minced	2 tsp.	
Tomatoes, ripe, peeled, chopped	4 lbs.	
White wine, dry	4 oz.	
Bay leaves	2	
Clove, ground	½ tsp.	
Salt and black pepper	to taste	

Fish fillet (cod or hake)	6–7 oz.	To prepare an individual serving, heat 3–4 oz. of sauce per serving in an individual, oven-proof baking dish. Place fish fillet on top and cover. Bake in a 400 degree F oven for 10–15 minutes, or until done. (Cooking time will vary, depending on the fillet's thickness.)

Peppers, green and red, roasted, peeled, julienned	as needed	Garnish with combination of julienned green and red peppers.

COD FILLET IN PAPRIKA AND MUSHROOM SAUCE   *Hungary*

Yield: 10 servings

Cod fillet	10, 6–8 oz. portions
Salt and white pepper	as needed
Bread crumbs	as needed

Salt and pepper the fish and roll in bread crumbs. Refrigerate.

Egg noodles, broad	1½ lbs.
Olive oil	as needed

Cook the noodles. When done, toss in a small amount of oil and reserve.

Slab bacon, small dice	6 oz.
Onion, diced	8 oz.
Paprika, Hungarian sweet	2 tbsp.
Stock, fish	12 oz.

In a large skillet, sauté the bacon until the fat begins to run. Add the onions and continue to sauté until the onions are soft. Add the paprika and cook for a minute. Add the fish stock and reduce by half.

Mushrooms, white, chopped	1½ lbs.
Sour cream	8 oz.
Green pepper, diced	4 oz.
Tomato, crushed	8 oz.
Parsley, chopped	5 sprigs
Salt and pepper	to taste

Add these ingredients and simmer for 20–30 minutes. Season with salt and pepper. Reserve.

Oil	as needed

To prepare an individual serving, fry a portion of the breaded fish on both sides in ¼ inch of oil until light brown. Do not cook through.

Sour cream	as needed
Parsley, minced	as needed

Put a bed of cooked noodles on an oiled individual, oven-proof serving dish. Place the fried fish on top and glaze with the paprika and mushroom sauce. Bake in a 400 degree F oven for 10–15 minutes or until golden brown. Garnish with sour cream and parsley.

For buffet service, any number of steaks can be prepared at the same time.

COD STEAMED IN BEER   *Belgium*

Yield: one serving

Onion, sliced, ⅛-inch-thick	2 slices
Butter, clarified	as needed

Sauté the onion in clarified butter until slightly brown.

Beer	4 oz.
Bay leaf	1 small
Salt and white pepper	pinch

Over high heat, add the beer, bay leaf, and a pinch of salt and white pepper. Boil for 1 minute.

Cod fillet	6 oz.
Salt and white pepper	as needed
Bread crumbs	as needed
Butter	as needed

Pour the onion/beer mixture into an individual, oven-proof dish. Place the cod fillet on top. Spoon some of the liquid on top of the fish, then sprinkle with bread crumbs. Dot the top of fish with butter and bake in a 400 degree F oven for 10–15 minutes, or until fish flakes easily. Remove the bay leaf before serving.

COD WITH TOMATOES AND OLIVES   *Southern France*

Yield: 10 servings

Although the recipe specifies fresh cod, this dish is traditionally made with salt cod. If using salt cod, cover it in water and soak for a least 24 hours. Change the water several times.

Sauce:

Olive oil	2 oz.	Heat the oil and sauté the leeks. When leeks are soft, add the garlic and sauté another minute over medium heat. Add the tomatoes, red pepper, olives, and capers and simmer for 30 minutes. Season with salt and pepper. Simmer for another 10 minutes. Let cool and reserve.
Leeks, white part only, washed, thin strips	1½ lbs.	
Garlic, chopped	1 tbsp.	
Tomatoes, plum, peeled, seeded, and chopped	3 lbs.	
Red pepper	1 tsp.	
Olives, Kalamata, pitted, chopped	20	
Capers	1 tbsp.	
Salt and black pepper	to taste	

Cod, fresh	6–7 oz. per serving	To prepare an individual serving, cut the cod into 1½-inch pieces. Dredge in flour and sauté in olive oil for 3–5 minutes per side, depending on thickness. Place a pool of tomato sauce on a warm plate. Place the cod on top of the sauce.
Flour	as needed	
Olive oil	as needed	

Parsley, fresh, chopped	as needed	Sprinkle with parsley and garnish with lemon wedges.
Lemon wedges	as needed	

PORTUGUESE FISH STEW   *Portugal*

Yield: 10–12 servings

Olive oil	2 oz.
Onion, diced	2 lbs.
Green pepper, seeded, diced	1 lb.
Garlic, minced	1 tbsp.
Tomatoes, crushed	2 lbs.

Over moderate to low heat, sauté the onion, pepper, and garlic until soft in the olive oil. Add the tomato and continue to cook for 10 minutes.

White wine	16 oz.
Stock, fish	16 oz.
Parsley, chopped	10 sprigs
Bay leaves	2
Salt and black pepper	to taste

Add these ingredients and simmer for 30 minutes. Season with salt and pepper. Let cool, remove bay leaves and reserve.

Fish fillets (cod, haddock, mackerel, tuna, or swordfish)*	3–4 oz.
Mussels, washed, debearded	4
Shrimp, medium, peeled, deveined	4

To prepare an individual serving, in a small pot, bring 5–6 oz. of the sauce to a boil. Lower heat to a simmer and add the fish fillets (which have been cut into three or four pieces). Simmer for several minutes, then add the mussels and shrimp. Cover and continue to simmer for several minutes or until the mussels have opened. Place in a large, heated bowl. Arrange the mussels and shrimp in an attractive pattern.

Coriander, fresh, chopped	as needed
Parsley, fresh, chopped	as needed

Garnish with coriander and parsley.

Serve with a good, toasted crusty bread.

---

* Cooking time should be adjusted according to variety and thickness of fish.

FILLET OF FLOUNDER WITH MUSHROOMS AND WINE *Southern France*

Yield: one serving

Olive oil	as needed
Flounder fillet	6–8 oz.
Flour	as needed

Heat the oil over moderate heat. Dredge fish fillet in flour and sauté on both sides until fish is lightly browned. Reserve in a warm place.

Olive oil	1 tbsp.
Onions, minced	1 tbsp.
Mushrooms, sliced	2 large
Garlic, minced	1 tsp.
Flour	1 tsp.

Wipe pan clean. Replace oil and sauté the onions, mushrooms, and garlic until the onions become soft. Add the flour, mix well, and continue to sauté for another minute or so.

White wine, dry	4 oz.
Clam juice	2 oz.
Heavy cream	2 oz.
Egg yolk	1 med.
Salt and white pepper	to taste
Lemon juice, fresh	to taste

Add the wine and deglaze the pan. Over high heat, reduce the liquid by half. Add the clam juice and heavy cream. Stir and simmer for a few minutes. Using a wire whisk, quickly stir in the egg yolk. Season with salt, pepper, and lemon juice and simmer for another minute. Adjust consistency with heavy cream, if necessary. Pour over fish.

Parsley, fresh, chopped	as needed

Garnish with parsley.

Serve with a medley of mixed vegetables.

FLOUNDER FILLETS WITH DILL *Russia*

Yield: 10 servings

Flounder fillets	4–5 lbs.

Select fillets that can be rolled and tied easily into 6–8 oz. portions.

Butter, clarified	as needed
Bread crumbs, fresh	2 cups
Parsley, flat, chopped	10 sprigs
Dill, fresh, chopped	equal in volume to the chopped parsley

Over medium heat, sauté the bread crumbs in the butter until crisp. Add parsley and dill and continue to sauté for another minute.

Butter, whole	as needed
Salt and white pepper	to taste

Add melted whole butter in sufficient quantity to bind the mixture. Season with salt and pepper.

Spread the bread crumb mixture over the fillets and roll up, starting with the tail end. Using butcher's twine, tie each fillet once around the middle. If you prefer, small skewers may be used instead. Fillets may be refrigerated at this point.

Sauce:

Flour	3 oz.
Butter	5 oz.
Stock, fish	16 oz.
Light cream	16 oz.
Dill, fresh, chopped	4 tbsp.
Lemon juice	to taste
Salt and white pepper	to taste
Egg yolks, beaten with 1 tbsp. water	2

Melt the butter and add flour to make a roux. Cook for 5–10 minutes, stirring, over low heat. Add stock and cream, stirring continuously, and cook over low heat until sauce begins to thicken. Season with dill, lemon juice, salt, and pepper. Simmer for 5 minutes. Remove from heat. Using a wire whisk, quickly beat in the the egg yolks. (This must be done very briskly or egg will coagulate.) Reserve.

Stock, fish	as needed

Poach fillets in fish stock for 3–5 minutes. Fillets may also be steamed over fish stock. Heat sauce through. Do not allow to boil. Remove fillets to a warm plate. Remove the string or skewers and ladle sauce around and over the fillets.

Serve with rice or boiled potatoes and a colorful medley of boiled or steamed vegetables.

FLOUNDER FILLET WITH TOMATOES AND ZUCCHINI   *Tunisia*

Yield: 10 servings

Sauce:

Olive oil	2 oz.
Onion, chopped	1 lb.
Garlic, chopped	1 tbsp.
Tomatoes, plum, halved	6 lbs.
Thyme, dried	1 tsp.
Rosemary, fresh	2 sprigs
Bay leaves	2
Harissa (see the recipe in the "Condiments" section)	1 tsp. or to taste
Salt and black pepper	to taste

Heat oil and sauté the onions until they are soft. Add the garlic and continue to cook for another minute. Add tomatoes to the onions along with the remainder of the ingredients. Cook over low heat for 30 minutes. Remove the bay leaves and the rosemary sprig. Put the remaining ingredients through a food mill to extract the pulp. Discard the tomato skins and seeds. Return the sauce to a very low heat. Season with the harissa, salt, and pepper. Cook for another 5 minutes. Let cool and reserve.

Olive oil	as needed
Flounder fillet	6–7 oz. each
Flour	as needed
Egg, beaten	as needed
Bread crumbs	as needed

To prepare an individual serving, heat the oil over moderate heat. Bread the fish using standard breading procedure (flour, beaten egg, bread crumbs). Fry in oil, turning once, until golden on both sides. Remove and place on towel to drain. Reserve in a warm place.

Zucchini, thin rounds	6–8 slices
Lemon juice, fresh	as needed
Reserved tomato sauce	as needed

In the same pan, quickly sauté the zucchini rounds until light brown on both sides. Add reserved tomato sauce, as needed, and heat through. Pour over fish and add a squeeze of lemon juice just before serving.

No garnish is necessary. Sautéed cubes of eggplant may be substituted for the zucchini or these vegetables may be used in combination.

FLOUNDER WITH SAUTÉED SHRIMP   *Sweden*

Yield: one serving

Flounder fillet	1, 6–7 oz.
Flour	as needed
Egg, beaten	as needed
Bread crumbs, fresh	as needed

Bread the fillet using standard breading procedure (flour, egg, then bread crumbs). Any number of fillets may be prepared in advance, then refrigerated, separated by waxed paper.

Butter, clarified	as needed

Fry the fillet for 2–3 minutes on each side. Transfer to heated plate.

Butter, whole	2 oz.
Shrimp, small	8–10
Lemon juice, fresh	1 tsp.
Parsley, fresh, chopped	1 tbsp.

Wipe pan. Add butter and, over medium heat, sauté cleaned shrimp for 1–2 minutes. Place in a line down the center of the fillet. Add lemon juice and parsley to pan and cook over high heat for just a few seconds. Pour over fillet.

Lemon wedges	as needed

Garnish with lemon wedges.

Serve with Swedish Browned Potatoes.

HALIBUT IN GREEN SAUCE   *Spain/Portugal*

Yield: 10 servings

Asparagus, tough ends removed	20 spears

Using a vegetable peeler, peel 1–2 inches of skin from the cut end. Wash thoroughly, then cook in boiling water until just done. Stalks should be slightly crisp. Plunge immediately into ice water and reserve.

(Continued)

Vegetable Stock:

Onion, diced	1 lb.
Carrot, peeled, sliced	8 oz.
Celery, diced	3 ribs
White wine, dry	16 oz.
Water	16 oz.
Salt	1 tsp.
White pepper	½ tsp.

In a soup pot, combine all ingredients and bring to a boil. Lower heat and simmer partially covered, for 45 minutes. Strain and discard vegetables. Reserve liquid.

Mussels	40
Stock, vegetable	

Remove beards and scrub. Bring stock to the boil and add the mussels. Cover pot and cook for a few minutes until the mussels open. Remove mussels and reserve. Decant stock to empty all sand and debris. Reserve.

Olive oil	as needed
Garlic, sliced	2 cloves
Halibut fillet	6–7 oz.
Flour	as needed

To prepare an individual serving, in a sauté pan, heat the oil over moderate heat and sauté garlic until golden. (Do not let garlic brown.) Mash with a fork to extract flavor and remove from pan. Dredge fish in flour and sauté on both sides until lightly browned.

Parsley and mint	2 tbsp.
Salt and white pepper	to taste

Add 4–5 oz. of stock, parsley, and mint. Simmer for 5 minutes, or until fish is no longer transparent inside. Remove fish to a hot platter. Bring pan liquid to a boil and reduce by half. Add 2 asparagus spears and 4 mussels to pan and toss in hot pan liquids just long enough to heat through. Garnish the fish fillet with the asparagus and mussels. Spoon pan liquids over all plated ingredients.

Accompany with a side dish of crisp, fried potatoes.

MARINATED MACKEREL FILLETS   *Southern France*

Yield: 10 servings

Mackerel fillets	4 lbs. (approx.)
Olive oil	as needed

Use mackerel that will yield 2 fillets per fish, weighing 6–7 oz. each. Remove skin and all bones. Wash fillets and pat dry. Brush with olive oil and sauté for a few minutes on each side. Place in a glass or stainless-steel pan in a single layer and cool.

Vinaigrette:

Olive oil	8 oz.
Red wine	3 oz.
Garlic, minced	2 tsp.
Onion, minced	2 tbsp.
Parsley, fresh, chopped	4 tbsp.
Capers	1 tbsp.
Salt	½ tsp.
Black pepper, coarse grind	1 tsp.
Sugar	½ tsp.
Mustard, dry	½ tsp.

Mix these ingredients together and pour over fish fillets. Cover and refrigerate for at least 4 hours before serving. Baste fish occasionally with the marinade.

Tomatoes, sliced	as needed
Cucumbers, sliced	as needed
Olives, black	as needed

Use these as garnish.

Serve cold, 1 fillet per serving, on a bed of lettuce as a warm weather entrée.
Slice fillets in smaller portions to serve as an appetizer. Garnish as directed.

BAKED MACKEREL IN CREAM   *Norway*

Yield: one serving

Mackerel fillet	6–8 oz.
Shallot, diced	1 tbsp.
Butter	1 tsp.
Salt and white pepper	as needed

If fillets are small, use 2 per serving. Sauté shallots in butter until soft. Transfer shallots to an individual, oval, baking dish. Salt and pepper fish and place on top of shallots. Bake for 10–15 minutes, depending on thickness of fillets, in 400 degree F oven.

Heavy cream	as needed
Paprika, sweet	as needed

Remove fish from oven. Add heavy cream to cover. Dust lightly with sweet paprika and return to oven for 10 minutes.

Parsley, fresh, chopped	as needed

Garnish with parsley.

Serve with broad egg noodles.

MUSSELS WITH PILAF   *Turkey*

Yield: 10–12 servings

Mussels	80–90
White wine, dry	12 oz.
Water	6 oz.
Oregano	1 tbsp.
Broth, clam, or fish stock	as needed

Scrub and debeard the mussels. Bring the wine, water, and oregano to a boil. Add the mussels, cover, and cook in a stainless-steel pot until the mussels open. Remove mussels and reserve with the shells. Decant the liquid and add enough clam broth or fish stock to make 1½ quarts of liquid. Reserve.

Olive oil	2 oz.
Onions, diced	2 lbs.
Rice, long-grain	1¾ lbs.
Tomatoes, plum, peeled, seeded, and chopped	1½ lbs.
Parsley leaves, chopped	4 tbsp.
Pine nuts	4 tbsp.
Currants	6 tbsp.

Heat the oil over moderate heat. Add the onions and sauté until they are soft. Add the rice and mix well. Sauté for a few minutes until the oil is absorbed by the rice. Add the tomatoes, parsley, pine nuts, and currants. Add the reserved stock and simmer, covered, until the rice is tender.

To serve, arrange the mussels that have been reheated quickly in hot fish stock or clam broth over a bed of the rice mixture. If using for buffet service, reheat mussels by adding them to the rice a few minutes before the rice has finished cooking. If rice is too dry, add a small amount of fish stock or clam broth.

MARINATED, GRILLED MONKFISH   *Spain*

Yield: 10–12 servings

Marinade:

Olive oil	8 oz.
Lemon juice, fresh	6 oz.
Thyme, fresh, chopped fine	2 tbsp.
Parsley, fresh, chopped fine	2 tbsp.
Salt and black pepper	½ tsp. each

Combine all ingredients for the marinade and mix thoroughly. Adjust oil or lemon juice to achieve a good balance of flavors.

Monkfish, 1½-inch cubes	4 lbs.

Place monkfish cubes in marinade, mix well, and refrigerate for 4 hours. Stir occasionally to redistribute the marinade.

Mushrooms caps	as needed
Pepper, green	as needed
Pepper, red	as needed

To prepare an individual serving, place 5–6 oz. per serving of monkfish cubes on a skewer, separated with mushroom caps or pieces of green or red pepper. Grill over charcoal or under broiler, 1–2 minutes per side. Brush fish with marinade once or twice while cooking.

(Continued)

Lemon wedges	as needed	Garnish with lemon wedges when serving.

Serve skewer on a bed of finely shredded mixed salad greens. Use arugula, radicchio, and escarole, along with any fresh herbs in season.

PORGIES WITH RED AND GREEN PEPPERS   *Spain*

Yield: 10 servings

Porgies, whole, gutted, gills, fins, and scales removed	10, ¾–1 lb. each	Wash the fish well. Make 3 diagonal incisions on both sides of each fish. Place fish in a glass pan or stainless-steel pan and add the lemon juice, oil, salt, and pepper to taste. Cover and refrigerate for 4 hours, turning fish occasionally.
Olive oil	2 oz.	
Lemon juice, fresh	8 oz.	

Olive oil	3 oz.	Over moderate heat, sauté in the oil the onions, garlic, and peppers until soft. Add the tomatoes, bay leaf, and thyme, and simmer for 30 minutes. Season with salt and pepper. Reserve.
Onion, diced	1 lb.	
Garlic, minced	1 tbsp.	
Peppers, sweet red, sliced thin	1 lb.	
Peppers, green, sliced thin	1 lb.	
Tomatoes, crushed	2 lbs.	
Bay leaf	2–3	
Thyme, dried	2 tsp.	
Salt and black pepper	to taste	

Olive oil	as needed	To prepare an individual serving, put 4–5 oz. per serving of sauce on the bottom of an individual, oven-proof serving dish. Place 1 porgy on top. Pour a small amount of olive oil on the fish and sprinkle with salt and pepper. Cover and bake in a 375 degree F oven for 10 minutes.
Salt and black pepper	as needed	

| Brandy | 2 oz. | Remove cover, add brandy, and bake for another 8–10 minutes, or until fish is done. |

| Lemons, thin sliced | as needed | Garnish with overlapping slices of lemon and parsley sprigs. |
| Parsley sprigs | as needed | |

Serve with rice.

POACHED SALMON WITH LEEKS   *Austria*

Yield: one serving

Carrots, julienned	2 oz.	Bring stock to a boil. Cook vegetables until barely tender. Remove vegetables, cover, and reserve in warm place.
Celery, julienned	1 oz.	
Stock, fish	8 oz.	

| Salmon steak | 6–8 oz. | Using a small sauté pan, pour boiling stock over fish and place in 400 degree F oven for 5–10 minutes, depending on thickness of fish and how well-done it should be. |

| Leek, julienned | 2 oz. | Sauté leek in clarified butter over high heat until slightly brown. On a very hot plate, place blanched vegetables, topped with fish fillet or steak. Place sautéed leek on top of fish and a small amount of the hot pan liquid. |
| Butter, clarified | as needed | |

| Watercress, sprigs | as needed | Garnish with watercress. |

Serve with small roasted potatoes. Hollandaise sauce or fresh lemon may be served on the side.

WHOLE FISH IN TOMATO AND GINGER   *Morocco*

Yield: 10 servings

Whole fish (porgy, croaker, or sea bass), gutted, gills, fins, and scales removed	10, ¾–1 lb. each
Chermoula (see the recipe in the "Condiments" section)	as needed

Wash the fish thoroughly, then pat dry. Slash each side diagonally 2 or 3 times, depending on size of fish. Rub each fish well with chermoula. Cover and refrigerate for 4 hours.

Sauce:

Tomatoes, peeled, seeded, and chopped	6 lbs.
Olive oil	4 oz.
Ginger root, minced	1 tbsp.
Garlic, minced	1 tbsp.
Cayenne pepper	½ tsp.
Parsley leaves, flat, chopped	10–12 tbsp.
Olives, green, pitted, halved	4 oz.
Chermoula	6–8 tbsp.

Combine these ingredients in heavy-bottomed saucepan and simmer for 30–40 minutes.

Olive oil	as needed
Lemon, thin sliced	as needed

Lightly oil the bottom of an individual, oven-proof serving dish large enough to hold a single fish. Then add a light layer of the reserved tomato sauce. Place the fish on top and spoon on a bit more of the tomato sauce. Arrange lemon slices in an overlapping row down the center of the fish. Cover and bake in a 400 degree F oven for 20 minutes, or until done.

SALMON WITH HERB SAUCE AND VEGETABLES
Northern France

Yield: 10 servings

Eggplant, ½-inch dice	1½ lbs.	Lightly salt eggplant and let stand, weighted, for 1 hour. Dry with towel and sauté in olive oil until brown.
Salt	as needed	
Olive oil	as needed	

Tomatoes, peeled, seeded, and chopped	3 lbs.	Mix with eggplant and reserve.

Herb Sauce:

Egg yolks	2 large	Beat egg yolks together with the salt and pepper. Slowly add the olive oil, beating continuously, until mixture is thick. Add fresh herbs and lemon juice. Adjust lemon, salt, and pepper. Reserve.
Salt	1 tsp.	
White pepper	½ tsp.	
Olive oil, virgin	16 oz.	
Tarragon, basil, or oregano, fresh, chopped fine	2 oz. or to taste	
Lemon juice	to taste	

Salmon steak	10, 6 oz. each	To prepare an individual serving, in an individual, oven-proof serving dish, place a layer of the eggplant and tomato mixture to cover. Place 1 salmon steak with a small piece of butter on top. Season with salt and pepper to taste. Add 2 oz. of white wine or fish stock and cover with foil.* Place in 450 degree F oven for 8–12 minutes, depending on thickness of steak. When done, place large dollop of herb sauce on top. Additional sauce may be served on the side.
Butter	as needed	
Salt and white pepper	to taste	
White wine or fish stock	as needed	

---

* If prepared in advance to this point and refrigerated, bring to room temperature before cooking. Otherwise, adjust cooking time to allow for chilled product.

FRESH SARDINES
Southern Italy

Yield: 10 servings

Sauce:

Tomatoes, plum	3–3½ lbs.	Plunge tomatoes into boiling water for a minute, or until the skins begin to split. When cool enough to handle, remove skins and seeds. Place the tomatoes in the bowl of a food processor along with the other ingredients and puree. Reserve.
Garlic, minced	3 tsp.	
Olive oil	4 oz.	
Italian parsley leaves	20 sprigs	
Salt and black pepper	to taste	

Sardines, fresh, gutted, heads and tails removed, filleted	6–7 oz. per serving	To prepare an individual serving, arrange 6–7 oz. of the sardiness (the number of fish will vary, depending on size) in an individual, oven-proof serving dish. Cover sardines with approximately 3 oz. of the tomato sauce and bake in a 400 degree F oven for 10–15 minutes.

May be baked in quantity for buffet service. Serve hot or at room temperature.

GRILLED SARDINES WRAPPED IN GRAPE LEAVES   *Southern France*

Yield: 10 servings

Thyme	1 tbsp.	Mix herbs together and crush to a fine consistency. If using fresh herbs, chop fine and triple the quantity. Add the salt and pepper and blend thoroughly.
Oregano	1 tbsp.	
Marjoram	1 tbsp.	
Salt and black pepper	1 tsp. each	

Sardines, fresh, gutted, heads and tails removed, filleted	7 lbs.	Place the sardines in a glass pan or stainless-steel pan and sprinkle generously with olive oil, then with the herb mixture. Turn fish to coat well. Cover and refrigerate for 2–3 hours.
Olive oil	as needed	

Grape leaves	as needed
Lemon halves	as needed
Olive oil	as needed

To prepare an individual serving, use 6–8 oz. (3–5 fish) per serving. Wrap each fish in 1 or 2 grape leaves. Place the leaves glossy side down and remove any stems. Position the fish at the leaf's stem end and roll toward the tip. Place the fish, open seam facing down, on a fish grill. Close the grill and place over hot coals for approximately 2 minutes per side, or until the grape leaves begin to char. Serve with lemon halves and olive oil.

To use as an appetizer, serve smaller portion sizes.

SCALLOPS IN CREAM AND SAFFRON   *Southern France*

Yield: one serving

Scallops, cleaned	6–7 oz.

If scallops are large, slice in half or thirds so that you have 2 or 3 thinner disks per scallop. Reserve.

Butter	1 tsp.
Garlic, minced	½ tsp.
Stock, fish	2 oz.
Heavy cream	4 oz.
Saffron	pinch
Salt and white pepper	to taste

Heat butter in a skillet large enough to hold the scallops. Sauté the garlic until just soft, then add the fish stock, heavy cream, and saffron. Simmer until the liquids begin to thicken and turns a rich, yellow color. Season with salt and pepper.

Add the scallops and simmer, covered, until the scallops are cooked through. Do not overcook.

Parsley, fresh, chopped	as needed

Garnish with parsley.

Serve on a bed of noodles.

SCALLOPS WITH HAM   *Southern Italy*

Yield: 10 servings

Olive oil	3 oz.
Onion, chopped	8 oz.
Garlic, minced	3 tsp.
Prosciutto, thin sliced, chopped	4 oz.
White wine	12 oz.

Heat oil; over low heat, sauté the onion and garlic until they are soft. Add the prosciutto and continue to cook for another minute. Add the wine and simmer for 5 minutes.

Bread crumbs	as needed
Parsley, chopped	3 tbsp.
Salt and white pepper	to taste

Remove wine mixture from heat. Add enough bread crumbs to absorb the liquid. Season with parsley, salt, and pepper. Reserve.

Butter, whole	as needed
Scallops	6–7 oz. per serving
White wine	as needed
Lemon juice, fresh	as needed

Place scallops in a large, buttered scallop shell or an individual, oven-proof dish. Cover scallops with bread crumb mixture, dot with butter, and add a small amount of wine to the dish. Bake in a 400 degree F oven for 8–10 minutes, depending on the scallops' size. Just prior to serving, top with a small amount of lemon juice.

Lemon wedges	as needed
Parsley, fresh, chopped	as needed

Garnish with lemon wedges and a sprinkling of parsley.

This entrée may be used in smaller portions as an appetizer.

CURRIED SHRIMP   *Portugal*   Yield: 10 servings

Sauce:

Butter, whole	4 oz.	Melt butter over medium heat. Add onions, red pepper, and garlic and sauté until soft. Do not allow to brown. Add the flour and incorporate thoroughly. Add the curry powder and continue to cook, stirring, for another minute.
Onions, small dice	1½ lbs.	
Pepper, red sweet, cored, diced	1 lb.	
Garlic, minced	1 tsp.	
Flour	3 tbsp.	Slowly add the fish stock and cream, stirring, and bring to a boil. Lower heat and simmer for 20–30 minutes. Season with salt and pepper. Let cool and reserve.
Curry powder	1½ tbsp.	
Stock, fish	20 oz.	
Light cream	12 oz.	
Salt and white pepper	to taste	

Shrimp, cleaned, de-veined, butterflied	5–6 oz. per serving (Number used will depend on size.)	To prepare an individual serving, heat 4–5 oz. per serving of sauce to the simmer, then add shrimp, incorporating them into sauce. Cook for several minutes, or until the shrimp are no longer translucent.

Serve on a bed of rice and accompany with a mixed green salad.

BROILED SHRIMP WITH TARRAGON   *Northern France*   Yield: one serving

Shrimp or small lobster tails (use 4 oz., not counting shells)	5 large	Slice shrimp lengthwise, leaving shell halves on. Devein and arrange on an oven-proof serving dish, shell side down.

(Continued)

Butter, room temperature	4 oz.
Tarragon	½ tsp.
Garlic, minced	1 sm. clove
Parsley, chopped	2 tsp.
Chives, chopped	½ tsp.
Salt and white pepper	to taste

Add together all ingredients and mix well. Spread enough of the butter mixture to cover each shrimp half.

Bread crumbs	as needed
Butter, clarified	as needed
Tomato halves	as needed

Sauté bread crumbs in butter. Sprinkle over buttered shrimp and broil for 2–3 minutes, or until shrimp are done. Do not over cook. Arrange shrimp around a large, grilled tomato half over which the melted herb butter has been poured

SHRIMP WITH OLIVES AND FETA CHEESE   *Greece*

Yield: 10 servings

Olive oil	2 oz.
Onion, diced	1 lb.
Green pepper, small dice	8 oz.
Carrot, diced	8 oz.

Heat oil and sauté the onion over medium heat until soft. Add the green pepper and carrot and continue to sauté for a few more minutes.

Tomatoes, crushed	2 lbs.
Stock, fish	6 oz.
Basil leaves, chopped	4 tbsp.

Add the tomatoes, fish stock, and basil and simmer for 20 minutes.

Kalamata olives, seeded, coarsely chopped	20
Salt and black pepper	to taste

Add olives and parsley. Simmer for 10 minutes. Season with salt and pepper. Let cool and reserve.

Shrimp, peeled, de-veined, butterflied	5–6 oz. per serving
Feta cheese, crumbled	2 tbsp. per serving
Olive oil	as needed

To prepare an individual serving, heat tomato sauce and pour 3–4 oz. in the bottom of an individual, oven-proof casserole. Arrange shrimp in an attractive pattern on top of the sauce. Sprinkle the crumbled feta cheese on top, along with a few drops of olive oil. Cover with foil and bake in a 400 degree F oven for 10 minutes, or until the shrimp are done. Do not overcook.

Serve in the casserole. Accompany with cucumber, tomato, and onion salad with a simple oil and vinegar dressing. If served as an appetizer, adjust portion size, prepare in a sauté pan, and serve on a plate along with other appetizers. Can be served at room temperature.

STUFFED SQUID IN WHITE WINE   *Northern Italy*

Yield: 10 servings

Squid, approx. 6 inches in length, excluding tentacles, head, viscera, ink sac removed	20

Cut off the tentacles just above the eyes and reserve. Remove the transparent backbone and any other material from inside the body. Wash under running water, peeling off the purple skin.

Bread crumbs	1 lb.
Oregano	2 tsp.
Parsley, chopped fine	8 tbsp.
Garlic, chopped fine	4 cloves
Eggs	3
Parmesan cheese, grated	6 oz.
Olive oil	3 oz.
Salt and white pepper	to taste

Thoroughly mix all ingredients and season with salt and pepper. Chop tentacles and add to mixture. Stuff squid and close open ends with small skewers or toothpicks. Do not overstuff.

(Continued)

Olive oil	6 oz.
Onion, small dice	2 lb.
Garlic, minced	3 lg. cloves
White wine	16 oz.
Tomatoes, crushed	2 lbs.

In a braising pan, heat oil, add onion and garlic, and cook over low heat until they are soft. Add wine and tomatoes and bring to a boil. Lower to a simmer and cook for 15–20 minutes.

Olive oil	as needed

In a separate pan sauté the stuffed squid lightly in olive oil, turning once. Place squid in simmering sauce and cook for 15–20 minutes, or until tender. Serve whole or sliced in rings and fanned out on the plate with the tomato sauce under the squid.

May also be served cut in rings and presented on a bed of spaghetti or linguine. If prepared in advance and cooled, reheat the squid in fish stock in the oven at low heat. Overcooking will toughen the squid. Reheat the sauce separately and combine the two when serving.

SQUID IN BLACK INK SAUCE   *Southern Italy*

Yield: 10 servings

Squid, head, viscera removed	5 lbs.

Cut off the tentacles just above the eyes and reserve. Squeeze out the beak at the base and discard. Reserve the ink sac. Remove the transparent backbone and any other material from inside the body. Wash under running water, peeling off the purple skin. Cut into rings ½-inch thick. Reserve.

White bread, crusts removed	5 slices
Garlic, peeled	10–12 medium cloves
Almonds, whole	8 oz.
Parsley, fresh, chopped	6 tbsp.

Soak the bread in water and squeeze it partially dry. Place the garlic, almonds, parsley, and bread in the bowl of a food processor and puree to a smooth paste. Add a few tablespoons of water, if necessary. Reserve.

Olive oil	6 oz.
White wine, dry	16 oz.
Stock, fish	24 oz.

Heat the oil in a heavy saucepan large enough to hold the reserved squid. Sauté the garlic/almond paste, stirring for 2 minutes. Add the squid and tentacles and sauté for another minute, then add the wine and fish stock. Simmer for 30–40 minutes.

Squid ink	
Salt and white pepper	to taste

Place the reserved ink sacs in a strainer held over a bowl. Mash the sacs to extract the ink. Add the ink to the sauce and bring to a boil. Season with salt and pepper and simmer for 10–15 minutes more.

Carrots, blanched, julienned	as needed
Scallions, blanched, julienned	as needed

Garnish with carrots and scallions.

Serve with rice or over pasta.

SQUID STEWED IN WINE AND TOMATO SAUCE   *Spain*

Yield: 10 servings

Squid, head, viscera, ink sac removed	5 lbs.

Cut off the tentacles just above the eyes and reserve. Squeeze out the beak at the base and discard. Remove the transparent backbone and any other material from inside the body. Wash under running water, peeling off the purple skin. Cut into rings ½-inch thick. Reserve.

Olive oil	4 oz.
Onion, diced	1½ lbs.
Garlic, minced	1 tbsp.
Parsley, fresh, chopped	6 tbsp.

Heat the oil and sauté the onion until soft. Add the garlic and parsley and continue to cook for 2 minutes more. Add the reserved squid and tentacles, and sauté over high heat for another minute.

(Continued)

Red wine	16 oz.	Add the wine and tomatoes. Season with salt and pepper. Lower heat, cover, and simmer partially covered for 45 minutes to 1 hour. Stir from time to time. Add wine if more liquid is needed.
Tomatoes, plum, peeled, seeded, and chopped fine	2 lbs.	
Salt and black pepper	to taste	

Serve in heated bowls and accompany with garlic toast.

SWORDFISH ON SKEWERS WITH SOUR CREAM   *Russia*

Yield: 10 servings

Marinade:

Sour cream	2 lbs.	Mix these ingredients well and set aside.
Lemon juice, fresh	4 oz.	
Parsley, chopped	4 oz.	
White peppercorns, coarsely cracked	2 tsp.	
Salt	to taste	

Swordfish, cut in 1½-inch cubes	4 lbs.	Put 6 oz. of fish on each skewer. Place the skewers in a nonmetallic pan and add the marinade. Thoroughly coat the fish. Refrigerate for 2–3 hours.

Butter, clarified	as needed	Broil or bake in a 450 degree F oven until fish is firm but has retained moist, slightly underdone centers. Top with a few drops of clarified butter just prior to serving and a generous dollop of the marinade, heated to just below boiling.
Parsley, chopped	as needed	

Lemon wedges	as needed	Garnish with lemon wedges and scallions, both white and green parts.
Scallions, chopped	as needed	

Serve with buttered kasha or other whole grains such as brown rice or pearl barley.

POACHED TROUT WITH WALNUT SAUCE   *Caucasus*

Yield: one serving

Sauce:

Walnuts, shelled	1 lb.	
Garlic, chopped	1 tsp.	
Lemon juice, fresh	4 oz.	
Mint leaves, fresh	¾ cup, loosely packed	
Olive oil	4 oz.	
Salt and white pepper	to taste	

Place all ingredients in a food processor and process until very smooth. Adjust seasonings to taste. Consistency should be somewhat thick, as it will be diluted with fish stock just prior to serving. If it is too thick, add a combination of oil and lemon juice. If it is too thin, add more nuts. (This recipe is sufficient for 10 servings.)

Trout, cleaned, filleted, head and tail on	1, 8–10 oz.

Bring the fish stock to a boil. Pour over fish, cover immediately and place in 325 degree F oven for 10–15 minutes, depending on the fish's thickness.

Stock, fish	as needed

Heat the walnut sauce with enough fish stock to make a sauce of desired consistency. Pour over fish and serve.

Parsley, fresh, chopped	as needed
Walnuts, chopped	as needed
Lemons, sliced	as needed

Garnish with parsley, a sprinkling of walnuts, and a lemon slice.

To serve cold: Use same method to cook the fish. (Any number may be done at the same time.) Let the fish cool in stock before refrigerating. Mix the sauce with fish stock to desired consistency and heat through, then refrigerate. Bring to room temperature before serving. For buffet service, split the fish and remove heads and tails prior to poaching. Use the same garnish and serve cold, with extra sauce on the side.

SAUTÉED TROUT WITH A SOUR CREAM/LEMON-DILL SAUCE   *Germany*

Yield: one serving

Trout, whole, filleted	8–10 oz.
Flour	as needed
Butter, clarified	as needed

Dredge the fish in flour. Shake off any excess. Heat butter and sauté the fish over medium heat for 3–4 minutes on each side. Transfer to heated plate and keep warm.

Butter, whole	1 oz.
Sour cream	4 tbsp.
Dill, fresh	1 tbsp. or as needed
Lemon juice, fresh	1 tsp.
Salt and white pepper	to taste

Wipe pan. Add whole butter and heat over low heat. Add dill and cook for 1 minute, then add sour cream. Cook for 2–3 minutes. (Do not boil.) Add lemon juice, stir well, and season with salt and pepper. Heat through and pour sauce over fish.

Lemon, sliced	as needed

Garnish with dill and lemon slice.

Accompany with steamed cauliflower florets sautéed briefly in clarified butter, chopped, fresh dill, and bread crumbs.

TROUT WITH HAM   *Spain*

Yield: one serving

Trout, filleted, head and tail on	8–10 oz.
Milk	as needed
Cornmeal	as needed
Salt and white pepper	as needed

Wash trout and pat dry. Dip fish in milk, then dredge in cornmeal, salt, and pepper. Reserve.

Slab bacon, rind off, diced	2 oz.

In a skillet large enough to hold the fish, render the fat from the bacon. Remove bacon pieces from pan and reserve.

Sauté the trout in bacon fat for 2–3 minutes on each side, or until done. Transfer the fish to a warm plate.

Proscuitto, diced	1 oz.
Onion, diced	2 tbsp.
Red wine vinegar	3 tbsp.

Pour off excess fat. Over medium to high heat, quickly sauté the ham, onion, and reserved bacon bits. (Garnish the fish with these ingredients.) Add vinegar to the pan and raise heat to high. When boiling, pour over fish.

Parsley, fresh, chopped	as needed

Sprinkle with parsley.

TUNA WITH FRESH TOMATO AND ANCHOVY SAUCE   *Southern Italy*

Yield: 10 servings

Sauce:

Olive oil	3 oz.
Onions, small dice	8 oz.
Garlic, minced	2 tsp.
Tomatoes, plum, peeled, seeded, and crushed	3½ lbs.
Anchovies, mashed	5–6 fillets

Heat oil over moderate heat. Sauté the onions until soft and slightly colored. Add the garlic and sauté for another minute. Add the tomatoes and simmer for 20 minutes. Add the anchovies and simmer for another 10–15 minutes. Let cool and reserve.

Bread crumbs	10–12 oz.
Red pepper flakes	1 tbsp.
Salt	½ tsp.
Black pepper	1 tsp.

Combine these ingredients, mix well, and reserve.

Olive oil	as needed
Tuna, fresh	6 oz.

To prepare an individual serving, brush each side of the tuna generously with olive oil, then dredge in the bread crumb mixture. Place 4–5 oz. of the reserved tomato sauce on the bottom of an individual, oven-proof casserole. Place the tuna on top and bake in a 400 degree F oven for 7–10 minutes, or until done.

(Continued)

Parsley, fresh, chopped	as needed	Garnish with lemon slices and parsley.
Lemons, sliced	as needed	

TUNA STEAKS *Portugal*   Yield: 10 servings

Marinade:

Garlic, minced	2 tbsp.	Combine these ingredients and mix thoroughly.
Coriander, fresh, chopped fine	6 tbsp.	
Italian parsley, fresh, chopped fine	6 tbsp.	
Olive oil	6 oz.	
White wine, dry	12 oz.	
Lemon juice, fresh	2 oz.	
Salt	1 tsp.	
Black pepper, coarse ground	1½ tsp.	
Tuna steaks ½- to ¾-inch thick	6 oz. each	Pour half of the marinade into a nonmetallic or stainless-steel pan. Place the tuna steaks on top in a single layer. Add the remaining marinade, cover tightly, and refrigerate overnight.
Olive oil	as needed	Brush steaks, 1 per serving, with olive oil. Grill or pan-fry for 2–3 minutes per side. Do not overcook. Fish should remain a bit rare in the center. Place fish on a warm platter and spoon a little olive oil on top.
Coriander leaves, fresh, chopped	as needed	Garnish with coriander leaves, almonds, and lemon slices.
Almonds, toasted, sliced	as needed	
Lemons, sliced	as needed	

POULTRY

CHICKEN SIMMERED IN BEER   *Northern France*

Yield: 10 servings

Chicken breast, boned and skinned	10, 5–6 oz. pieces	Heat the oil and butter over low heat and lightly brown the chicken. Remove and keep warm.
Peanut oil	2 oz.	
Butter	2 oz.	
Onions, diced	2 lb.	Add the onions and garlic to the pan and cook over low heat until soft.
Garlic, minced	2 tsp.	
Flour	4 tbsp.	Sprinkle flour over onions and garlic and mix well. Cook over low heat for 5 minutes.
Beer	16 oz.	Add beer and deglaze pan. Return chicken to pan.
Thyme	1 tsp.	Add seasonings and simmer, covered, for 20 minutes. Remove chicken breasts and keep in warm place. Over high heat, reduce liquid by half.
Bay leaf	2 large	
Salt and white pepper	to taste	
Sugar	1 tbsp.	
Mushroom caps	2 lbs.	Sauté caps in clarified butter. Return chicken breasts to reduced liquid and heat through.
Butter, clarified	as needed	
Parsley, fresh, chopped	as needed	Garnish with mushroom caps and parsley.

Serve on a bed of buttered rice with an accompaniment of steamed butternut squash.

BREAST OF CHICKEN WITH CAMEMBERT   *Northern France*

Yield: one serving

Chicken breast, butterflied	1, 5–6 oz.
Camembert cheese	as needed
Salt and white pepper	to taste
Flour	as needed
Egg, beaten	as needed
Bread crumbs	as needed

Salt and pepper the breast. Cover half the breast with a piece of Camembert cheese ¼-inch-thick. Fold other half of breast over the cheese. Dip first in flour, then egg, then bread crumbs.

Butter, clarified	as needed

Over medium heat, sauté the breast on one side until brown. Turn, drain excess fat, and finish in a 400 degree F oven for 5–8 minutes, or until the chicken is done. Alternate method: Sauté on both sides until cooked through.

CHICKEN WITH CORIANDER   *Algeria*

Yield: 10 servings

Chickens	5, 2 lbs. each

Split each chicken down the backbone. Remove excess fat and skin; trim ¼-inch of bone from the ends of the drumsticks.

Olive oil	6 oz.
Aniseed, ground	1 tbsp.
Salt	2 tsp.
Black pepper	2 tbsp.

Mix these ingredients together, then rub over all the chicken's surface. Cover and refrigerate for several hours.

Stock, chicken	4 oz.
Saffron threads	¾ tsp.

Heat 4 ounces of chicken stock and add the saffron threads. Let steep for 20–30 minutes.

Stock, chicken	as needed
Coriander leaves, chopped	6 tbsp.

In a heavy skillet, sauté the chicken on all sides until browned. Transfer to a shallow roasting pan. Deglaze the skillet with the chicken/saffron stock. Add stock, along with the chopped coriander leaves and enough additional chicken stock to just cover, to the roasting pan. Cover pan and place in a 350 degree F oven for 30 minutes. Remove cover and cook for another 15 minutes. Remove chicken and reserve in a warm place. Strain, degrease, and reduce pan liquids until they begin to thicken.

Scallions, julienned	as needed
Coriander leaves, chopped	as needed
Lemon wedges	as needed

Garnish with scallions, coriander, and lemon wedges.

Serve with a puree of celeriac and potatoes.

CHICKEN BREASTS WITH EGG CRÊPE   *Morocco*

Yield: 10 servings

Butter	2 oz.
Onion, small dice	2 lbs.
Garlic, minced	1 tbsp.
Ginger root, grated	2 tsp.
Saffron threads	1 tsp.
Black pepper	1 tsp.
Stock, chicken	1½ qts.
Salt	to taste

In a saucepan large enough to hold the chicken breasts, melt the butter and sauté the onion and garlic over low heat until soft. Add the ginger root, saffron, and black pepper and continue to cook for another minute. Add the chicken stock and simmer for 20–30 minutes. Season with salt.

Chicken breasts, skin off, bone out	10, 6–7 oz. portions

Add the chicken breasts, cover pot, and poach very gently for 15–20 minutes, or until tender. Do not overcook. Remove breasts and reserve. Reduce pan liquids until thickened and reserve.

(Continued)

Butter	as needed	To prepare an individual portion, heat a 50/50 mixture of butter and oil that is approximately ¼-inch-deep in a small skillet. Over medium to high heat, sauté one poached chicken breast on both sides until it is golden.
Oil	as needed	

Olive oil	as needed	Heat the oil over medium heat in a nonstick or well-seasoned omelette pan. Combine all ingredients with the beaten egg. Pour into pan, lifting the sides of the set egg and tilting the pan to make a thin crêpe.
Egg, beaten	1	
Paprika	½ tsp.	
Cumin	⅛ tsp.	
Parsley leaves, fresh, chopped	1 tbsp.	Place sautéed chicken breast in the center of a warm plate. Spoon some of the reserved sauce over the chicken. Drape the chicken with the egg crêpe and spoon a little more of the sauce on top.
Salt and black pepper	to taste	

Almonds, toasted, sliced	as needed	Garnish with almonds.

CHICKEN WITH KOHLRABI   *Ukraine*

Yield: one serving

Kohlrabi*	1, approx. 2 inches in diameter	Peel and slice ⅛ inch thick. Cook in salted, boiling water until just barely tender. Place in ice water and reserve.

Chicken breast, skin off, boned	6 oz.	Flatten the breast a little between sheets of waxed paper and sauté in butter on both sides until lightly browned. Remove from pan and reserve in a warm place.
Butter, clarified	2 oz.	

Flour	1 tsp.	In same pan, add flour and paprika and cook for a minute or so, stirring with a wire whisk.
Paprika	1 tsp.	

* If the leaves are very fresh and have good color, shred and steam them at the same time and use as a garnish. A small quantity may be added to the sauce for added color and texture. Any number of kohlrabi can be prepared in advance.

Stock, chicken	4 oz.
Garlic, crushed	¼ tsp.

Add stock and garlic and incorporate thoroughly. Return chicken to pan and add the slices of kohlrabi. Simmer over low heat until chicken is cooked through and the sauce begins to thicken slightly.

Sour cream	1 tbsp.
Salt and white pepper	to taste

Add sour cream, salt, and white pepper and heat through. Adjust seasonings.

Serve with potato dumplings and a dandelion salad garnished with chopped hard-boiled egg and an oil, vinegar, and chopped, fresh dill dressing.

CHICKEN KIEV   *Russia*   Yield: 10 servings

Butter*	5 oz.

Divide into 10 sticks approximately 3 inches by ½ inch by ½ inch, weighing ½ oz. Place on a sheet of waxed paper, keeping pieces separate, and freeze until needed.

Chicken breasts, boned, skin off	10 whole, 10–12 oz.
Salt and white pepper	to taste

Split breasts down the middle. Remove the fillets. Place breasts and fillets between sheets of waxed paper and pound with a mallet or heavy cleaver until the breast meat is a uniform ⅛-inch-thick. Be careful not to tear meat. Pound edges of the larger pieces a bit thinner. Lightly salt and pepper each piece.

Place 1 piece of frozen butter on each of the larger pieces of chicken. Cover the butter with the fillets. Fold the smaller sides of the bottom piece of chicken over the fillet sections. Roll up, starting at the narrow end and refrigerate, seam side down, for 1 hour.

(Continued)

* For interesting variations, garlic, fresh herbs, or finely chopped cashew nuts may be mixed with the butter prior to freezing.

Flour	as needed
Egg, beaten	as needed
Bread, coarse crumb	as needed

Dredge chicken in flour, then dip in egg and roll in bread crumbs. Place in refrigerator until needed.

Deep-fry for 6–8 minutes in 350 degree F oil. For large quantities, hold finished pieces in warm oven after deep-frying. This preparation is best, however, when served immediately after deep-frying.

Tomato, fresh, sliced	as needed

Garnish with tomato slices.

Serve with buttered, fresh green peas and matchstick potatoes or thin potato pancakes.

FOUR DIFFERENT WAYS TO MARINATE CHICKEN   *Egypt*

Yield: 10 servings

Version 1:

Yogurt	4 oz.
Garlic puree	1 tsp.
Mustard powder	1 tsp.
Tumeric	1 tsp.
Cardamom, ground	½ tsp.
Curry powder	1 tsp.
Lemon juice	2 oz.
Vinegar, wine	2 tsp.

Combine these ingredients and reserve.

Version 2:

Onions, grated	1½ lbs.	Combine these ingredients and reserve.
Olive oil	2 oz.	
Oregano	2 tbsp.	
Lemon juice	2 tbsp.	
Garlic, puree	1 tsp.	
Mustard powder	1 tsp.	
White pepper	½ tsp.	

Version 3:

Onions, grated	1½ lbs.	Combine these ingredients and reserve.
Lemon zest	2 tbsp.	
Olive oil	2 oz.	
Rosemary leaves, fresh, chopped	2 tbsp.	
White pepper	½ tsp.	

Version 4:

Onions, grated	1½ lbs.	Combine these ingredients and reserve.
Orange rind, grated	4 tbsp.	
Orange juice	12 oz.	
Olive oil	2 oz.	

These marinades can be used for grilled or fried chicken parts or deboned chicken meat.

MARINATED CHICKEN GRILLED ON SKEWERS   *Egypt*

Yield: 10 servings

Chicken breast, meat only	4–4½ lbs.	Cut breast meat into 1-inch-square pieces. Toss well in marinade version 1. Cover and marinate for 3–4 hours in the refrigerator.

Onion, sliced	as needed	Thread the chicken on skewers, alternating 2 pieces of chicken with 1 piece of onion or tomato. Grill slowly over coals or under the broiler. Brush frequently with the marinade.
Tomatoes, small halves	as needed	

Mint, fresh	as needed	When serving, garnish with mint.

Serve with an assortment of fresh salad vegetables.

GRILLED CHICKENS MARINATED IN LEMON AND GARLIC   *Egypt*

Yield: 10 servings

Marinade:

Onion puree	8 oz.	Using a food processor, puree the onion until almost liquid. Add the remaining ingredients and, using pulsing action, mix thoroughly. Reserve.
Olive oil	8 oz.	
Garlic, peeled, minced	1 head	
Lemon juice, fresh	8 oz.	
Parsley leaves, flat, chopped	3 tbsp.	

Chickens, halved, fat and skin removed	5, 2 lbs. each	Fold wing under and place in a single layer in a glass pan or stainless-steel pan. Pour the marinade over the chicken, cover, and refrigerate for at least 4 hours.

Salt and black pepper, coarsely ground	as needed

Wipe off the marinade and grill the chicken over coals or under the broiler. Baste frequently with the marinade and cook until the chicken is well-browned on both sides. Do not cook too close to the coals; the chicken should not become charred. Sprinkle with salt and pepper just prior to serving.

Serve on a bed of parsley. This recipe can also be done with squab. Calculate approximately 1 lb. per serving, including the bones.

CHICKEN BRAISED WITH OLIVES AND LEMON   *Morocco*

Yield: 10 servings

Olive oil	2 oz.
Butter	2 oz.
Chickens, split in half	5, 2½ lbs. each

Heat olive oil and butter over medium heat and brown the chicken halves on both sides. When done, transfer the chicken to a casserole. Discard excess fat.

Onion, thin sliced	2 lbs.
Garlic, minced	1 tbsp.
Saffron threads, ground	1 tsp.
Paprika	2 tsp.
Ginger root, minced	1 tsp.
Red pepper flakes	½ tsp.
Stock, chicken	16 oz.

In the same pan, sauté the onions over medium to low heat until soft. Add the garlic and other spices and cook for another minute. Add the chicken stock and mix. Cook for 5 minutes, then pour over the chicken. Cover and place in a 350 degree F oven for 30–40 minutes, or until the chicken is almost done.

Preserved lemons (see the recipe in the "Condiments" section)	2
Olives, green, pitted, coarsely chopped	1 lb.

Rinse the preserved lemons under running water. Discard the pulp and cut the peel into thin strips. Add the lemon and olives to the chicken and continue to cook, uncovered, for another 10–15 minutes.

(Continued)

Preserved lemon pieces	as needed
Olives, green, coarsely chopped	as needed
Parsley leaves, fresh, chopped	as needed

Use ½ chicken per serving. Degrease and then spoon some of the pan liquids over the chicken. Garnish with a few pieces of the lemon, olives, and a sprinkling of parsley leaves on top. Add a squeeze of fresh lemon juice just prior to serving.

Serve with slices of fried eggplant and fried potatoes.

CHICKEN BREASTS IN ORANGE SAUCE— VERSION 1   *Israel*

Yield: 10 servings

Chicken breasts, bone out, skin on	10, 5–7 oz. each
Lemon juice, fresh	6 oz.

Trim breasts of excess fat and skin, then place in a glass pan or stainless-steel container and marinate in the lemon juice for 2–3 hours. Reserve the lemon juice.

Mustard, Dijon	as needed
Orange juice, fresh	1 pint
Salt and white pepper	to taste

Remove the breasts from the marinade and coat each side with mustard. Place the breasts in a small roasting pan, skin side down, in a single layer. Season lightly with salt and pepper and add the reserved lemon juice and orange juice. Cover pan and place in a 375 degree F oven for 15 minutes.

Brown sugar	4–5 oz.
Salt and pepper	as needed

Uncover the chicken and turn, skin side up. Sprinkle the chicken with the brown sugar, salt, and pepper. Continue to roast, basting frequently, for another 30 minutes, or until the chicken is done and the skin has browned. Remove the chicken to a warm place. Pour the sauce into a saucepan, degrease, and reduce over high heat until it thickens. Adjust salt, pepper, and sugar, then pour sauce over the chicken.

This is a good preparation for buffet service. For greater economy, substitute chicken quarters. For individual service, reheat the breasts, as needed, in the sauce.

CHICKEN BREASTS IN ORANGE SAUCE— VERSION 2   *Spain*

Yield: one serving

Butter, clarified	as needed
Chicken breast	5–7 oz.
Flour	as needed
Stock, chicken	4 oz.

In a sauté pan, heat the butter over medium heat. Flatten chicken breast between sheets of waxed paper, using a mallet or heavy cleaver. Dredge breasts in flour and sauté until one side is slightly browned. Turn breast over. Add chicken stock and simmer until stock is reduced by half.

Orange juice, fresh	3 oz.
Mint, fresh, chopped	1 tsp.
Salt and white pepper	to taste

Add juice and simmer, covered for 5–7 minutes, or until the chicken is done. Remove chicken to a warm plate. Season with the mint, salt, and pepper. Reduce pan liquids to a light, syrupy consistency. Pour over chicken and serve.

Orange or tangerine segments	as needed
Mint leaves, fresh	as needed

Garnish with orange or tangerine segments and mint leaves.

CHICKEN BREASTS EN PAPILLOTE   *Southern France*

Yield: 10 servings

Chicken breasts, boned, skin off	10, 5–7 oz. each
Stock, chicken	as needed

Place the chicken breasts in a small pot and add enough chicken stock to cover. Bring to a boil, then lower heat and simmer for 8–10 minutes, or until just tender. Remove from stock and let cool. Reduce stock to 8 oz., strain, and reserve.

(Continued)

White wine, dry	8 oz.
Milk	8 oz.
Butter	3 oz.
Flour	2 oz.
Egg yolks, beaten	2
Chives	2 tbsp.
Nutmeg, ground	½ tsp.
Salt and white pepper	to taste

Heat the reserved chicken stock and wine and let simmer. In a separate pan, melt the butter and add the flour. Stir well and cook for a few minutes to make a smooth roux. Add the milk, stirring with a wire whisk and cook over low heat until the mixture begins to thicken. Add this to the chicken stock and wine and mix well. Remove a ladle of the hot liquid and beat in the egg yolks. Lower heat and return this to the rest of the liquid, stirring constantly until thickened. Keep below the boiling point. Season with the chives, nutmeg, salt, and pepper. Remove from heat. Reserve.

Asparagus	20 spears
Mushroom caps	20
Butter	as needed

Wash, trim, and peel asparagus ends and blanch until just tender. Sauté mushrooms caps in butter. Reserve.

Butter	as needed

Cut 10 squares of aluminum foil large enough to make package for each breast. Brush softened butter over foil, then place a single portion of chicken in the middle. Place an asparagus stalk on either side. Pour a small amount of sauce over the chicken, then place a mushroom cap on top. Fold the foil to make a tight envelope. Refrigerate until needed.

Put packet(s), as needed, on a baking sheet and place in a 400 degree F oven for 10–15 minutes or until heated through.

Serve directly in the packet or snip foil in an attractive pattern prior to serving to make a more decorative presentation. Serve with glazed carrots and small, roasted potatoes.

CHICKEN PAPRIKASH—VERSION 1   *Austria*

Yield: 10 servings

Chicken breasts, skin off, boned	10, 6 oz. each
Butter, clarified	as needed

Flatten the breasts slightly, using a heavy cleaver. Sauté in clarified butter until lightly colored. Remove and keep warm.

Onions, small dice	2 lbs.

In same pan, sauté onions until soft; do not allow to brown.

Paprika, sweet Hungarian	4 tbsp.

Add paprika and sauté until it begins to darken.

Tomato pulp	8 oz.
Sour cream	24 oz.
Salt and white pepper	to taste

Add tomato and simmer for 5 minutes. Add sour cream and blend well. Season with salt and pepper and heat through. Do not let boil. Place chicken breasts in a baking dish and pour sauce on top. Cover and finish in 350 degree F oven for 15 to 20 minutes, depending on thickness of breasts.

Serve with buttered noodles or dumplings and bibb salad with lemon/oil dressing.

CHICKEN PAPRIKASH—VERSION 2   *Hungary*

Yield: 10 servings

Butter, clarified	4 oz.
Onions, minced	1 lb.
Paprika, sweet Hungarian	1 tbsp.
Flour	1 tbsp.
Stock, chicken	as needed
Salt	1 tsp.

Sauté onions until soft. Add paprika and flour and continue to sauté until well-incorporated. Add enough stock to make a pasty consistency. Cook for a few minutes until the mixture begins to brown.

(Continued)

Chicken breast, meat only	10, 5 oz. pieces	Add chicken breasts, cover, and braise for 10 minutes. Add peppers and tomatoes, cover, and continue to braise for another 10–15 minutes, or until the chicken is tender.
Peppers, green bell, large dice	2	
Tomatoes, peeled, large dice	2	

Butter, whole	2 oz.	Remove chicken and reserve in a warm place. Bring pan juices to a boil, remove from heat and strain through a fine sieve. Return to heat, add butter, and adjust salt and pepper. Return chicken breasts and heat through.
Salt and white pepper	to taste	

Sour cream	as needed	Top each serving with a dollop of sour cream at room temperature and garnish with green pepper and tomato.
Pepper, green, thin sliced	as needed	
Tomato, thin sliced	as needed	

Accompany with spätzle or noodles.

HORTOBAGY PALAÇINTA   *Hungary*

Take left-over Chicken Paprikash and grind, using fine setting on grinder. Sauté in clarified butter with a little salt, white pepper, and minced onion for 5–10 minutes, or until slightly brown. Place appropriate amount on crêpes and roll up. Place rolls in oven-proof dish with the paprikash sauce and heat through. Garnish the same way as Chicken Paprikash.

CHICKEN WITH RED PEPPERS   *Southern Italy*

Yield: 10 servings

Marinade:

Lemon juice, fresh	8 oz.
Olive oil	12 oz.
Italian parsley leaves, chopped	10 sprigs
Basil leaves, fresh, chopped	15–20
Salt and black pepper, coarsely ground	1 tsp. each

Using a wire whisk, mix the lemon juice, and the olive oil together. Add the remaining ingredients and reserve.

Chicken breasts, skin off	10, 6 oz. each

Place breasts between sheets of waxed paper and flatten slightly, using a mallet or heavy cleaver. Using a glass or stainless-steel pan, place the chicken breasts in a single layer and add the marinade. Cover the pan and refrigerate for at least 4 hours.

Peppers, sweet red	3 lbs.

Remove stems, core, and seeds. Cut into rings ¼ inch thick. Reserve.

Remove the chicken from marinade and sauté on 1 side until lightly browned. Turn breast(s) over, add 2 oz. of the marinade per serving. Place pepper rings on top, cover, and finish cooking in a 400 degree F oven for 10–12 minutes, or until done. Cooking time will vary, depending on thickness of breast(s).

Place chicken in the center of a warm plate, surrounded by pepper slices. A combination of red and green peppers may also be used. Accompany with saffron rice.

CHICKEN BREAST WITH
FRESH ROSEMARY
Northern Italy

Yield: one serving

Five or six large fresh sage leaves may be used instead of the rosemary. These must be removed before serving.

Oil	1 tbsp.	Heat oil. Sauté garlic over low heat until it begins to lightly brown. Mash garlic pieces with a fork and remove from oil. Add rosemary leaves and continue to sauté over low heat for 1 minute.
Garlic, sliced	½ tsp.	
Rosemary leaves, fresh	1 tsp.	

Chicken breast, skin off	5–6 oz.	Salt and pepper the chicken, then dredge lightly in flour. Raise the heat to medium and sauté for a few minutes on each side until the meat begins to brown. Remove and reserve.
Flour	as needed	
Salt and white pepper	to taste	

White wine, dry	4 oz.	Add wine, bring to a boil, and deglaze pan. Return chicken to pan, lower heat and simmer, covered, 5–8 minutes, turning once. Place chicken on a warm plate. Bring pan liquids to a boil and reduce to 4–5 tablespoons. Add butter and season with salt and pepper
Salt and white pepper	to taste	
Butter	1 tsp.	

Lemon slices	as needed	Garnish with lemon slices and pan liquids.

Serve with fresh, steamed spinach dressed with oil and lemon and a grating of fresh black pepper.

CHICKEN BAKED WITH SESAME SEEDS   *Israel*

Yield: 10 servings

Chicken legs	10 pieces
Chicken thighs	10 pieces
Lemon juice, fresh	6 oz.
Salt	1 tsp.
Black pepper	2 tsp.

Trim excess fat and skin. Mix the lemon juice, salt, and pepper together and pour over the chicken. Place in a glass pan or stainless-steel container, cover, and refrigerate for at least 4 hours.

Flour	8 oz.
Sesame seeds	8 oz.
Paprika	2 tbsp.
Salt and pepper	as needed

Combine these ingredients and blend thoroughly. Reserve.

Eggs, beaten with 2 tbsp. water	4 or as needed
Salt and black pepper	to taste
Oil	as needed

Dip the chicken pieces in the egg, then dredge in the flour/sesame mixture. Sauté the chicken pieces over medium to high heat in ½ inch of oil until lightly browned. Transfer to a baking sheet and finish cooking in a 350 degree F oven for 20–25 minutes.

Lemon wedges	as needed

Garnish generously with lemon wedges.

A good buffet item to prepare in quantity. Individual portions can also be prepared easily.

CHICKEN SPANISH
STYLE   *Spain*

Yield: 10 servings

Chicken breasts, skin off, boned	10, 6 oz. each
Prosciutto, fat removed	10 slices

Place breasts between waxed paper and flatten, using a mallet or heavy cleaver. Place a slice of prosciutto on each breast and fold over. Close open side with a small skewer or toothpick. Refrigerate until needed.

Sauce:

Olive oil	2 oz.
Onion, diced	1 lb.
Tomato, crushed	2 lbs.
Stock, chicken	8 oz.
Red wine, dry	8 oz.
Garlic, minced	2 tsp.
Parsley, flat, chopped	4 tbsp.
Basil, fresh, chopped	4 tbsp.
Salt and black pepper	to taste

Sauté onions and garlic in olive oil over low heat until soft. Do not allow to brown. Add tomato, chicken stock, wine, garlic, parsley, basil, and bay leaf. Simmer, partially covered, for 45 minutes. Season with salt and black pepper. (Do not use too much salt. The prosciutto used in the second cooking process will add additional saltiness.) Remove bay leaf. Let cool and reserve.

Olive oil	as needed
Pine nuts	1 tsp.
Salt and black pepper	to taste

To prepare an individual serving, sauté a chicken breast on one side over medium heat until lightly browned. Turn and add 3–5 oz. of the tomato sauce. Add the pine nuts and simmer, covered, until chicken is cooked through, about 6–7 minutes, depending on thickness of the breast. Season with salt and pepper.

Pine nuts	10 tsp.
Salt and black pepper	to taste

For buffet service, sauté 10 breasts, then place in baking pan. Add tomato sauce and pine nuts. Cover and bake in 350 degree F oven for 30 minutes or until chicken is cooked through. Season with salt and pepper.

Serve with boiled rice or a simple pasta dressed with butter.

STEAMED BREAST OF CHICKEN   *Morocco*

Yield: 10 servings

Butter, whole, softened	4 oz.
Saffron threads, ground fine	1 tsp.
Salt	2 tsp.
Cayenne pepper	½ tsp.

Combine the saffron, salt, and cayenne with the softened butter. Blend these ingredients thoroughly.

Chicken breasts, skin on	4 lbs., 6–7 oz. each

Rub the butter mixture on all sides of the chicken breasts. Refrigerate for several hours.
   Place chickens in a steamer and cook for 20 minutes, or until done.

Coriander, fresh, chopped	as needed
Mint leaves	as needed

Garnish with coriander and mint leaves.

Serve with rice. Accompany with side dish containing a mixture of ground cumin and salt.

CHICKEN WITH TARRAGON   *Southern France*

Yield: one serving

Chicken breast, boned, skin off	1, 5–7 oz.
Salt	as needed
White pepper	as needed
Flour	as needed
Butter, clarified	as needed

Salt and pepper the chicken breast, then dredge in flour. Over medium heat, lightly brown the chicken on both sides in clarified butter. Remove to a warm plate and reserve.

(Continued)

Butter, whole	1 oz.
Shallots, chopped	1 tsp.
White wine, dry	3 oz.
Flour	1 tsp.
Tarragon leaves	1 tsp.
Stock, chicken	4–5 oz.

Wipe pan and add whole butter. Over low heat, sauté the shallots until soft. Add the wine and reduce over high heat until almost evaporated. Add the flour, mix well, and cook for a minute. Add the tarragon and chicken stock. Return chicken breast to pan, cover, and cook, over low heat, for 10–12 minutes, or until chicken is done.

Heavy cream	as needed
Salt and white pepper	to taste

Remove chicken from pan to a warm dinner plate. Reduce pan liquids until they begin to thicken. Add a splash of heavy cream. Season with salt and pepper. Bring to the boil, stirring. Strain sauce and then pour over chicken.

Serve with fresh, steamed asparagus or buttered carrots and parsley potatoes.

CHICKEN STEAMED WITH ZUCCHINI   *Italy*

Yield: one serving

A number of variations can be created using this method of preparation. Flavorings such as fresh or dried herbs can be used, singly or in combinations. Other miniature vegetables or vegetables such as sweet red or green peppers, celery, fennel, or leafy greens such as mustard or kale can be used to create colorful, well-balanced presentations. Be sure to cut individual vegetables to a size and shape that will enable the desired degree of cooking to take place. Fish fillets may also be prepared in this manner. The cooking time will vary according to the ingredients used.

Olive oil	1 tsp.
Chicken breast, boned, flattened to uniform thickness	1, 6 oz.
Zucchini	6 miniature

Oil an oven-proof china plate large enough to hold the ingredients and deep enough to hold the liquids. Place the chicken in the center and arrange the miniature zucchini around the edge of the plate.

Lemon juice, fresh	½ lemon	Spoon on a mixture of lemon juice, white wine, salt, and pepper. Wrap in foil and place in steamer for 20–30 minutes.
White wine, dry	4 tbsp.	
Salt and white pepper	to taste	

Parsley, fresh, chopped	as needed	Unwrap and garnish with parsley.

The plate used to cook the chicken is also used for serving, so it will be very hot. Use a slightly larger plate underneath when serving.

BASTYA   *Morocco*   Yield: 8–10 servings

Chicken:*

Cornish hens	5	Wash hens and rub inside and out with salt and pepper. Heat butter in a large casserole and brown them lightly on all sides over medium heat. Add the onions and cook until they are soft. Add the garlic, spices, and 1 qt. water and bring to the boil. Skim liquid. Lower heat, cover, and simmer for 45 minutes to 1 hour, until the hens are very tender. The meat should separate easily from the bones. When done, remove hens. When cool enough to handle, remove the meat, shred, and reserve. Discard the skin and bones. Reduce the pan liquids to ⅓ of volume. Strain, degrease, and reserve.
Salt and pepper	as needed	
Butter, whole	2 tbsp.	
Onions, chopped	1½ lbs.	
Garlic, unpeeled, crushed	1 large	
Saffron	1½ tsp.	
Red pepper, dried	1	
Parsley	6 sprigs	
Black peppercorns, crushed	¼ tsp.	
Cinnamon sticks	2, 2 inches long	
Coriander seeds, crushed	1 tsp.	

(Continued)

---

* Traditionally made with squab.

Almond-Cinnamon Mixture:

Olive oil	as needed
Almonds, blanched	5 oz.
Sugar, confectioner's	4 tbsp.
Cinnamon	1 tsp.

Heat oil and toast the almonds until they are evenly browned. Drain on absorbent towels and crush them coarsely.

Blend with the sugar and cinnamon and reserve.

Egg Mixture:

Eggs	4 large
Lemon juice	1 tbsp.

Beat eggs together with the lemon juice and 6 oz. of reserved pan liquids.

Butter, whole	2 tbsp.

Heat the butter in a skillet until it foams. Add the egg mixture and cook, scraping the sides and bottom as you would for scrambled eggs. Cook until the eggs are fairly firm but not dry. Some of the liquid may separate. Remove eggs from pan and reserve. Discard any liquid that remains.

To Assemble as Two Round Cakes

The following directions are for one cake, approximately 9 inches in diameter, using half of the reserved ingredients.

Phyllo dough*	18–20 sheets
Butter, melted	as needed

On a buttered, 12-inch pizza pan, arrange overlapping sheets of phyllo dough. Brush each sheet liberally with melted butter on both sides, 1 at a time, so that they form a circle. Imagine the spokes of a wheel when laying this out. Use 5–6 sheets of phyllo. Repeat this again, adding another layer.

Starting 3 inches from the outside of the pan, spread a thin layer of the shredded chicken meat. Top this with a layer of the egg mixture (include any liquid), then sprinkle evenly with the almond mixture. Repeat this until all of the ingredients have been used. Fold phyllo inward over the top of the filling. Butter more sheets, and, again, arrange them in a circle to cover the top. Using a large spatula, lift the sides and tuck the top layers of phyllo dough under to form a neat, round cake. (At this point the Bastya can be frozen for future use).

To bake, place Bastya in a 475 degree F oven for 20 minutes. Remove from oven and drain any butter that has accumulated. Place another pizza pan on top, invert, and return the Bastya to the oven and bake for another 20 minutes, or until well-browned.

Sugar, confectioner's	as needed

Sprinkle with confectioner's sugar and serve hot.

The above recipe will make 2, 9-inch Bastya serving 8–10. Individual servings, either pie-shaped or rectangular, may also be prepared following the same procedure. Use phyllo dough to form envelopes containing a proportionate amount of the filling. Appetizer- or entrée-sized portions may be prepared in advance and frozen.

* Keep phyllo under a damp cloth to keep it from drying out. Work quickly, using melted butter generously, as dough has a tendency to become brittle when exposed.

CORNISH HENS WITH APPLE AND VEAL STUFFING
Germany

Yield: 10 servings

	8 oz.
Slab bacon, diced	4 oz.
Onion, minced	1½ lbs.
Veal, ground	1 lb.
Apples, tart, peeled, cored, small dice	4 oz.
Golden raisins	to taste
Salt and white pepper	

Sauté bacon and reserve. Leave small amount of fat in pan and sauté onion, over low heat, until it begins to color slightly. Add ground veal and cook until meat begins to brown. Add apples and raisins, cook for 5 minutes, and add bacon bits. Season with salt and pepper. (Keep in mind that the bacon will add saltiness to the stuffing.) Let cool.

Cornish hens	10 very small
Salt and white pepper	as needed
Lemon juice, fresh	as needed

Rub hens with a mixture of salt, pepper, and lemon juice.

Bread crumbs, toasted	4 oz.
Egg, beaten	1 large
Port wine	as needed
Salt and white pepper	to taste
Chicken stock	as needed

Add bread crumbs and egg to stuffing and enough port wine to keep the mixture slightly moist. Season with salt and pepper.

Stuff hens. Truss and sauté slowly in clarified butter on all sides until skin is golden. Arrange in roasting pan breasts up. Add enough chicken stock to cover bottom of pan one inch. Cover and braise in 350 degree F oven for 30–40 minutes or until done.

Apples, spiced	as needed
Apricot, brandied	as needed

Garnish with spiced apple or brandied apricot.

Serve with glazed baby carrots and a puree of potatoes.

CORNISH HENS WITH CALVADOS *Northern France*

Yield: 10 servings

Cornish hens	5, halved
Butter	2 oz.
Olive oil	2 oz.

Brown Cornish hen halves in butter and oil. Remove from pan and keep in warm place.

Carrots, diced	1 lb.
Shallots, whole, peeled	10 small

Remove excess fat from pan and sauté vegetables until they begin to brown.

Calvados	8 oz.

Add calvados, cover, and cook over medium heat for 3–4 minutes.

Apple cider	24 oz.
Parsley	4 sprigs
Bay leaf	3 large
Salt and black pepper	to taste
Nutmeg	to taste

Add cider, herbs, salt, pepper, and nutmeg and bring to a boil. Lower heat to a simmer and return hens to pan. Cook for 20 minutes, or until hens are tender.

Heavy cream	4 oz.
Lemon juice, fresh	to taste

Remove hens to a warm place. Reduce pan liquids by half. Remove bay leaf and add heavy cream and return hens to sauce and heat through. Do not boil. Prior to serving, add a small squeeze of lemon juice.

Serve with buttered green beans and small potato pancakes or with small potatoes that have been sautéed in clarified butter and roasted in the oven.

GRILLED CORNISH HENS   *Morocco*

Yield: 10 servings

This is a small dinner entrée that should follow a rather substantial course of appetizers.

Butter:

Butter, clarified	1 lb.	Add all ingredients to the butter and cook over very low heat for 5 minutes. Do not brown garlic. Mash the garlic in the butter and remove. Let cool.
Garlic, minced	2 tsp.	
Paprika, sweet	1 tbsp.	
Cayenne pepper	½ tsp.	
Salt	½ tsp.	
Black pepper	½ tsp.	

Cornish hens	5	Split hens in two. Remove the breast bone and rib cage. Rub the flavored butter mixture on all sides. Refrigerate overnight.

Cornish hens	½ per serving	Let hens come to room temperature. Grill or broil over charcoal for 10–12 minutes per side. Do not place hens too close to heat. Surfaces should be browned not charred.

Lemon wedges	as needed	Garnish with lemon wedges.

Serve with fried potatoes that have been lightly salted and peppered.

CORNISH HENS WITH RED WINE AND SAFFRON RICE   *Germany*

Yield: 10 servings

Chicken giblets, chopped fine	1 lb.	Brown giblets in olive oil. Add vegetables, mix well, and cook over medium heat until vegetables are soft and begin to color slightly.
Celery root, small dice	1 lb.	
Carrot, small dice	1½ lbs.	
Leek, white only, thin slice	1 lb.	
Olive oil	2 oz.	
Tomato paste	12 oz.	Add and cook for 5 minutes.
Red wine, dry	1 qt.	Add these ingredients, mix well and cook, uncovered, over medium to low heat for 1 hour. Strain through double cheesecloth. Return strained liquid to heat and reduce until sauce begins to thicken. Reserve.
Stock, chicken	1 qt.	
Black peppercorns	15	
Bay leaf	4	
Parsley, whole sprigs	10	
Cornish hens	10	Truss hens and brown evenly on all sides. Roast in 375 degree F oven for 25–35 minutes or until done. Remove from oven and keep warm.
Olive oil	2 oz.	
Sherry	2 oz.	Heat reduced sauce and season with these ingredients.
Brandy	to taste	
Salt and black pepper	to taste	
Mushrooms, whole, sautéed	as needed	Garnish with mushrooms.

To serve, place hen on bed of saffron rice. Spoon a small amount of the red wine sauce over the hen.

ROAST DUCK WITH APPLES AND SAUERKRAUT   *Germany*

Yield: 12 servings

Ducks, cut into quarters	3, 4 lbs. each

Place duck quarters in small roasting pan. Rub salt and pepper on all surfaces. Roast in 450–500 degree F oven for 10–15 minutes to render fat and crisp skin. Remove from oven and keep warm. Reserve rendered fat.

Onion, diced	1 lb.

In a large skillet, sauté onions in rendered fat until they begin to brown.

Apples, tart, peeled, cored, and diced	6 large
Sauerkraut, washed of brine	2 lbs.

Add apples and sauerkraut, mix well, and continue to cook until apples begin to soften.

White wine, dry	16 oz.
Caraway seeds	2 tbsp.
Salt and white pepper	to taste
Brown sugar	2 oz.

Add caraway, salt, pepper, brown sugar, and enough wine to keep mixture fairly moist. (More wine may be added during cooking, if necessary.) Adjust seasonings to taste.

Put apple/sauerkraut mixture on bottom of a small roasting pan. Arrange duck quarters on top. Cover and place in a 350 degree F oven for ½ hour. Remove cover and return to oven for another 10–15 minutes.

Remove duck and keep warm. Adjust seasonings in sauerkraut/apple mixture. (The taste should be a good balance of sweet and sour.)

Serve 1 or 2 duck quarters on top of the apples and sauerkraut. A simple boiled potato is a good accompaniment.

GRILLED QUAIL "LATHOLEMONO" *Greece*

Yield: 10 servings

The marinade can also be used for fish or lamb.

Marinade:

Olive oil	10 oz.
Lemon juice, fresh	10 oz.
Oregano, dried	1 tbsp.
Salt and black pepper	to taste

Mix the olive oil, lemon juice, oregano, salt, and pepper together with a wire whisk. There should be a good balance of flavors. If either oil or lemon predominates, balance it with an addition of the other ingredient. Reserve.

Quail	20

Split each quail down the center of the backbone. Flatten with a heavy cleaver or mallet. Place in one layer in a glass pan or stainless-steel pan and add the marinade. Toss well to insure that the quail are well coated. Cover and refrigerate overnight.

Olive oil	as needed

Grill the quail, 2 per serving, over coals or under a broiler, brushing with olive oil or the marinade, until they are browned on both sides.

Lemon wedges	as needed

Garnish with lemon wedges.

Serve on toast rounds.

STUFFED QUAIL WITH POLENTA OR RICE   *Northern Italy*

Yield: 10 servings

Stuffing:

Olive oil	2 oz.
Onion, minced	8 oz.
Garlic, minced	2 tsp.
Veal, ground	2 lbs.
Thyme, dried	1 tsp.
Bread crumbs	4 oz.
Egg, beaten	1 lg.
Water	2 oz.
Parsley, chopped	6–8 large sprigs
Salt and pepper	to taste

Heat oil and sauté onions and garlic over low heat until soft. Add veal and other ingredients and continue to cook until meat is lightly browned. Remove from heat. Add these ingredients and mix well. Sauté a small amount of the ground meat mixture and adjust seasonings.

Quail, washed and patted dry	20

Stuff the quail with the veal mixture. Cross legs of birds at lower joints and truss. Any stuffing that remains may be added to the roasting pan to enrich the sauce.

Olive oil	2 oz.

In a skillet, brown birds on all sides. Transfer birds to a roasting pan just large enough to hold them and reserve.

Sauce:

Onions, thin slice	1 lb.
Flour	3 oz.
Marsala wine	8 oz.
Stock, chicken	1 qt.
Salt and pepper	to taste

Using the same skillet, sauté the onions until soft. Add the flour, mix well, and continue to cook for 3–4 minutes, making sure that the flour and fats are thoroughly blended. Add the wine and deglaze the skillet. Add the chicken stock, salt, and pepper, bring to a boil, and pour over birds.

Salt and pepper	to taste

Cover the roasting pan and place in a 350 degree F oven for 25–30 minutes. Remove quail and keep in warm place. Degrease pan liquids, strain, and discard onions. Bring pan liquids to a boil. Season with salt and pepper.

Serve 2 quail per plate set on polenta rounds cut to size and sautéed in clarified butter. Sauce lightly with pan liquids. An alternate presentation would be to surround the quail with saffron rice.

QUAIL IN POTATO NESTS   *Southern France*

Yield: 10 servings

Quail, washed, patted dry	20
Lemon juice, fresh	as needed
Olive oil	as needed
Salt and black pepper	as needed

Rub the quail with lemon. Tuck wing tips under, cross the legs, and secure them with a small skewer or toothpick. Lightly salt and pepper. Heat the olive oil and sauté the quail on all sides over medium to high heat. When quail are nicely browned, place them in a roasting pan just large enough to hold them.

Onion, diced	1 lb.
Garlic, minced	1 tbsp.
White wine, dry	16 oz.
Parsley leaves	5 sprigs
Bay leaf	2 large
Salt and pepper	to taste

In the same sauté pan, sauté the onions and garlic. When soft, add the wine and deglaze the pan. Add the parsley, bay leaf, salt, and pepper. Simmer for 15 minutes, then pour over the quail. Cover pan and place in a 350 degree F oven for 30 minutes, or until the quail are done. Remove quail and reserve in a warm place. Strain, degrease, and reserve pan juices.

(Continued)

Potato Nests*:

Potatoes, peeled, shredded	5–6 lbs.

Blanch potatoes for 1 minute. Place immediately in cold water. Drain and dry potatoes just prior to deep-frying. Dip potato nest fryer into cooking oil. Line the larger frame with shredded potatoes. Insert the smaller frame over the potatoes and secure. Deep-fry at 350 degrees F until potato nests are lightly browned. Make 20 nests and hold, inverted, in a 150–200 degree F oven until needed.

For each serving, place 2 potato nests on a bed of watercress. Remove skewers from the quail. Place 1 quail in each basket. Spoon some of the pan juices on top.

Tomatoes, sliced	as needed
Eggs, hard-boiled, sliced	as needed

Garnish plate with tomato and egg slices.

---

* Potato tulips may also be used. Slice potatoes lengthwise in thin slices. Do not blanch. Place slightly overlapping potato slices vertically in potato nest fryer with an additional slice on the bottom. Deep-fry at 350 degrees F. These "tulips" may also be used as containers for a variety of cooked vegetables.

QUAIL STUFFED WITH PROSCIUTTO AND BASIL   *Southern Italy*

Yield: 10 servings

Quail, washed, patted dry	20
Butter, softened	4 oz.
White pepper	1 tsp.
Basil leaves	40
Prosciutto	20 slices

Mix the butter and pepper together. Trim the fat from the prosciutto and lay out the slices. Place 2 basil leaves, lengthwise, on each slice. Top with a scant teaspoon of the butter/pepper mixture. Roll up each slice and stuff one into the cavity of each quail. Truss the quail by tucking the wings under the backbone and passing a toothpick or small skewer through the legs just above the bottom joint.

Olive oil	as needed	Brush quail with olive oil, then lightly salt and pepper them. Refrigerate until needed.
Salt and white pepper	as needed	

Olive oil	1 tsp.	To prepare an individual serving, heat the oil in a skillet just large enough to hold the quail. Sauté 2 quail per serving on all sides over medium heat until browned. Add the wine and simmer until half of the wine has evaporated. Cover and cook over low heat for another 5–6 minutes, or until the quail are done.
White wine, dry	4 oz.	

Parsley or watercress sprigs, fresh	as needed	When serving, remove the skewers and place each quail on a thick slice of eggplant that has been lightly floured and sautéed in olive oil. Spoon the pan juices on top of the quail and garnish with parsley or watercress sprigs.

QUAIL BRAISED IN TOMATOES AND OLIVES *Russia*

Yield: 10 servings

Olive oil	2 oz.	In a large sauté pan, heat the oil and sauté onions until they are translucent. Remove from oil and reserve.
Onions, diced	1½ lbs.	

Quail*	20	Truss quail and dust with flour. Add oil to pan if necessary and, over medium high heat, sauté on all sides. When lightly browned, place the quail in a roasting pan just large enough to hold them.
Flour	as needed	

(Continued)

* For interesting variations, the quail may be stuffed with a variety of bread-based stuffings or with 1 blanched pearl onion per bird.

Red wine, dry	8 oz.
Tomatoes, peeled, chopped	2 lbs.
Olives, Kalamata or Alphonso, pitted, chopped	20
Thyme	½ tsp.
Salt and black pepper	to taste

Return onions to sauté pan and add the wine. Over high heat, reduce the liquid by half. Add the tomatoes, olives, and thyme and return to a boil. Lower heat and simmer for 10 minutes. Season with salt and pepper. Pour the sauce over the quail and place in a 400 degree F oven for 20–25 minutes, or until done.

To serve, place each quail on a toast round that has been sautéed in olive oil or clarified butter. Pour the tomato sauce around the perimeter of the plate. Use 2 quail per serving.

MEATS

BEEF POACHED IN BEER   *Austria*

Yield: 10–12 servings

Slab bacon, small dice	8 oz.	Sauté bacon until crisp. Remove and reserve.

Turnips, diced	1 lb.	Sauté vegetables in rendered bacon fat until slightly browned.
Onions, diced	2 lbs.	
Carrots, diced	1 lb.	

Juniper berries	½ oz.	Add these ingredients to vegetables, mix well, and continue to cook for a few minutes.
Black peppercorns	1 tsp.	
Bay leaves	4	
Marjoram	½ oz.	

Beef brisket or rump, fat removed	5 to 6 lbs.	Rub well with salt and pepper mixture. Tie with butcher's twine to insure uniform slices. Place in deep pot with vegetables. Add bacon bits and beer to cover. Simmer until tender, about 2 hours.
Salt and black pepper	as needed	
Beer	as needed	

Salt and black pepper	as needed	When done, remove meat to a warm place. Remove bay leaves and degrease cooking liquid. Use this as a sauce for the meat. If too thin, thicken with roux. Adjust salt and pepper.

Serve with medley of boiled or steamed potatoes and other seasonal vegetables dressed with butter and chopped parsley. Serve cold with marinated beet or cucumber salad as a side dish.

BEEF STEWED IN BEER   *Belgium*

Yield: 10 servings

Slab bacon, ½-inch dice	1 lb.
Beef, top round, in 2-inch cubes	5 lbs.
Flour	as needed

In a large skillet, sauté bacon until crisp. Remove and place in a stew pot. Discard excess fat. Dredge meat in flour and sauté in the bacon fat until browned. Remove and place in the stew pot.

Onions, thinly sliced	3 lbs.
Beer, dark	1 qt.
Thyme	1 tsp.
Bay leaves	3
Sugar	1 tbsp.
Mustard, whole grain	1 tbsp.
Bread, crusts removed	4–5 slices
Salt and black pepper	to taste

Using the same skillet, sauté the onions until soft. Add the beer and bring to a boil. Deglaze the pan and add the remainder of the ingredients, mix well, and add to the meat. Bring to a boil, lower heat, then simmer for 1–1½ hours, or until meat is tender.

Vinegar, red wine	to taste
Salt and black pepper	to taste

When meat is done, add a small amount (1–1½ tbsp.) of wine vinegar. Season with salt and pepper.

Serve with a potato and celery root puree and marinated beet salad. Cold beer is the beverage of choice.

BEEF ROLLS   *Czechoslovakia*   Yield: 10 servings

Beef, top round	20, 3 oz. slices	Pound thinly sliced beef so that thickness of meat is uniform, about ⅛ inch thick.

Bacon	20 slices	Place 1 slice of bacon and 1 strip of pickle on each slice of beef.
Dill pickle, 3 inches by ¼ inch by ¼ inch	20 strips	

Capers	1 tbsp.	Mix all other ingredients and spread equal amounts on each piece of beef. Roll up each slice and secure with a small skewer or toothpick. In a heavy pan, brown the rolls over high heat, remove and set aside in a warm place.
Mustard	2 tbsp.	
Onions, minced	12 oz.	
Pepper, coarse ground	to taste	
Vegetable oil	as needed to bind ingredients	

Slab bacon, diced	8 oz.	In same pan, sauté bacon until fat begins to run. Add vegetables and continue to sauté until lightly colored. Add wine and deglaze pan. Add beef rolls and enough wine to just cover. Simmer for 1 hour, or until tender.
Carrots, sliced	1 lb.	
Onions, diced	1 lb.	
Celery, sliced	1 lb.	
Red wine	as needed	

Flour	3 tbsp.	Remove beef rolls and place in a warm place. Strain liquid and degrease. Puree vegetables in a food processor. Mix degreased liquid and pureed vegetables and return to heat. Bind with the mixture of flour and sour cream. Adjust seasonings, then simmer for 5 minutes. Add the beef rolls and heat through.
Sour cream	6 tbsp.	
Salt and black pepper	to taste	

Serve with buttered broad noodles garnished with poppy seeds.

BOEUF EN DAUBE
Southern France

Yield: 10 servings

This braised beef dish is usually served with macaroni and vegetables.

Chuck or stewing meat	5–5½ lbs.	Trim meat and cut into 2-inch cubes. Combine with these ingredients and let marinate overnight in the refrigerator.
Wine	16 oz.	
Olive oil	1 oz.	
Carrots, sliced	2 lbs.	
Onion, diced	2 lbs.	
Celery, chopped	6 ribs	
Thyme, dried	1 tsp.	
Bay leaf	2	
Juniper berries, crushed	6	
Salt and pepper	to taste	

Slab bacon, ½-inch cubes	1 lb.	Blanch the bacon for 5 minutes, then drain. Place half of the bacon on the bottom of a heavy casserole, then add the marinated vegetables in a layer. Place the marinated beef on top of the vegetables. Add the tomatoes, the remaining bacon, and enough marinade to barely cover. (If the marinade is insufficient, add more wine or beef stock.) Cover the casserole and start the cooking on top of the stove. When the liquid starts to boil, transfer the pot to 300 degree F oven for 4–5 hours. Add liquid from time to time, if necessary. Pot liquids should barely simmer during the cooking process.
Tomatoes, canned Italian plum	2 lbs.	
Wine or stock	as needed	

To serve, remove bay leaf and degrease the cooking liquids. Place a portion of meat on a hot plate. Surround the meat with cooked macaroni and the pot vegetables. Spoon some of the cooking liquid over the macaroni. Any vegetable in season can be served as an accompaniment to this dish.

CALF'S LIVER SAUTÉ WITH SHALLOTS   *Northern France*

Yield: one serving

Calf's liver, membrane removed	4–5 oz. slice
Flour	as needed
Salt and black pepper	to taste
Butter, clarified	as needed

Dredge the liver in flour and shake off all excess flour. Lightly salt and pepper. Heat clarified butter over medium-high heat. Sauté liver until brown—about 1 minute per side. Cook longer for well done. Remove liver to warm place.

Onions, minced	2 tbsp.
Butter, whole	1 tsp.
Parsley, chopped	2 tsp.
Red wine	2 oz.

Pour off pan liquids and add butter. Over medium heat, sauté onions until slightly colored. Add wine, raise heat to high, and add parsley. Return liver to pan to heat for a few moments to heat through. Pour sauce over liver and serve.

Pear, poached, thin slices	as needed
Watercress sprigs	as needed

Garnish with slices of poached pear placed on top of the liver and watercress.

Serve with boiled parsley potatoes.

MARINATED CALF'S LIVER   *Morocco*

Yield: 10 servings

Marinade:

Onion, minced	12 oz.
Coriander, fresh, chopped	6 sprigs
Cumin, ground	3 tsp.
Paprika, mild	2 tbsp.
Vinegar, white	3 tbsp.
Water	as needed

Mix all ingredients together with enough water to bind the mixture. Reserve.

(Continued)

Calf's liver	4 lbs.

Remove all membrane and the outer skin. Slice thin, then cut into strips. Mix together with the marinade and refrigerate for 3–4 hours.

Olive oil	as needed
Flour	as needed

To prepare an individual portion, remove 6 oz. of liver from the marinade. Pat dry and dredge in flour. Sauté in hot olive oil for 1–2 minutes on each side. Do not overcook.

Lemon wedges	as needed
Parsley, fresh, chopped	as needed

Garnish with lemon wedges and parsley.

Another way to serve this dish is to remove the liver from the pan and reserve in a warm place. Make a pan sauce by combining a few pitted, chopped green olives, chopped fresh parsley, 1 oz. of fresh lemon juice, and a julienne of preserved lemon peel with 4 ounces of chicken or vegetable stock. Simmer this mixture, stirring, for a few minutes, then return the liver to the pan briefly to heat through.

STUFFED FLANK STEAK   *Spain*

Yield: 10–12 servings

Flank steaks, butterflied	2, 2½ lbs. each
Garlic, minced	1 tbsp.
Salt, kosher	1 tsp.
Black pepper	1 tbsp.

Using a meat mallet or a heavy cleaver, pound the steaks to a uniform thickness. Mix the salt, pepper, and garlic together and apply to all sides of the meat. Refrigerate for several hours.

Filling:

Olive oil	as needed
Eggs, beaten with 2 tbsp. water	5 large

Heat oil in a nonstick pan that is a little smaller than each of the pounded pieces of meat. Add half of the eggs and cook slowly to form an egg pancake. When done, remove from pan. Repeat this process with the remaining egg. Place 1 pancake on top of each piece of meat.

Pork, ground	1 lb.
Olives, green, pitted, chopped	4 oz.

Mix the pork and olives together. Divide in 2 parts and spread evenly over the egg pancake.

Red peppers, roasted, peeled, and cut in strips	1½ lbs.
Carrots, julienned and blanched	1 lb.

Place equal amounts of peppers and carrots in rows over the pork mixture on both steaks. Roll and tie the meat securely.

Olive oil	as needed
Flour	as needed
Onion, chopped	1 lb.
Garlic, chopped	1 tbsp.
Tomato paste	2 oz.
Beef stock	as needed

Heat oil in a casserole just large enough to hold the rolled flank steaks. Dust the meat with flour and brown on all sides. Add the onion and garlic and cook for 2–3 minutes over medium heat. Mix the tomato paste with enough beef stock to barely cover the meat. Add and bring to the boil. Lower heat, cover, and place in a 350 degree F oven for 1½ hours or until tender. When done, strain and degrease the pan liquids. Let meat rest for 20–30 minutes before slicing and serve with pan juices.

This dish may also be served cold. When cool, wrap flank steak rolls in foil and refrigerate under weights overnight. This will facilitate making very thin slices. Accompany with grilled eggplant and tomatoes.

KÖNIGSBERGER
KLOPSE   *Germany*

Yield: 10 servings

This recipe title translates literally as "Meatballs from the King's Mountain."

Ingredient	Amount	Instructions
Onions, minced	1 lb.	Heat butter and sauté onions until soft. Do not allow to brown.
Butter, clarified	as needed	
Stale white bread, crusts removed	6 slices	Soak in a small amount of warm milk, then squeeze almost dry.
Anchovies	10–12	Chopped fine.
Beef, ground twice	2 lbs.	Mix all of the ingredients listed above with the ground meat and eggs. Season with salt and pepper. Cook a small sample in simmering water and adjust seasonings. Form mixture into round balls 2 inches in diameter and refrigerate.
Pork, ground twice	2 lbs.	
Eggs	5	
Salt and white pepper	to taste	
Butter, whole	6 oz.	In a pan large enough to hold the meatballs, melt butter over medium heat and add flour. Mix well and cook the roux over low heat until it begins to turn a very light brown. Add stock and bring to a boil, stirring. Lower heat, add meatballs, and let simmer for 20 minutes.
Flour	8 oz.	
Stock, veal	2 qts.	
Capers	3 tbsp.	Add capers and simmer for another 20 minutes. Before serving, add the sour cream. Mix well and heat through. Season with salt and pepper.
Sour cream	8 oz.	
Salt and white pepper	to taste	

Serve with a red beet salad and with small, peeled, boiled potatoes garnished with bread crumbs browned in butter or warm sauerkraut.

SAUERBRATEN   *Germany*   Yield: 10 servings

Onion, sliced	2 lbs.
Carrot, sliced	1 lb.
Celery root, sliced	1 small
Lemon, sliced	1
Bay leaves	2
Black peppercorns	1 tsp.
Cloves	1 tsp.
Juniper berries	1 tbsp.
Allspice	1 tsp.
Cider vinegar	24 oz.
Water	8 oz.

Combine ingredients and bring to boil. Simmer for 10 minutes. Cool.

Beef, rump, top round, or eye round, in 1 piece	5–6 lbs.
Salt	as needed

Tie meat into uniform shape. Rub with salt and place in a glass or enamel container just large enough to hold the meat. Pour marinade over meat. If liquid is insufficient to cover, add equal parts vinegar and water. Marinate 3–5 days in refrigerator. Turn meat each day.

Slab bacon, diced	4 oz.

Render bacon and reserve bacon bits. Brown marinated beef in bacon fat. Place beef in a small roasting pan and add enough marinade to half cover the meat. Braise in 350 degree F oven for 2–3 hours, or until very tender. Baste frequently and add more of the marinade, if necessary.

Gingersnaps	10
Brown roux	as needed
Tomato puree	2 oz.
Salt and pepper	to taste

Remove meat and keep warm. Degrease cooking liquid. Add crumbled gingersnaps and tomato puree and simmer for 20 minutes. Season with salt and pepper. If sauce is too thin, add roux as needed.

Serve with potato dumplings, wide noodles, or boiled potatoes and steamed, buttered cabbage or squash.

STEAK ROMAN STYLE   *Southern Italy*

Yield: 10 servings

Marinade:

Garlic, pureed	3 tbsp.
Rosemary leaves, fresh, chopped fine	3 tbsp.
Black pepper, coarsely ground	1 tbsp.
Olive oil	as needed

Combine all ingredients except olive oil, using a mortar and pestle or blender. Add enough olive oil to make a thin paste. Reserve.

Sirloin or rib	10, 8–10 oz. each

Trim excess fat. Place each steak between sheets of waxed paper and pound lightly with a mallet or heavy cleaver to flatten steaks slightly. Spread the marinade over all the steaks' surfaces and refrigerate overnight.

Pat steaks dry. Grill over coals or broil until done as desired.

Serve with fried potatoes and grilled tomatoes.

STUFFED CABBAGE   *Poland*

Yield: 10 servings

Cabbage	2 large leaves per serving

Remove the core from cabbage and cook in boiling, salted water until leaves are soft enough to roll up easily. If leaves are small, 2 may be combined for each cabbage roll. The number of rolls per serving will vary, depending on the size of the finished cabbage roll. Partially remove very thick veins from the large, outer leaves, taking care not to separate the 2 sides of the leaf completely.

Rice	8 oz.

Parboil rice until just barely done. Grains should still be very firm.

Onion, diced	12 oz.
Beef, ground	1 lb.
Veal, ground	8 oz.
Pork, ground	8 oz.
Dill, fresh, chopped	2 tbsp.
Marjoram, dried	1 tsp.
Salt and black pepper	to taste

Sauté onion until lightly browned and add to the raw meat. Add the partially cooked rice, dill, marjoram, salt, and pepper. Sauté a small amount of the mixture and taste. Adjust seasonings.

To stuff the cabbage leaves, place 1–2 tbsp. of the meat on each leaf. The amount will depend on the size of the leaf. Do not overstuff. Turn the leaf so that the stem end is toward you. Fold the sides over the meat first, then roll forward so that the stem end is inside the roll. Use leftover cabbage leaves or veins to line the bottom of a braising pan just large enough to hold all the cabbage rolls. Place the rolls seam side down, close together, in the pan. Cover top with a layer of cabbage leaves.

Olive oil	1 oz.
Tomato paste	8 oz.
Stock, beef	8 oz.
Salt and black pepper	to taste

Mix these ingredients well and bring to the boil. Pour over cabbage rolls. Cover pan and braise in a 350 degree F oven for 1½ hours.

Serve with boiled, buttered potatoes and a side dish of sour cream sauce. (One part pan liquids to 3 parts sour cream heated almost to the boiling point and garnished with chopped, fresh dill.) Cold beet or cucumber salad may be served on the side.

TRIPE ROMAN STYLE *Northern Italy*

Yield: 10 servings

Honeycomb tripe, washed	5 lbs.

Place tripe in enough boiling water to cover. Reduce heat to simmer and cook for 10 minutes. Rinse under cold water. Trim and cut into ribbons ¼ to ½ inch thick. Wash again.

(Continued)

Salt pork, small dice	8 oz.

In boiling water, blanch pork for 2–3 minutes and drain.

Onion, small dice	1 lb.
Garlic, minced	4 medium cloves
Celery, small dice	8 oz.
Carrot, small dice	8 oz.
Tomatoes, crushed	1 lb.
White wine	8 oz.
Stock, chicken	16 oz.

In a pot just large enough to hold all the ingredients, sauté salt pork over medium to high heat until the fat begins to run. Add onions, garlic, celery, carrots, and cook over low heat until vegetables are soft. Add tripe, tomatoes, wine, and chicken stock and mix well.

Salt and white pepper	to taste

Cover and simmer for 4–5 hours* or until tripe is tender. Use pot with tightly fitting lid so that a minimum of moisture escapes. Season with salt and pepper and stir occasionally. If needed, add a bit more chicken stock from time to time.

Mint leaves, fresh, chopped	to taste

When tripe is tender, add mint and simmer for another 5 minutes.

Parsley, fresh, chopped	as needed
Parmesan cheese, grated	as needed

Garnish with chopped parsley and serve with grated Parmesan cheese.

May be served as an appetizer or as a main course.

---

* If pressure cooker is used, cut cooking time to 1½ hours.

VIENNESE GOULASH   *Austria*   Yield: 10–12 servings

The addition of an appropriate amount of beef stock will create a hearty Goulash Soup.

Onions, sliced	5 lbs.	Using a deep braising pan, sauté onions until slightly soft.

Paprika, sweet Hungarian	4 tbsp.	Mix these ingredients together and add to onions. Sauté for a few minutes over moderate heat until the paprika begins to brown slightly.
Caraway seeds	2 tbsp.	
Marjoram	1 tsp.	
Garlic, minced	3 cloves	

Tomato paste	4 oz.	Add tomato paste and cook for 2–3 minutes.

Beef, rump, in ½-inch pieces	5 lbs.	Dust meat cubes with flour. In a separate pan, brown meat in lard or oil. Add to onion mixture. Deglaze pan with beef stock. Season with salt and pepper. Cook approximately 1½–2 hours over slow heat or until meat is tender.
Flour	as needed	
Lard or oil	as needed	
Stock, beef	8 oz.	
Salt and black pepper	to taste	

Potatoes, ½-inch dice	2 oz. per serving	Boil potatoes and reserve. Add to goulash prior to service. Heat through.

Peppers, red and green, thin sliced	as needed	Sauté in advance. May be used as a garnish.
Butter, clarified	as needed	

Serve with wide, buttered noodles sprinkled with poppy seeds and a bibb lettuce or cucumber salad. May be garnished with a dollop of sour cream and finely chopped parsley.

VIENNESE STEAK AND ONIONS   *Austria*

Yield: one serving

| Onions, thinly sliced | 6 oz. | Fry onions in hot oil until brown and crisp; drain and set aside. Onions should have the appearance of angel-hair pasta. |

| Sirloin steak | 8–10 oz. | Pan-fry steak either rare, medium, or well done. Place it on a very hot platter. |

Stock, beef	4 oz.	Add beef stock to sauté pan, bring to a boil, and reduce by half. Add the butter and stir. Season with salt and pepper. Pour reduced stock over steak and top with a mound of crisp onions. (Reheat onions in hot oil for a few seconds if they have lost crispness.)
Butter, whole	1 tsp.	
Salt and black pepper	to taste	

| Lemon wedges | as needed | Garnish with lemon wedges and a watercress sprig. |
| Watercress sprigs | as needed | |

Serve with shoestring potatoes and a cucumber or green salad.

RABBIT IN CREAM SAUCE   *Czechoslovakia*

Yield: 12 servings

| Slab bacon, diced | 1 lb. | In a heavy skillet, sauté bacon until fat is rendered. Reserve bacon bits. |

| Rabbits, quartered | 3, 3 lbs. each | Dredge quartered rabbit pieces in flour. Discard excess bacon fat and sauté the rabbit on both sides until lightly browned. Remove and reserve in a warm place. |
| Flour | as needed | |

| Carrot, diced | 1 lb. | In the same pan, sauté the vegetables over low heat until they are soft and slightly browned. |
| Onion, diced | 1 lb. | |

Marjoram	1 tbsp.
Thyme	1 tsp.
Allspice	1 tsp.
Salt and white pepper	to taste
Veal or chicken stock	16 oz.

Add seasonings and continue to cook for several minutes. Add stock and deglaze the pan. Return rabbit to pan and simmer, covered, over low heat for 45 minutes.

Sour cream	1½ lbs.
Lemon rind, grated	2 lemons

Remove rabbit and reserve in a warm place. Strain pan liquids and degrease. Discard the vegetables and reduce the pan liquids by a third. Add the sour cream and lemon rind and bring to just below a simmer over low heat. Adjust seasonings. Prior to serving, return the rabbit to the sauce and heat through. Do not allow to come to the boil.

Serve with potato dumplings.

GRILLED LAMB AND KIDNEYS   *Southern Italy*

Yield: 10 servings

Marinade:

Olive oil	8 oz.
Onion, grated	1 lb.
Red wine	4 oz.
Rosemary leaves, fresh, chopped	2 tbsp.
Salt and black pepper	to taste

Mix these ingredients together. Other fresh herbs may be substituted or used in combination. Reserve.

Lamb loin or leg, in 2-inch cubes	4 lbs.
Lamb kidneys	20

Trim fat from the kidneys. Place both the lamb and the kidneys in the marinade for 4 or more hours, turning frequently.

(Continued)

Lemon juice, fresh	as needed

Thread lamb and kidneys, alternately, on a skewer. Broil over coals or under the broiler, basting frequently with the marinade. Cook until done as desired. Add a squeeze of fresh lemon just prior to serving.

Serve on a bed of buttered rice. Accompany with small tomatoes and peppers that have been grilled on separate skewers and basted with oil that has been flavored with fresh herbs such as basil, rosemary, or oregano.

LAMB WITH ALMONDS   *Morocco*

Yield: 10–12 servings

Olive oil	2 oz.
Butter	2 oz.
Onion, diced	2 lbs.
Ginger root, minced	1 tbsp.
Garlic, minced	1 tbsp.
Tumeric	1 tsp.
Cinnamon	1 tsp.
Saffron	½ tsp.

In a heavy skillet, heat the oil and butter over medium heat and sauté the onions until soft. Add the ginger, garlic, tumeric, saffron, and cinnamon, stir, and cook for another minute. Transfer these ingredients to a casserole large enough to hold the lamb.

Lamb, shoulder, trimmed, in 2-inch cubes	6 lbs.

In the same skillet, sauté the lamb cubes until lightly browned. Add the lamb to the casserole.

Stock, lamb or water	as needed
Coriander leaves, chopped	10 sprigs
Salt and black pepper	to taste

Add stock or water to cover. Bring to a boil, skim, then cover the casserole. Lower heat and simmer for 2 hours or until the meat is very tender. Fifteen minutes before completion, add the coriander leaves and season with salt and pepper.

Remove meat to a warm place. Degrease the pot liquids, then reduce to thicken. Return the meat to the pot and reserve until needed.

Eggs, hard-boiled, peeled, quartered	10	Sauté the almonds in oil until golden. Drain and reserve. Reheat meat as needed. Place in center of a heated plate and garnish with egg quarters, a sprinkling of toasted almonds, and some of the pot liquid.
Almonds, whole, blanched	1½ lbs.	
Oil	as needed	

BRAISED LAMB WITH BEANS   *Southern France*

Yield: 10 servings

Pea beans	1½ lbs.	Soak beans over night. Rinse well and place in a saucepan, with enough cold water to cover to a depth of 3–4 inches above the level of the beans. Bring to the boil and let cook for 2–3 minutes. Drain water and begin process once again, using boiling water.

Onion, peeled, whole	4 oz.	Add onion, bacon, and herbs. Simmer for 40 minutes or until the beans are tender but not mushy. Discard the onion and herbs. Remove the bacon, cube, and reserve. Place beans in cold water and reserve.
Slab bacon	4 oz., one piece	
Thyme, parsley, bay leaf	4–5 sprigs, tied together	

Peanut oil	as needed	In a heavy casserole, heat the oil and sauté the cubed bacon. Remove when rendered and reserve. Trim excess fat from lamb cubes, then sprinkle with salt, pepper, and a little sugar and sear over high heat until well-browned on all sides. Remove to a platter and reserve.
Sugar	as needed	
Salt and black pepper	as needed	
Lamb shoulder, in 2-inch cubes	4–5 lbs.	

Onion, chopped	1 lb.	Pour out excess fat and sauté onions until they are soft. Add the garlic and sauté for another minute. Sprinkle with flour, and mix well. Cook for another minute. Add the wine and deglaze the pan. Add the tomato paste and blend thoroughly. Add the reserved bacon bits and season with salt and pepper.
Garlic, chopped	1 tbsp.	
Flour	2–3 tbsp.	
Wine, white	16 oz.	
Tomato paste	2 tbsp.	
Salt and black pepper	to taste	

(Continued)

Carrots, thick slices	8 oz.
Herb bundle (see first step)	
Stock or water	as needed

Return the lamb to the casserole. Add the carrots and the herbs. Simmer, covered, 1½–2 hours, or until the meat is tender. Add water or stock, if needed to keep liquid at the same level as the meat while cooking. When done, discard the carrots and herbs. Let cool and reserve.

For a single serving, place a layer of the beans on the bottom of an individual, oven-proof casserole. Add 4–6 oz. of the lamb and another layer of beans. Moisten with a small ladle of the cooking liquid and reheat in a 350 degree F oven.

Garlic cloves, peeled, then blanched or roasted	as needed
Parsley, fresh, chopped	as needed

Garnish with small cloves of garlic and top with a sprinkling of parsley.

GRILLED, MINCED LAMB   *Morocco*

Yield: 10 servings

Olive oil	4 oz.
Onion, small dice	1 lb.
Paprika	3 tbsp.
Cumin	1 tbsp.
Cinnamon	1 tsp.
Red pepper flakes	1 tsp.

Sauté the onions in olive oil over low heat until very soft. Add the paprika, cumin, cinnamon, and red pepper flakes. Mix well and sauté for another minute.

Lamb shoulder, ground twice	5 lbs.
Mint leaves, fresh, chopped	6 tbsp.
Coriander leaves, fresh, chopped	6–10 tbsp.
Salt and black pepper	to taste

Add the sautéed onion mixture to the meat. Add the mint, coriander, salt, and pepper. Mix well. Sauté a sample in a little oil and adjust the seasonings, if necessary. Form into patties weighing 3–4 oz. each and refrigerate until needed.

Olive oil	as needed	Use 2 patties per serving. Brush with oil and grill over coals until done as desired.

Cumin, powdered	as needed	Sprinkle with a dusting of powdered cumin before serving.

Serve with fried potatoes and tomato salad. May be used as an appetizer or buffet item if formed into small meatballs and sautéed. Serve hot or at room temperature.

BOILED LAMB WITH DILL SAUCE   *Sweden*

Yield: 12–15 servings

Lamb leg, bone out	5 lbs.	Trim the fat and tie the leg with butcher's twine. Place in boiling water for several minutes and scald. Drain and discard the water.

Bay leaves	3	Place lamb and these ingredients in a small soup pot and cover with boiling water. Simmer, covered, for 1 hour or until internal temperature of lamb reaches 140 degrees. Remove lamb to a warm place and reserve the stock.
Salt	2 tbsp.	
Dill, fresh	10 sprigs	

Dill Sauce:

Butter	4 oz.	Melt butter and add the flour, stirring, to make a smooth roux. Cook over low heat for 5 minutes. Add the dill and cook for another minute. Remove the bay leaf and heat 1½ qts. of the reserved lamb stock and using a wire whisk, add it to the roux. Add the sugar, vinegar, and salt. Let simmer for 15 minutes and taste again. Adjust the seasonings, if necessary. Remove from heat and quickly beat in the egg yolks.
Flour	3 oz.	
Dill, fresh, chopped	15 sprigs	
Sugar	4 tbsp.	
Vinegar, white	to taste	
Salt	to taste	
Egg yolks	3	

Serve with boiled potatoes dressed with melted butter and chopped, fresh dill.

LAMB CHOPS PARMESAN   *Northern Italy*

Yield: one serving

Lamb chops, single rib	2–4 chops per serving, depending on size	Remove all bones except the rib bone. With a mallet or heavy cleaver, flatten the eye of the chop slightly.
Parmesan cheese, grated	as needed	Bread chops, first with the cheese, then with eggs, then with bread crumbs. Any number of chops can be prepared to this point and refrigerated for later use. Separate layers of chops with waxed paper.
Eggs, beaten with small amount of water	as needed	
Bread crumbs	as needed	
Olive oil	as needed	Sauté chops over medium-high heat in olive oil, turning once. Grate small amount of fresh pepper on top of chops just prior to serving.
Lemon wedges	as needed	Garnish with lemon wedges.

Serve with sautéed zucchini and roasted sweet red peppers, cut julienne.

LAMB CHOPS WITH PORCINI AND CAPERS   *Southern Italy*

Yield: 10 servings

Mushrooms, dried porcini*	4 tbsp.	Soak the mushrooms for at least 30 minutes in a generous amount of water. Remove the mushrooms from the water, taking care not to disturb the sediment on the bottom. (Strain the liquid and reserve for other uses.) Chop the mushrooms and mix them with the tomatoes, capers, and mashed anchovies. Reserve.
Tomatoes, plum, peeled, chopped	2 lbs.	
Capers, chopped	2 tbsp.	
Anchovy fillets, mashed	10	

---

* If fresh porcini are available, slice them thin, then sauté in clarified butter over high heat for a few minutes and mix with the tomatoes, capers, and anchovies.

Olive oil	as needed
Lamb chops	2, 5 oz. each
Pepper, coarse ground	as needed

To prepare an individual serving, over high heat, sear chops on both sides in olive oil. Transfer chops to oiled parchment paper or aluminum foil. Place 2 oz. of reserved sauce and several grindings of black pepper on top and fold over edges to make a tightly sealed package. Bake in a hot oven at 400–450 degrees F for 15 minutes.

Serve in the parchment or remove and place on a warm plate. If aluminum foil is used and you wish to present this, use a scissors to snip open the packet in an attractive, leaflike pattern.

LAMB SHANKS WITH EGGPLANT   *Turkey*

Yield: 10 servings

Butter, clarified	5 oz.
Lamb shanks	7–8 lbs.
Onion, diced	1 lb.
Stock, beef, veal, or lamb	1 qt.
Lemon juice	4 oz.

Heat butter and sauté the lamb shanks and onion over medium heat until they begin to turn light brown. Add the stock and lemon juice. Bring to a boil, then lower heat and simmer for 40 minutes. Remove the shanks. Strain and degrease the stock and reserve.

Peppers, green, diced	2 lbs.
Onion, cut in crescents	8 oz.
Eggplant, in 1-inch cubes	3 lbs.
Tomatoes, plum, peeled, chopped	2 lbs.
Heavy cream	6 oz.
Salt and black pepper	to taste

In a clean pot, place the lamb shanks and the vegetables. Add the reserved stock and the heavy cream. Bring to a boil, then lower heat and simmer for 30–40 minutes. Season with salt and pepper.

Use 1–2 shanks per serving, depending on size. Accompany with rice pilaf.

LAMB WITH PILAF   *Turkey*   Yield: 10 servings

Lamb leg, bone out, tied	5 lbs.	Trim excess fat from lamb leg.

Olive oil	as needed	Mix the olive oil and the garlic, oregano, pepper, and salt to make a thin paste. Rub this over the the lamb and place in a small roasting pan. Add stock and roast in a 350 degree F oven for 1 hour. (Cooking time may vary, depending on the meat's thickness.) When done, remove the lamb and reserve in a warm place. Strain stock and degrease. Add enough stock to make a total of 2 qts. Reserve.
Garlic, mashed	3 tsp.	
Oregano	1 tbsp.	
Black pepper	1 tsp.	
Salt	1 tsp.	
Stock, beef, veal, or lamb	1 qt.	

Pilaf:

Butter, whole	4 oz.	In a small soup pot, heat butter over medium heat until it foams. Add the liver and sauté until the liver loses its red color. Remove from the pot and reserve. Add the pine nuts and the rice. Sauté, stirring occasionally, until the pine nuts begin to brown.
Lamb liver, small dice	8 oz.	
Pine nuts	5–6 tbsp.	
Rice, long-grain	1½ lbs.	

Tomato paste	2 tbsp.	Add the reserved stock, liver, tomato paste, currants, and salt. Mix well, cover, and cook over low heat until the rice is done. If the rice appears to be dry, add a little more stock.
Currants	2 tbsp.	
Salt	1 tsp.	

Dill, fresh, chopped	15 sprigs	Add dill to the rice and heat through.

Eggplant slices, sautéed	as needed	Serve with 2 eggplant slices per plate. Garnish with lemon wedges.
Lemon wedges	as needed	

Serve sliced lamb on a bed of the pilaf.

MARINATED LAMB SHANKS   *Morocco*

Yield: 10 servings

Lamb shanks	10 or more (the number will vary depending on size) Each serving should contain 5–6 oz. of meat.*

Place shanks in enough water to cover and simmer for 45 minutes, or until just tender. Remove from heat and reserve. (Reserve the stock for other uses).

Marinade:

Onion, grated	1 lb.
Garlic, minced	2 tsp.
Parsley leaves, flat, chopped	4 tbsp.
Coriander leaves, chopped	4 tbsp.
Olive oil	6 oz.
Red pepper flakes	1 tsp.
Cumin, ground	1 tsp.
Paprika	1 tbsp.
Salt	1 tsp.
Black pepper	1 tsp.

Combine these ingredients and mix well. Reserve.

Rub the marinade all over the cooked shanks. Refrigerate for at least 4 hours. Grill shanks over charcoal or under a broiler until well-browned. Shanks may be prepared as needed.

Serve with rice or cracked wheat garnished with fresh, chopped coriander and/or parsley and chopped, raw onions.

---

* Be sure to subtract the weight of the bone.

LAMB SHASHLIK   *Russia*   Yield: 10–12 servings

Marinade:

Red wine	4 oz.	Mix all ingredients together and bring to a boil. Let cool.
Pomegranate juice	8 oz.	
Onions, thin sliced	1 lb.	
Cilantro, fresh, stems and leaves chopped	½ cup, loosely packed	
Basil leaves, fresh, chopped	½ cup, loosely packed	
Lemons, thin sliced	2	
Salt	2 tsp.	
Black pepper, coarse ground	2 tsp.	
Olive oil	4 oz.	

Lamb, leg or shoulder, 1½-inch cubes	5 lbs.	Trim meat of excess fat. Place cubes in a glass or enameled container and pour marinade on top. Mix well, cover, and refrigerate overnight.

Using skewers of appropriate length (depending on size of portion), thread lamb cubes as tightly as possible and broil to desired doneness. For best results, use charcoal grill. While broiling, brush shashlik with reserved marinade several times.

Basil or cilantro, fresh, chopped	as needed	Garnish with basil or cilantro and lemon halves.
Lemon halves	as needed	

Serve with a medley of vegetables, brushed with olive oil, threaded on separate skewers, and grilled. This allows control of the individual cooking times for each of the vegetables. Arrange grilled meat and vegetables over a bed of simple rice or a rice pilaf.

STUFFED LEG OF LAMB   *Southern France*

Yield: 10–12 servings

Stuffing:

Olive oil	1 oz.
Onion, diced	12 oz.
Mushrooms, sliced	8 oz.
Garlic, minced	1 tsp.
Rosemary leaves, fresh, chopped	1 tbsp.
Thyme leaves, fresh, chopped	1 tsp.
Parsley leaves, fresh, chopped	2 tbsp.
Pork butt, ground twice	12 oz.
Bread crumbs, toasted	2 oz.
Egg, beaten	1
Salt and black pepper	to taste

Heat oil and sauté the onions over low to medium heat until soft. Add the mushrooms and garlic and sauté for another minute. Add the remaining ingredients and mix well. Remove from heat. Combine pork butt, bread crumbs, egg, salt, and pepper with the onion and herb mixture. Blend well and reserve.

Lamb leg, boned and butterflied	5 lbs.

Trim lamb of excess fat. Spread the stuffing over the meat's cut side, leaving edges large enough to fold over and close. Reshape the leg and tie with butcher's twine.

Slab bacon, small cubes	1 lb.
Salt and black pepper	as needed
Garlic cloves, peeled	25–30
White wine	8 oz.
Stock, veal	8 oz.

Place cubed bacon on the bottom of a roasting pan just large enough to hold the lamb leg. Place the lamb, cut side down, over the bacon and salt and pepper the entire surface. Scatter the whole garlic cloves around the lamb. Add the wine and the stock. Place in a 450 degree F oven for 30 minutes, then baste meat and lower heat to 350 degrees F and continue to roast for another 1½ hours. Baste frequently. If pan juices evaporate add more wine and/or stock.

When done, let lamb rest in a warm place for at least 20–30 minutes before carving. Degrease the pan liquids and serve over the meat.

(Continued)

| Garlic cloves, roasted | as needed |
| Bacon bits | as needed |

Garnish with cloves and bacon.

Serve with roasted potatoes. If potatoes are to be roasted in the same pan as the meat, cut them in quarters. Otherwise, quarter the potatoes and blanch until barely fork-tender. Toss in a mixture of olive oil, salt, pepper, and some chopped, fresh rosemary leaves and roast in a separate pan until lightly browned.

QUINCE STUFFED WITH LAMB   *Armenia*

Yield: 10 servings

Onions, fine dice	1 lb.
Butter, clarified	as needed
Rice	4 oz.
Cilantro, fresh, chopped	4 tbs.

Sauté onions in butter until soft. Add rice and sauté until butter has been absorbed. Add cilantro, mix, and remove from heat.

Lamb, ground	2 lbs.
Bread crumbs	4 oz.
Water	2 oz.
Eggs, beaten	2
Salt and black pepper	to taste

Add these ingredients to the onion and rice and mix thoroughly. Sauté a small amount and adjust salt and pepper.

| Quince or tart apples | 20 |

Select fruits that are as uniform as possible. Cut a ½-inch slice from the stem end and reserve in cold water to which a small amount of lemon juice has been added. If fruits are uneven, trim the opposite ends so that the fruits have a flat surface upon which to stand. Scoop out cores, leaving a uniform ½-inch shell. Remove seeds and chop the rest of the cores. Reserve.

Spoon the meat mixture into the quince shells and cover with the reserved slices.

Apricots, dried, chopped	2 oz.
Prunes, dried, pitted and chopped	2 oz.
Stock, beef	as needed
Butter	as needed
Sugar	1 tbsp.

Place stuffed quince in a braising pan just large enough to hold them. Heat enough stock to fill the pan about half way up the sides of the quince. Dissolve the sugar in the stock and add to the pan. Scatter the dried fruits and the chopped quince, dot with butter, and braise in a 350 degree F oven for 40 minutes. Be careful not to overcook. Quince should be tender but not mushy.

Cilantro or parsley, fresh, chopped	as needed

When serving, garnish with Cilantro or parsley.

Serve with the pan liquids. Use the fruit as a base, with the stuffed quince arranged on top.

LAMB WITH HONEYED TOMATOES AND ALMONDS   *Morocco*

Yield: 10–12 servings

Olive oil	2 oz.
Butter	2 oz.
Lamb shoulder, trimmed, 2-inch cubes	6 lbs.
Salt and pepper	as needed

In a large casserole, heat the oil and butter. Salt and pepper the lamb cubes and sauté until lightly browned.

Onion, diced	2 lbs.
Ginger root, minced	1 tbsp.
Cinnamon sticks	2
Garlic, minced	1 tbsp.
Saffron threads	1 tsp.

Add these ingredients, stir well, and cook until the onions are soft.

(Continued)

Stock, lamb	12 oz.	Mix the lamb stock with the tomato paste. Pour over the lamb, cover casserole, and simmer for 1½ hours. When done, remove meat and reserve. Remove and discard the cinnamon sticks.
Tomato paste	2 oz.	

Tomatoes, peeled, seeded, and chopped	5 lbs.	Add the tomatoes to the casserole. Cook, uncovered, over medium heat, stirring frequently, until most of the liquid has evaporated. Add the honey, cinnamon, salt, and pepper. Return meat to casserole and reserve.
Honey	6 tbsp.	
Cinnamon, ground	to taste	
Salt and black pepper	to taste	

Almonds, whole, toasted	as needed	At service, reheat meat as needed. Garnish with toasted almonds.

LAMB STEW, BASQUE STYLE   *Spain*

Yield: 10–12 servings

Lamb, leg or shoulder, 1½-inch cubes	5 lbs.	Trim excess fat from lamb. Dredge meat in flour and sear in olive oil over high heat in a large skillet. When done, transfer browned meat to a stew pot.
Flour	as needed	
Olive oil	2 oz.	

Prosciutto, ⅛-inch-thick slices, diced	8 oz.	In the same skillet, sauté prosciutto along with the onions, garlic, and red pepper, until the vegetables are soft. Use low to medium heat.
Onion, diced	2 lbs.	
Garlic, chopped	1 tbsp.	
Pepper, red sweet, diced	1 lb.	

Cumin	¾ tsp.	Add the cumin, marjoram, and cayenne pepper and mix well.
Marjoram	2 tsp.	
Cayenne pepper	½ tsp. or to taste	

Red wine, dry	12 oz.
Stock, beef	as needed
Salt and black pepper	as needed

Add the wine and bring to a boil. Deglaze the pan and add enough beef stock to barely cover the lamb. Simmer until the lamb is tender, about 1 hour. Season with salt and pepper.

Serve with boiled potatoes or rice.

LAMB AND VEGETABLES ON SKEWERS   *Greece*

Yield: 10 servings

Marinade:

Lemon juice, fresh	8 oz.
Olive oil	6 oz.
Salt	1 tbsp.
Black pepper, coarse ground	1 tbsp.
Oregano, dried	2 tbsp.
Thyme, dried	1 tbsp.
Garlic, sliced	4–5 cloves

Combine these ingredients and mix well. Reserve.

| Lamb leg, 1½-inch cubes | 5 lbs. (after trimming excess fat and deboning) |

Marinate meat overnight. Turn meat several times.

Tomatoes, firm, wedges	as needed
Pearl onions, peeled, blanched	as needed
Green pepper, 1-inch squares	as needed

To prepare an individual serving, use 7–8 oz. of marinated lamb. Skewer the lamb cubes. On a separate skewer, place tomato wedges, alternating with pearl onions and green pepper. Brush with the marinade or oil and grill over hot coals. (Start the skewer with the meat first, because it will require longer cooking time.)

(Continued)

| Pita bread | 1 | Lightly brush pita bread with oil and place on grill to warm for 10–15 seconds on each side. Place pita on a plate and top with a skewer of meat and a skewer of grilled vegetables. |
| Olive oil | as needed | |

Parsley, fresh, chopped	as needed	Garnish with a sprinkling of parsley, a few olives, and a large dollop of yogurt.
Olives, Kalamata	as needed	
Yogurt, unflavored	as needed	

MOUSSAKA   *Greece*

Yield: 10–12 servings

Eggplant	3 large	Remove stem end of eggplant and cut, unpeeled, into slices ¼ inch thick. Sprinkle lightly with salt and place in a colander for 30 minutes to drain. Rinse the slices and dry with a towel. Brush slices with oil and place in a 400 degree F oven until lightly browned. Reserve.
Salt	as needed	
Olive oil	as needed	

| Lamb, ground | 4 lbs. | Sauté until brown. Remove from pan and place in colander to drain. |

| Onions, diced | 1½ lbs. | Using the same pan, discard excess fat and sauté onions until soft. Return meat to pan. |

Tomato paste	4 oz.	Add these ingredients, mix well, and cook for 5 minutes, stirring, over medium heat. Season with salt and pepper.
Cinnamon, ground	1 tbsp.	
Parsley leaves, flat, chopped	6 tbsp.	
Sugar	2 tsp.	
Salt and black pepper	to taste	

Béchamel Sauce:

Butter	5 oz.
Flour	5–6 oz.
Milk, scalded	2 qts.

Melt butter. Add flour and stir well. Cook over low heat for 5 minutes. Remove from heat. Gradually add the hot milk to the roux and simmer, stirring for 20–30 minutes, or until it thickens. If the béchamel becomes too thick, add a little more milk. Remove from heat.

Eggs, beaten	2

Stir eggs briskly into the sauce. Reserve.

Olive oil	as needed
Potatoes	as needed
Parmesan cheese, grated	as needed

Oil baking pan. Peel potatoes and cut them into uniform, thin slices. Cover the bottom of pan with a layer of potato slices, overlapping slightly. Then lay alternate layers of meat and eggplant. Reserve nicest slices of eggplant for the top. Pour the sauce evenly over meat and eggplant. Sprinkle with the cheese and bake at 350 degrees F about 45 minutes, or until the top is golden.

This dish may be cooked in advance and reheated for service in individual, oven-proof dishes. It may also be served at room temperature. Let stand for 20–30 minutes before slicing. Smaller portions may be used for buffet service.

LAMB KIDNEYS WITH TARRAGON BUTTER   *Southern France*

Yield: 10 servings

Tarragon Butter:

Butter, unsalted	1 lb.
Lemon juice, fresh	2 oz.
Salt	½ tsp.
White pepper	¼ tsp.

Let butter come to room temperature. Add the lemon juice, salt, and pepper, and using a heavy whisk, mix thoroughly.

(Continued)

Tarragon leaves, chopped	3 tbsp.
Parsley leaves, chopped	4 tbsp.
Chives, chopped	4 tbsp.
Shallots, diced	2 tbsp.

Blanch the herbs and shallots in boiling water for 1 minute. Place them in a clean kitchen towel and wring out all excess moisture. Chop the herbs and shallots as fine as possible and incorporate them thoroughly with the butter. Reserve.

Lamb kidneys	4 lbs.
Water	1 qt.
Wine vinegar	4 oz.

Slit the kidneys lengthwise, cutting on outside edge away from the small, fatty section. Do not cut all the way through; the two halves should remain joined. Soak the kidneys in water and vinegar overnight.

Olive oil	as needed
Salt and black pepper	as needed

To prepare an individual serving, skewer the kidneys so that they remain opened. Use 5–6 oz. per serving. Brush with olive oil and season with salt and pepper. Place on a grill over coals or under a broiler for 1–2 minutes on each side. Be careful not to overcook. Arrange the kidneys in a circle on a warm plate and place a small amount of tarragon butter on each kidney.

Parsley leaves, fresh, chopped	as needed

Garnish with parsley.

Serve with a mound of shoestring potatoes in the center of the plate.

FRESH HAM IN BEER   *Belgium*   Yield: 10 servings

Pork leg, fresh, boned	4–5 lbs.
Salt	1 tbsp.
Black pepper, coarse ground	1 tbsp.
Olive oil	2 oz.

Remove excess fat, score skin, and tie with butcher's twine to assure uniform shape. Mix salt and pepper with the oil. Rub mixture on all sides of the meat. Brown meat over high heat, then place in a braising pan deep enough to hold the pork and enough liquid to cover.

| Onions, sliced | 2 lbs. |
| Garlic, chopped | 5 cloves |

In pan used to brown meat, sauté onions and garlic until translucent. Place over and around pork.

Beer, dark	as needed
Sugar	2 oz.
Caraway seeds	2 tbsp.

Use enough beer to cover meat. Add sugar and caraway seeds. Bring to a boil, then lower heat. Simmer, covered, for 2 hours.

| White bread, crusts removed | 4–6 slices |
| Salt and black pepper | to taste |

Remove meat to a warm place. Degrease pan liquids. Add diced bread to liquid, a little at a time, using a heavy whisk. Continue until sauce has reached a smooth consistency, but is not too thick. Return to heat and season with salt, pepper, and sugar. Simmer for a few minutes. Adjust seasonings so that a good balance is obtained.

Serve with a potato and celery root puree and other root vegetables, such as carrots or beets.

PORK WITH CLAMS   *Spain*

Yield: 10 servings

Garlic, minced	3 tbsp.
Paprika	3 tbsp.
Salt	¾ tsp.
Black pepper, coarse ground	¾ tsp.
Olive oil	as needed

Mix these ingredients together with enough olive oil to make a thin paste.

| Pork loin | 4–5 lbs. |

Cut the pork into 1-inch slices, then cut into bite-sized pieces. Rub the garlic paste on the pork so that it is thoroughly coated. Place in a glass or stainless-steel bowl.

(Continued)

Marinade:

White wine, dry	16 oz.
Parsley leaves, flat, chopped	4 tbsp.
Bay leaves	2 large

Add the wine, parsley, and bay leaves. Cover and refrigerate 6–8 hours, turning the pork from time to time.

Remove the pork and strain the marinade in a colander. Reserve the marinade.

Olive oil or lard	as needed
Onion, diced	2 lbs.

Heat the oil and sauté the pork pieces over high heat until browned. Transfer the pork to a clean casserole. Sauté the onions over medium heat, adding a little more oil if necessary, until they are soft and beginning to color. Transfer the onions to the casserole.

Deglaze the frying pan with the reserved marinade. Add this to the casserole and simmer, covered, for 30–40 minutes, or until the pork is tender. Remove from heat, let cool, and reserve.

Clams, small	50–60

Scrub the clams. If they are sandy, place with 2–3 ounces of cornmeal in water to cover for 1 hour. To prepare an individual serving, place 6–8 ounces of the reserved pork in a small saucepan with 2–3 oz. of the pork's cooking liquid. Cover pan and bring to the boil. Lower heat and add 5–6 clams. Cover and simmer until the clams open.

Serve with rice or fried potatoes. Accompany with a green salad.

PORK CHOPS WITH HAM AND GARLIC   *Russia*

Yield: 10 servings

Butter, clarified	as needed
Pork chops	10 double, 10 oz. each
Black pepper	as needed

Heat butter. Trim chops of excess fat and lightly pepper them. Over high heat, brown the chops on both sides and reserve.

Onions, thin sliced	2 lbs.
Garlic, chopped	1 tbsp.

In same pan, sauté onions until they have a golden color. Add the garlic and continue to sauté for 1–2 minutes. Do not let the garlic brown. Remove from pan and reserve.

Canadian bacon or smoked ham, cut to size	10 slices, ⅛ inch thick
Stock, veal	as needed

In a braising pan just large enough to hold the chops, place the slices of bacon or ham and put a chop on top of each. Place equal amounts of onions on top of each chop. Add about a half inch of stock to the pan, cover, and place in a 350 degree F oven for 30–40 minutes, or until the chops are tender.

Serve the chops on a toast round. Cut the rounds slightly larger than the slices of bacon. Place the toast round on the center of a warm plate. The toast will be topped by the bacon, then the chop and, finally, the onions. Surround with a potato puree spooned or piped onto the plate. Serve with a cucumber salad.

PORK CHOPS STUFFED WITH APPLES AND CURRANTS   *Germany*

Yield: 10 servings

Stuffing:

Butter, clarified	as needed
Onion, small dice	8 oz.
Apples, peeled, cored, and diced	2 lbs.
Currants	3 tbsp.
Butter	as needed
Bread crumbs	8 oz.
Cinnamon	to taste
Sugar	to taste
Salt and black pepper	to taste

Sauté the onion in the butter until soft. Add the apples and continue to cook until the apples are soft. Add the currants, mix well, and reserve. Sauté the bread crumbs in the butter until they are brown and add to the apple mixture. Add the seasonings and let cool.

(Continued)

Pork, loin chops, 1½ inches thick, center cut	10	Trim fat and cut a pocket through the eye of the chop to the bone. Salt and pepper the chop inside and out. Stuff pocket and close opening partially with small skewers or toothpicks.
Salt and pepper	as needed	

Oil	as needed	Sauté chops on both sides to give them a light-brown color. Place chops in a roasting pan in a single layer and add ½ inch of stock. Cover pan and braise in a 350 degree F oven for 30–40 minutes, or until the chops are tender.
Stock, veal or chicken	as needed	

Serve with a puree of celeriac and potatoes.

BRAISED PORK LOIN WITH CIDER SAUCE   *Northern France*

Yield: 10 servings

Pork loin, boned and tied	5 lbs.	In a heavy skillet, heat butter and brown meat on all sides.
Butter, clarified	2 oz.	

Apple cider	1 qt. or as needed	Heat cider and cloves. Place pork in a roasting pan and pour in enough cider to reach halfway up the sides of the meat. Braise in a 350 degree F oven for 45 minutes. Baste every 10–15 minutes. Add more cider, if needed.
Cloves	8	

Carrots, diced	1 lb.	Skim as much fat from pan liquids as possible. Add vegetables and other ingredients. Continue cooking for 30–45 minutes. Remove meat and keep warm. Skim any remaining fat from pan, then put vegetables and pan juices through a food mill. Season with salt and pepper.
Onions, diced	1 lb.	
Thyme	½ tsp.	
Salt and black pepper	to taste	

Watercress sprigs	as needed

To serve, put a small amount of the vegetable puree on a very hot plate. Arrange pork slices on top. Garnish with a sprig of watercress.

Potato dumplings make a good accompaniment.

PORK ROAST WITH CARAWAY   *Hungary*

Yield: 10–12 servings

Pork loin, boned	5 lbs.

Trim excess fat and tie with butcher's twine to ensure round, uniform slices.

Paprika	3 tbsp.
Salt	1 tbsp.
Black pepper, coarse ground	1 tbsp.
Caraway seeds	2 tbsp.
Garlic, crushed	1 tbsp.
Olive oil	as needed

Mix all ingredients, except oil. Then add enough olive oil to bind ingredients and make a smooth paste. Rub mixture evenly over pork's entire surface.

Onion, diced	1 lb.
Carrots, sliced	1 lb.
Celery root, diced	1 medium
Stock, veal or chicken	16 oz.

Place vegetables in roasting pan just large enough to hold the pork. Place pork on top. Add veal or chicken stock. Place in 350 degree F oven for 1 hour and 15 minutes, or until internal temperature reaches 160 degrees F. Remove meat, wrap in aluminum foil, and set aside in warm place.

Stock	as needed
Salt and pepper	as needed

Degrease pan juices, puree vegetables, and combine. Return to heat and simmer for 10 to 15 minutes. Add stock and adjust seasoning if needed.

Serve with potato dumplings and julienned leeks poached in white wine.

PORK ROAST WITH EGGPLANT AND PEPPERS   *Southern Italy*

Yield: 10–12 servings

Olive oil	as needed
Garlic, minced	3 tsp.
Thyme leaves, fresh, chopped	2 tbsp.
Salt	1 tsp.
Black pepper, coarse ground	1 tsp.

Mix these ingredients together, using enough olive oil to bind them. (The mixture should be moist enough to spread easily.)

Pork loin, trimmed, boned, and tied	5 lbs.
Stock, veal	as needed

Spread the mixture over the entire surface of the pork loin. Place on a rack and roast in a 325 degree F oven until thermometer registers 175 degrees F. Keep ½ inch of veal stock on the bottom of the roasting pan during the roasting period. (Cooking time will vary, depending on the meat's thickness.)

Peppers, sweet red	2½ lbs.
Peppers, green	2½ lbs.

Cut peppers in half, remove the seeds, and place on a baking sheet, cut side down. Roast in a 450 degree F oven until the skins begin to blister. Remove from oven and cover. When cool enough to handle, remove the skins and cut into narrow strips. Reserve.

Olive oil	as needed
Eggplant, large cubes	2 lbs.
Parsley leaves, flat, chopped	4 tbsp.

In hot olive oil, sauté the eggplant cubes until tender, but not mushy. They should have a rich, brown color. Combine the eggplant and the cooking oil with the roasted peppers and reserve.

Let the roast stand for at least 10–15 minutes in a warm place before slicing. To prepare an individual serving, degrease the pan juices and reheat 6 oz. of the meat and 6–7 oz. of the vegetables with some of the reserved pan juices. Surround the slices of meat with the vegetables.

PORK CHOPS WITH ORANGE AND GINGER   *Spain*

Yield: one serving

Pork chops, loin, center cut	2
Oil	as needed

Trim chops of excess fat and pound lightly. Dredge in flour and quickly brown on both sides in hot oil. Reserve in a warm place.

Sherry, dry	2 oz.
Stock, chicken	4 oz.
Ginger, fresh, pureed	½ tsp.
Orange rind, grated	2 tsp.
Salt and white pepper	to taste

Discard any excess oil in the pan. Add the sherry, deglaze the pan, and reduce by half. Add the chicken stock, ginger, and orange rind. Bring to the boil then lower heat, return the chops to the pan, and simmer, covered, for 10–15 minutes, or until the chops are tender. Add salt and pepper to taste.

Cornstarch	½ tsp.

Remove the chops to a warm plate. Mix the cornstarch with a little cold water and add this to the pan liquids. Cook, stirring, until the sauce thickens. Or, after removing the chops, reduce the pan liquids over high heat and pour over the chops.

Serve with a salad and rice or fried potatoes.

STUFFED BREAST OF VEAL   *Hungary*

Yield: 10 servings

Veal breast, boned	5–6 lbs.

On the thin side of the breast, separate the layers of meat connected by the thin membrane to form a pocket for the stuffing. Extend the pocket as far as possible. Be careful not to tear through the meat. If a small break does occur, sew it or seal it with a skewer.

Salt	2 tsp.
White pepper	2 tsp.
Paprika, Hungarian rose	2 tsp.

Mix these ingredients together and rub the breast inside and out. Set aside.

(Continued)

Stuffing:

White bread rolls or slices	¾–1 lb.	Soak bread in milk.
Milk	6 oz.	

Onions, minced	8 oz.	Sauté onions in clarified butter over low heat until soft.
Butter, clarified	as needed	

Butter, whole	4 oz.	Beat the whole butter with the raw eggs. Squeeze excess liquid from bread and combine with onions, butter, and beaten eggs. Add hard-boiled eggs and parsley and mix well.
Eggs, raw	2	
Eggs, hard-boiled and chopped	2	
Parsley, flat, chopped fine	3 tbsp.	

Salt and white pepper	to taste	Add salt, white pepper, and nutmeg.
Nutmeg, ground	to taste	

Stock, veal	as needed	Stuff veal breast. Close open end with a large skewer(s). Place mirepoix on the bottom of a small roasting pan. Put veal on top and add stock to cover bottom of pan to a depth of 2 inches. Braise in a 350 degree F oven for 1½ hours, basting occasionally. Add stock if needed. Remove and keep warm.
Mirepoix (carrots, onions, and celery)	8 oz. each	

Sour cream	6 tbsp.	Mix sour cream and flour thoroughly. Strain pan juices. Press vegetables in a strainer to extract the juices. Degrease the liquid and add the sour cream and flour mixture. Return to heat and simmer for 10 minutes. Adjust seasonings.
Flour	3 tbsp.	
Salt and white pepper	to taste	Place a small pool of sauce on a very warm plate. Place slices of stuffed breast on top.

Accompany with rice and peas or small, caramelized potatoes.

NATURSCHNITZEL   *Austria*

Yield: one serving

Veal cutlet, cut from leg, ¼ inch thick	4–5 oz.

Remove all fat and other connecting tissue. Do not pound. Make small incisions around edges to prevent curling.

Flour	as needed
Butter, clarified	as needed

Dredge cutlet in flour and shake off excess. Sauté in clarified butter, turning once, until nicely browned. Do not overcook. Place on a warm plate and hold in a warm place.

Stock, veal	6 oz.
Butter	1 oz.
Lemon juice	to taste
Salt and white pepper	to taste

Add these ingredients to pan juices. Bring to boil and reduce by a third. Return cutlets to pan, reduce to simmer, and heat through, approximately 15 or 20 seconds. Overcooking will toughen the meat.

Lemon wedges	as needed
Pasrley, chopped, fried	as needed

Garnish with lemon wedges and parsley.

Serve with whole, boiled potatoes.

VEAL CUTLETS WITH CREAM AND MUSHROOMS   *Austria*

Yield: one serving

Veal cutlet, cut from leg, ¼ inch thick	4–5 oz.

Remove all fat and other connective tissue. Pound lightly with mallet and make small incisions around edges to prevent curling.

Flour	as needed
Butter, clarified	as needed

Dredge cutlet in flour and shake off excess. Sauté in clarified butter, turning once, 1–2 minutes per side. (Do not overcook.) Place on a warm plate and hold in a warm place.

(Continued)

Mushrooms, thin sliced	2 large	Sauté mushrooms for a few minutes. (This may be done in advance.)

| Heavy cream | 4 oz. | Add cream and bring to boil; reduce by a third. Return cutlets to pan; reduce heat. Season with salt and pepper. Cook just long enough to heat through. Sauce should lightly coat spoon. |
| Salt and white pepper | to taste | |

Parsley, fresh, chopped	as needed	Serve on a warm plate and garnish with parsley.

Accompany veal with wide, lightly buttered noodles and fresh, steamed peas.

VEAL CUTLETS ZURICH   *Switzerland*

Yield: one serving

| Veal cutlet | 5 oz. | Remove all membrane and fat. Slice against the grain into ¼-inch by 2-inch strips. Heat butter and sauté veal over medium-high heat until veal loses all color (approximately 2 minutes). Remove veal and place in a basket strainer and let drain. Reserve juices. |
| Butter, clarified | as needed | |

| Shallots, minced | 1 tbsp. | Sauté shallots until soft. Add brandy and flame. |
| Brandy | 2 oz. | |

Flour	as needed	Sprinkle shallots lightly with flour and mix. Cook for 1 minute. Do not allow to brown.

White wine	2 oz.	Add these ingredients, lower heat, stirring, until sauce thickens. Season with salt and white pepper. Return veal to heat through. Do not allow to come to the boil.
Heavy cream	3 oz.	
Reserved veal juices		
Salt and white pepper	to taste	

Parsley, fresh, chopped	as needed	Garnish with parsley.

Serve with wide, buttered noodles or Rosti potatoes.

WIENER SCHNITZEL   *Austria*   Yield: one portion

Veal cutlet, cut from leg, ¼ inch thick	4–5 oz.	Remove all fat and other connective tissue. Pound lightly with mallet and make small incisions around edges to prevent curling.

Flour	as needed	Place each ingredient in a separate, flat container. Dip veal in the following order: flour, egg, bread crumbs. Shake off any excess. (Cutlets may be refrigerated at this point for later use. Store, separated by waxed paper, in refrigerator.)
Bread crumbs, toasted, coarse ground	as needed	
Flour	as needed	

Butter, clarified	To cover sauté pan to depth of ⅛ inch	Sauté cutlet a few minutes on each side until golden. Serve immediately.

Lemon halves	as needed	Garnish with lemon and parsley.
Parsley, fresh, chopped, sautéed in clarified butter	as needed	

Serve with buttered, boiled potatoes, parsley, and steamed spinach.

SCHNITZEL HOLSTEIN   Yield: one serving

See the recipe for Wiener Schnitzel and follow the same procedure. Garnish each cutlet with a fried egg crossed with anchovies. Caviar, capers, minced onions, and pickles may also be placed around egg yolk.

When preparing individual servings, it is recommended that a small nonstick pan be used for the fried egg.

VEAL SCALLOPS WITH MUSHROOMS, HAM, AND CHEESE   *Austria*

Yield: 10 servings

| Mushrooms | 1½ lbs. | Clean mushrooms, using slightly damp cloth. Trim stem ends. Put mushrooms through grinder, using a fine blade. Sauté over high heat until liquid evaporates. Reserve for future use. |
| Butter, clarified | as needed | |

| Veal cutlets, membrane removed | 10, 5 oz. each | Pound slices to ¼-inch thickness. Make small incisions around the edges to prevent curling. Flour each cutlet and set aside, separated by waxed paper. |
| Flour | as needed | |

| Boiled ham, thin sliced | 10 slices | Trim to size of 5 oz. veal cutlets. |

| Gruyère cheese, thin sliced | 10 slices | Trim to size of 5 oz. veal cutlets. |

| Lard or clarified butter | as needed | To prepare an individual serving, sauté a cutlet over medium-high heat for about 1–2 minutes on each side. Do not overcook. Using the same skillet, top the cutlet with the mushroom puree, a slice of ham, and the cheese. Place in a 450 degree F oven for a minute or so until the cheese is melted. |

Serve with grilled tomatoes and a saffron rice.

SCALLOPINE WITH WILD MUSHROOMS   *Northern Italy*

Yield: one serving, 10 servings sauce

Mushrooms, dried porcini	4 oz.
Stock, veal	1 qt.

Soak the mushrooms in warm stock for 1 hour. Remove mushrooms and discard any tough stems. Rinse and chop. Let stock settle, then strain or decant through cheesecloth to eliminate any sandy residue. Add to stock. Bring the stock to a boil and reduce to 16 oz.

Garlic, mashed	2 large
Parsley leaves, flat, chopped	2 tbsp.
Olive oil	3 oz.
Tomato paste	1 tbsp.
Red wine, dry	8 oz.
Butter	4 oz.
Salt and pepper	to taste

Over moderate heat, sauté mushrooms, garlic, and parsley in olive oil until garlic is just soft. Add tomato paste and continue to cook for several minutes. Add the red wine and the veal stock and simmer until reduced by a third. Add butter, strain, and season with salt and pepper. Reserve until needed.

Veal scallope, cut from leg, ¼ inch thick	4–5 oz.
Flour	as needed

Place scallope between waxed paper and pound with a mallet or heavy cleaver to ⅛ inch thickness. Make a few incisions around the edges to prevent curling. Dredge in flour and shake off excess.

Butter, clarified	as needed

Sauté in clarified butter over moderately high heat for 1–2 minutes on each side. Remove to a warm plate.

Using the same sauté pan, place sauce sufficient for 1 serving and bring to a boil. Pour over the veal.

Parsley, fresh, chopped	as needed

Garnish with chopped, fresh parsley.

Usually served without an accompaniment.

ROLLED VEAL SCALLOPS WITH PORK STUFFING   *Northern Italy*

Yield: 10 servings

Stuffing:

Pork, ground	1 lb.	Mix well and sauté a small sample to taste. Adjust seasonings. Shape into finger-sized pieces.
Sage, dried	½ tsp.	
Basil, dried	½ tsp.	
Thyme, dried	½ tsp.	
Salt and black pepper	to taste	

Veal scallops	10, 5 oz.	Pound veal. Place 1 piece of the pork mixture on a scallop. Fold sides of scallop in toward the center, then roll up and tie with butcher's twine. Do not overstuff. Make sure that sides remain tucked in.

Onion, small dice	12 oz.	Over medium heat, sauté vegetables in olive oil until they begin to brown slightly. Add veal rolls and sauté for 5 minutes on all sides. Remove and keep warm.
Garlic, small dice	2 cloves	
Carrot, small dice	8 oz.	
Celery, small dice	8 oz.	
Olive oil	2 oz.	

White wine	12 oz.	Add wine to vegetables and cook over medium heat for 5 minutes. Add tomatoes, bring to a boil, then reduce heat and simmer for ½ hour. Puree this mixture.
Tomatoes, ground	2 lbs.	

Salt and black pepper	to taste	Season with salt and pepper. Return to heat, add the veal rolls, and simmer for 20 minutes.

Remove string prior to service. May be reheated slowly in sauce for individual portions.

VEAL KIDNEYS WITH SHERRY   *Spain*

Yield: 10 servings

Veal kidney, washed, fat and membrane removed	5 lbs.	Cut the kidney in half lengthwise, then cut each half into bite-sized pieces. In a glass pan or stainless-steel pan, soak the kidneys overnight, refrigerated, in the vinegar and enough water to cover.
Wine vinegar	6 oz.	
Water, cold	as needed	

Flour	as needed	To prepare an individual serving, place 6–7 oz. of kidney in a small strainer. Shake off liquid and then dust with flour, shaking strainer to remove excess.

Olive oil	as needed	Sauté the kidneys over moderately high heat for 1 minute, or until they are lightly browned. Add the sherry, stir well, and bring to the boil. Add the stock and simmer for 3–5 minutes. Season with salt and pepper.
Sherry, dry	2 oz.	
Stock, beef	4 oz.	
Salt and black pepper	to taste	

Serve kidneys and sauce over a bed of boiled rice. Accompany with grilled tomato and a sprinkling of fresh, chopped parsley.

ONIONS FILLED WITH MEAT AND MUSHROOMS   *Belgium*

Yield: 10 servings

Onions, red or Spanish, peeled	10, 10–12 oz. each	Take a small slice off the flat end of the onions so they will not roll when placed on plate. Place in steamer for 5–7 minutes, depending on size. Remove and place immediately in ice water. When cool, drain, dry, and slice off 1 inch from the top. Reserve slices. Remove center core of onion, leaving an outer shell of approximately ½ inch.

(Continued)

Butter, clarified	as needed
Mushrooms, white, chopped	8 oz.

Chop the onions removed from the shell and the mushrooms and sauté in clarified butter until slightly brown.

Veal, ground	8 oz.
Pork, ground	8 oz.
Salt and black pepper	to taste
Nutmeg	to taste
Bread crumbs	2 oz.
Egg	1

Add meat and sauté until slightly brown. Season with salt, pepper, and a few grindings of nutmeg. Add bread crumbs and egg and mix well. Sauté a small amount, taste, and adjust seasonings. Stuff mixture into onions. Reserve.

Butter, whole	2 oz.
Bread crumbs	2 oz.

Sauté the bread crumbs. Sprinkle over tops of stuffed onions. Place in baking pan containing 1 inch of water and bake in a 350 degree F oven, covered, for 15 minutes. Remove cover and continue baking for another 15–20 minutes. Onions should remain firm but tender.

Serve with a potato puree and a mixed green salad.

VEAL SCALLOPS IN A FRESH TOMATO SAUCE   *Southern Italy*

Yield: 10 servings

Sauce:

Olive oil	2 oz.
Onions, diced	1½ lbs.
Garlic, minced	2 tbsp.
Tomatoes, plum, peeled, seeded, and chopped	4 lbs.
Parsley, chopped	4 tbsp.
Salt and black pepper	to taste

Heat oil and, over low heat, sauté the onions and garlic until very soft but not browned. Add tomatoes and parsley, and season with salt and pepper. Simmer for 30 minutes. Reserve.

Veal:

Italian parsley leaves, chopped	5 tbsp.	Mix these ingredients together.
Garlic, minced	5 tsp.	
Flour	10–12 oz.	
Salt and white pepper	to taste	

Veal scallops	3 lbs., 4–5 oz. each	Using the heel of your hand, press the parsley/garlic mixture onto the meat. Cover each portion with waxed paper and refrigerate until needed.

Olive oil	2 tbsp.	To prepare an individual serving, in a sauté pan, heat the oil over high heat. Dip veal scallop in beaten egg and sauté quickly on both sides. Reserve in a warm place. Discard excess oil and add 3–5 oz. of tomato sauce to the pan. Heat over medium-high heat. Pour the sauce onto a very warm dinner plate and place the scallop on top.
Eggs, beaten	as needed	

Watercress sprigs	as needed	Garnish with watercress and lemon slices.
Lemon slices	as needed	

Serve with crisp, fried potatoes.

BRAISED VEAL SHANKS— VERSION 1   *Austria*

Yield: 10 servings

Veal shanks, cut across bone, 1½–2 inches thick	10, 12 oz. each	Brush with oil and roast for 10 minutes in 500 degree F oven. Use a heavy braising pan, just large enough to hold the pieces of veal.

(Continued)

Slab bacon, small dice	8 oz.	Sauté until fat is rendered; remove bacon bits and reserve. Discard excess fat.

Onions, diced	1 lb.	Sauté vegetables until slightly browned.
Carrots, diced	8 oz.	
Celery, diced	8 oz.	
Parsnips, diced	4 oz.	
Turnips, diced	4 oz.	

Flour	4 oz.	Add flour to vegetables, mix well, and sauté for a few minutes until the flour has been completely incorporated. Add other ingredients.
Thyme	1 oz.	
Bay leaves	4	

Stock, veal	1 qt.	Add stock and seasonings to vegetables, mix well, and bring to boil. Add bacon bits. Pour over shanks. If necessary, add more stock to cover. Cover and braise in 350 degree F oven about 1 hour, or until tender.
Salt and black pepper, coarse ground	to taste	

Remove shanks to a warm place. Strain braising liquid and degrease. Reduce by a third and adjust seasonings. Sauce with braising liquid and garnish each serving with a few of the reserved bacon bits.

Serve with braised red cabbage and dumplings, noodles, or a potato puree.

BRAISED VEAL SHANKS— VERSION 2   *Northern Italy*

Yield: 10 servings

Veal shanks, cut across bone, 1½–2 inches thick	10–12 oz. each serving	Tie each piece around the perimeter so that meat does not separate from the bone during cooking.

Olive oil	4 oz.
Butter, whole	2 oz.
Flour	as needed

Lightly flour the shanks and brown on all sides in moderately hot oil and butter. Remove from pan and reserve in a warm place.

Onions, small dice	2 lbs.
Carrots, small dice	8 oz.
Celery, small dice	8 oz.
Garlic, minced	1 tbsp.
Marjoram	1 tsp.

In the same skillet, sauté all vegetables over low heat until soft.

Flour	4 tbsp.
White wine	16 oz.
Tomatoes, Italian plum, drained, chopped	24 oz.
Stock, veal	8 oz., reduced to 4 oz.
Salt and white pepper	to taste

Add flour and incorporate thoroughly. Add wine, deglaze pan, and boil until wine is reduced by half. Add tomatoes and stock and simmer for 10 minutes. Season with salt and pepper.

Lemon peel, grated	1 lemon

Place veal shanks in a roasting pan and pour the liquids and vegetables on top. Add lemon peel and braise in a 350 degree F oven for about 1 hour or until tender. When done, remove meat and degrease pan liquid. Adjust seasonings. (You may wish to add a bit more fresh lemon juice to brighten flavor of sauce.)

Parsley, fresh, chopped	as needed
Lemon wedges	as needed

To serve, remove the string and place 1–2 pieces (including the bone) on a hot plate. Meat portion should be 4 to 5 oz., excluding the weight of the bone. Surround the shanks with a liberal amount of the sauce. Provide an extra small fork to facilitate removal of marrow from the bone. Garnish with parsley and lemon wedges.

Customarily served with a saffron rice or Risotto Milanese.

VEAL JARDINIÈRE
Northern France

Yield: 10 servings

Veal shoulder, fat and cartilage removed, 1-inch cubes	5 lbs.
Onion, diced	1 lb.
Butter, clarified	as needed

In a large, heavy skillet, heat the butter, then sauté the meat and onions until the onions are soft. Do not brown.

Flour	2 oz.
Stock, veal	1 qt.
White wine	8 oz.

Dust the meat and onions lightly with flour. Stir to incorporate the flour thoroughly. Cook for 1–2 minutes. Add the stock and wine. Deglaze the pan and bring to a boil. Cover, lower heat, and simmer for 1 hour, or until meat is tender.

Peas, fresh, shelled	1 lb.
Onions, pearl, peeled	2 lbs.
Carrots, sliced in rounds	2 lbs.
Sugar	2 tbsp.
Salt and black pepper	to taste

Add vegetables and seasonings. Simmer for 15 minutes, or until vegetables are just tender.

Butter, whole	4 oz.

Add butter, stir well, and adjust seasonings, if necessary.

Serve in a deep plate with crusty bread. Accompany with a salad made from mixed greens such as romaine, escarole, and chicory. Dress salad with a garlic-flavored vinaigrette.

Vegetables and Salads

STRING BEANS WITH ANCHOVIES AND GARLIC   *Northern Italy*

Yield: 10 servings

String beans, trimmed	2 lbs.
Water	as needed
Salt	to taste

If the beans are very fresh, trim only the stem ends. Cook them in boiling salted water for a few minutes until just fork-tender. When done, place the beans immediately in iced water. Reserve.

Olive oil	4 oz.
Butter	2 oz.
Garlic, chopped	1 tsp.
Parsley leaves, flat, chopped	20 sprigs
Anchovy fillets, chopped	4 oz.
Black pepper	to taste

In a small, heavy-bottomed saucepan, heat the oil and butter over medium heat. Add the rest of the ingredients and sauté until the garlic just begins to soften. Remove from heat and reserve.

To prepare an individual serving, in a small sauté pan, heat enough of the oil/anchovy mixture to coat 3 oz. of the cooked beans. When the oil is hot, add the beans. Toss to coat them, then quickly heat through and serve.

STRING BEANS WITH CORIANDER   *Portugal*

Yield: 10 servings

This dish may be used as a buffet item or a side dish.

Marinade:

Garlic, minced	2 tsp.
Olive oil	6 oz.
Coriander, fresh, leaves chopped fine	6 tbsp.
Salt	½ tsp.
Black pepper, coarse ground	1 tsp.

In a nonmetallic bowl large enough to hold 2½ lbs. of beans, combine these ingredients and reserve.

(Continued)

String beans, trimmed	2½ lbs.
Water	as needed
Salt	to taste

If the beans are very fresh, trim the stem ends only. If beans are large, cut on the diagonal into 2 or 3 pieces each. Cook them in rapidly boiling, salted water until done, but still crisp. Drain, and pour the marinade over the warm beans. Mix well, let cool, then refrigerate for at least 4 hours. Toss beans occasionally.

Lemon juice, fresh	3–4 tbsp.

At service, let the beans come to room temperature. Add the lemon juice and toss well.

GREEN BEANS WITH HAM   *Spain*

Yield: 10 servings

Green beans, trimmed	2½ lbs.
Vinegar	4 oz.
Water	as needed

If the beans are very fresh, trim the stem ends only. Bring to a boil enough water to cover the beans and the vinegar. Add the beans and vinegar and cook until tender, but still firm. When done, place them immediately into iced water.

Olive oil	4 oz.
Garlic, minced	2 tsp.
Ham, small dice, or Prosciutto	4 oz.
Onion, small dice	8 oz.

In a pan large enough to hold the beans, heat the oil over medium heat and sauté the garlic, ham, and onion for a few minutes. (Do not let the garlic or onions brown.) When done, remove pan from heat and let cool.

Black pepper	to taste

Drain the beans and add them to the pan. Toss well and sauté for 1–2 minutes. Add a few grindings of pepper. Let cool and reserve.

If beans are to be served hot, reheat the necessary amount over high heat in a little olive oil. This recipe may also be served at room temperature as an accompaniment for cold meats, as part of a salad plate, or as a buffet item.

GREEN BEANS PROVENÇAL   *Southern France*

Yield: 10 servings

Green beans, fresh, small, ends trimmed	2½ lbs.
Water	as needed

Blanch the beans in boiling water until done, but still crisp. Plunge immediately into iced water and reserve.

Olive oil	3 oz.
Onion, diced	1 lb.
Garlic, minced	1 tsp.
Tomatoes, peeled, seeded, and chopped	4 lbs.
Basil leaves, fresh, chopped	1 tbsp.
Parsley leaves, flat, chopped	1 tbsp.
Salt and black pepper	to taste

Heat the olive oil and sauté the onions over medium heat until soft. Add the garlic and sauté for another minute. Add the tomatoes, basil, and parsley. Lower heat and simmer uncovered for 20 minutes. Season with salt and pepper. Cook for another 10 minutes.

Add the beans and simmer for 5 minutes, or until the beans are heated through.

To avoid overcooking, reserve the sauce and the beans separately when they are done. Combine the sauce with the beans to prepare individual servings as needed.

GREEN BEANS AND MUSHROOM SALAD
Southern France

Yield: 10 servings

Green beans, fresh, small, ends trimmed	3½ lbs.
Water	as needed

Blanch the beans in boiling water until done, but still crisp. Plunge immediately into iced water and reserve.

Mushrooms	1 lb.
Lemon juice	2 oz.
Salt and white pepper	to taste

Trim and discard any tough ends from the mushroom stems. Slice them thinly and toss with the lemon juice, salt, and pepper. Reserve.

(Continued)

Dressing:

Onion, red, minced	2 tbsp.
Heavy cream, slightly beaten	12 oz.
Lemon juice	1 oz.
Salt and white pepper	to taste

Combine the onion, heavy cream, and lemon juice. Season with salt and pepper.

To prepare an individual serving, drain the beans and place 5 oz. of beans and 1½ oz. of mushrooms in a small mixing bowl. Add enough dressing to lightly coat the vegetables. Toss well and place on a chilled plate.

Serve as an individual first course or as part of a varied appetizer presentation. It also may be used as part of salad plate accompanying cold fowl or fish.

GREEN BEANS WITH RED PEPPER SAUCE   *Portugal*

Yield: 10 servings

Pepper Sauce:

Peppers, red, sweet, washed, halved, seeds removed	2½ lbs.
Garlic, peeled	1 head
Olive oil	as needed
Oregano	as needed
Salt and black pepper	to taste

Place the peppers, cut side down, on a baking sheet along with the peeled garlic cloves. Brush peppers with olive oil. Add a sprinkling of oregano and roast in a 400 degree F oven until the pepper skins begin to char. Remove peppers and garlic from oven, cover, and when cool enough to handle, peel the peppers. Place the peppers and garlic in the bowl of a food processor and puree with 2 oz. of olive oil. Season with salt and pepper. Reserve.

String beans, trimmed	3 lbs.
Water	as needed

Cook the beans in boiling water until barely tender. Plunge them immediately into iced water and reserve.

Olive oil	as needed

To prepare an individual serving, reheat 4–5 oz. of beans quickly in the hot oil. Place them on a warm plate. Add approximately 2–3 oz. of the peppers to the pan and heat through. Pour over beans and serve hot.

Serve as a separate vegetable course or as an accompaniment for any meat, fish, or fowl entrée. Yellow peppers can be used to create another variation.

CARROT SALAD WITH ORANGES AND WALNUTS   *Morocco*

Yield: 10 servings

Dressing:

Orange juice, fresh	16 oz.	Mix these ingredients together. Reserve.
Lemon juice	2–3 oz.	
Salt	½ tsp.	
Confectioner's sugar	2 tbsp.	
Orange flower water	2 tbsp.	

Oranges, navel	4	Peel, remove membranes, and separate into sections.

Carrots, shredded	2¼ lbs.	Combine the shredded carrots and the oranges. Add the dressing and chill for several hours. Before serving, sprinkle with the walnuts.
Walnuts, chopped	as needed	

SALAD NIÇOISE   *Southern France*

Yield: 10–12 servings

This can be a complete summer meal when served with a crusty French or Italian bread.

Dressing:

Olive oil	9 oz.	Using a wire whisk, combine these ingredients. Reserve.
Vinegar, wine	3 oz.	
Mustard, Dijon	1 tbsp.	
Garlic, minced	1 tsp.	
Salt and black pepper, coarse ground	to taste	
Herbs, fresh (thyme, oregano, rosemary, etc.)	2 tbsp.	

(Continued)

Green beans, fresh, small, trimmed	2 lbs.
Water	as needed
Celery	4 ribs
Potatoes, red-skinned	2 lbs.

In boiling water, blanch the beans until they are done, but still crisp. Place in iced water and reserve. Using a vegetable peeler, remove the celery strings, then cut in pieces about 3 inches long. Cut these pieces lengthwise into strips ¼ inch wide. Blanch the celery briefly, then place them in iced water and reserve. Cook the potatoes until they are fork-tender. When cool enough to handle, peel and slice. Place the beans, celery, and potatoes in 3 separate containers and toss lightly with the salad dressing. Reserve.

Peppers, green, halved, seeds and cores removed	3
Tomatoes, cherry, washed, stems removed	1 lb.
Tuna, canned	2 lbs.
Anchovy fillets	6 oz.
Olives, green and black, brine-cured	8 oz.
Onions, red, sliced thin	1 lb.
Eggs, hard-boiled, halved	5–6

Slice the peppers thin. Depending on the number of servings, arrange a proportional amount of all the ingredients in a symmetrical pattern in a salad bowl with the tuna, anchovies, hard-boiled egg halves, and olives on top. Add more dressing as needed.

Basil, fresh, chopped	as needed
Parsley, fresh, chopped	as needed
Scallions, chopped	as needed

Sprinkle the top with the basil, parsley, and scallions.

CUCUMBER AND YOGURT SALAD   *Greece and Turkey*

Yield: 10–12 servings

Yogurt	2 lbs.

Place a double layer of cheesecloth in a colander large enough to hold the yogurt. The cheesecloth should extend beyond the rim of the colander by 3–4 inches. Pour the yogurt into the colander. Tie the overlapping corners of the cheesecloth together. Suspend the yogurt over a deep, narrow pot and let drain in the refrigerator overnight. (Tie a wooden spoon to the top of the cheesecloth and place across the top of the pot).

Cucumber, peeled, seeded, and chopped fine	6
Garlic, minced	4 tsp.
Olive oil	3 oz.
Dill leaves, fresh, chopped	4 tbsp. or to taste
Salt and white pepper	to taste

Add these ingredients to the thickened yogurt. Mix well and chill for several hours before serving.

Cucumbers, sliced thin	as needed

Garnish with cucumber slices.

Serve with an assortment of other appetizers. This dish may be used as a dip for raw vegetables. Serve it with pita bread.

PUREE OF CELERIAC AND APPLES   *Northern France*

Yield: 10 servings

Celeriac, washed, peeled, 1-inch dice	3 lbs.
Flour	3 tbsp.
Milk	3 tbsp.
Water	as needed

Bring to a boil the milk, flour, and enough water to cover the celeriac. Add the celeriac and cook for 20 minutes, or until tender. Drain and reserve.

(Continued)

Apples, tart, peeled, cored, 1-inch dice	1½ lbs.
Butter	4 oz.

Over low heat melt the butter and sauté the apples for 5 minutes.

Place the celeriac and apples in a food processor. Using a pulsing action, puree the vegetables.

Sugar	as needed
Nutmeg	½ tsp.
Salt and white pepper	to taste
Heavy cream	if needed

Add the sugar, nutmeg, salt, and pepper. Pulse once or twice to mix again. Add a small amount of cream, if the consistency is too thick.

Serve as an accompaniment for any roasted meats or fowl.

PUREE OF CELERIAC AND POTATOES   *Austria*

Yield: 10 servings

Potatoes, washed, peeled	2 lbs.
Celeriac, washed, peeled	2 lbs.
Water	as needed
Butter	4 oz.
Salt and white pepper	to taste
Heavy cream	4–6 oz.

Cut the potatoes and celeriac into uniform pieces and boil in salted water until tender. Place in a food processor, along with the butter, salt, and pepper. Puree, using a pulsing action. Add enough heavy cream to obtain the desired consistency.

The puree may be served directly or may be placed into a pastry bag and piped onto a baking sheet. Brushed with clarified butter. Place for a few moments in a very hot oven or under the broiler to brown.

SWEET AND SOUR RED CABBAGE   *Norway*

Yield: 10 servings

Cabbage, red, shredded	3 lbs.
Apples, cored, diced	8 oz.
Lemon juice	½ lemon

Mix these ingredients and reserve.

Butter	4 oz.
Vinegar, cider	6 oz.
Water	4 oz.
Salt	1 tbsp.
Sugar	3 tbsp.
Caraway seeds	2 tsp.

Melt the butter. Add the other ingredients and bring to a boil, lower heat and simmer for 5 minutes. Taste for balance between sugar and vinegar. Adjust, if necessary. Pour over cabbage and apples and toss. Cover, place in 300 degree F oven, and braise for 2 hours.

Jelly, red currant	4 oz.
Red wine	4 oz.

Dissolve jelly in wine and add to the cabbage, distributing mixture thoroughly. Return to oven for 15–20 minutes. Adjust seasonings to achieve a good sweet and sour balance.

Serve as part of a buffet hot food presentation. Also may be served as an accompaniment for roast pork, smoked meats, and flavorful sausages.

SAUTÉED CELERY
Northern Italy

Yield: 10–12 servings

Celery stalks, large, inner portions	2 lbs.

Reserve outer stalks for other purposes, such as stocks or sauces. Using a vegetable peeler, remove the stringy outer side of the stalks. Trim the edges of the bottom portions so that there are straight edges along the entire length of the stalks. Cut into julienned strips about 2 inches long.

Water	as needed
Salt	as needed

Bring water to a boil. Add the salt and cook celery for a few minutes, or until barely tender. Place in iced water immediately and reserve until needed.

Olive oil	1 tbsp.
Garlic, chopped	½ tsp.
Salt and white pepper	to taste

In a small skillet, heat the oil and add garlic. Sauté for a few minutes until the garlic becomes soft and just begins to turn golden. Add 2–3 oz. of the blanched celery. Toss to coat well with the oil and heat through. Sprinkle with salt and a few grindings of black pepper.

EGGPLANT PUREE   *Turkey*   Yield: 10 servings

Eggplant, washed	4 lbs.

Prick each eggplant 4 or 5 times with a fork. Place them on a baking sheet and bake at 400 degrees F until they become very soft. When cool enough to handle, remove the pulp and place in a colander. Cover with a heavy dinner plate and weight down to extract the juices. Reserve.

Butter	2 oz.
Flour	3 oz.
Milk	1 pint

Heat butter until it foams. Remove from heat and, using a wire whisk, add the flour. Blend well and cook over low heat for 3–5 minutes, or until the mixture becomes light brown. Add the milk and continue to cook until the milk begins to thicken.

Parmesan cheese, grated	4 oz.
Salt and white pepper	to taste

Add the cheese and the reserved eggplant. Cook over low heat for 10 minutes. Season with salt and white pepper.

Serve hot or at room temperature as an accompaniment for grilled or roasted meats. May also be served as part of a platter of assorted appetizers.

EGGPLANT SALAD   *Turkey*   Yield: 10–12 servings

Eggplants, washed	2–3 lbs.

Prick each eggplant four or five times with a fork. Place them on a baking sheet and bake at 400 degrees F until they are soft and the skins are slightly charred. When cool enough to handle, remove the pulp and place in a colander. Cover with a heavy dinner plate and weight down to extract the juices. When the pulp has drained, chop fine.

Onion, minced	8 oz.	Add these ingredients to the eggplant pulp and, using a food processor, blend by using the pulsing action. Do not overmix. Texture should be slightly lumpy.
Parsley leaves, chopped	4 tbsp.	
Scallions, chopped (include the green parts)	6	
Olive oil	4 oz.	

Lemon juice, fresh	to taste	Add these ingredients and pulse a few more times to mix.
Salt and white pepper	to taste	

Feta cheese crumpled into small bits may be added after recipe has been completed to create an interesting variation. Mix by hand to incorporate the cheese.

PILAF WITH EGGPLANT AND ONION   *Greece*

Yield: 10–12 servings

A vegetarian preparation, this pilaf makes a good accompaniment for batter-dipped, deep-fried vegetables.

Eggplant, washed, stem end removed	2 lbs.	Leaving the eggplant's skin on, cut it into ½-inch cubes. Lightly sprinkle with salt. Place in a colander with a heavy plate on top and let sit for 30 minutes.
Salt	as needed	

Olive oil	as needed	Heat oil over medium to high heat. Rinse salt off the eggplant and dry with a towel. Sauté eggplant until well browned. Remove from pan and reserve.

Onion, diced	1 lb.	In the same pan, adding more oil if necessary, sauté the onions until they begin to brown. Add the rice and continue to cook until all of the oil has been absorbed.
Rice, long-grain	1½ lbs.	

(Continued)

Water or vegetable stock	2 qts.
Cinnamon	2 tsp.
Salt and black pepper	to taste
Pine nuts	4 tbsp.
White raisins or currants	5 tbsp.
Dill, fresh, chopped	4 tbsp.

Add liquid, cinnamon, salt, and pepper and stir well. Add the pine nuts, white raisins or currants, and dill. Cover and bring to a boil. Lower heat to simmer and cook until the rice is tender. Remove from heat. Remove the lid and add the reserved eggplant and mix well. Then cover the pot with a clean towel. Return the lid and let sit for 15 minutes before serving.

Serve hot or at room temperature as an accompaniment to any roasted meats or fowl.

OKRA STEWED WITH TOMATOES   *Greece*

Yield: 10–12 servings

Okra, small, fresh, washed	2–2½ lbs.
Water	as needed
Salt	1 tsp.
Vinegar, red	4 tbsp.

Trim the okra's cone-shaped end, retaining the cone shape and leaving the pod intact. Place pods in water to cover to which the vinegar and salt have been added. Let stand for at least 1 hour.

Sauce:

Olive oil	2 oz.
Onion, sliced	1 lb.
Tomatoes, peeled and chopped	1½ lbs.
Thyme, dried	2 tsp.
Sugar	2 tsp.
Parsley leaves, flat, chopped	6 tbsp.
Salt and black pepper	to taste
Lemon juice, fresh	to taste

Heat the oil over moderate heat and sauté the onion until soft. Add the tomatoes and the thyme and simmer for 30 minutes. Add the sugar, parsley, salt, pepper, and lemon juice and simmer for 10 minutes.

Drain the okra and rinse under cold water. Add to the tomato sauce and simmer for 20–30 minutes, or until the okra is tender but not mushy. Adjust seasonings, if necessary.

This dish may be served hot or at room temperature as an accompaniment to broiled chicken or fish. It also may be served on an appetizer or luncheon plate with a thin slice of feta cheese that has been garnished with virgin olive oil and a sprinkling of oregano.

RATATOUILLE   *Southern France*   Yield: 10–12 servings

Eggplant, washed, sliced lengthwise ¼ inch thick	1½ lbs.	Sprinkle the eggplant with salt, place in a colander, and weight down for 30 minutes to express juices.
Zucchini, washed, ends trimmed	1 lb.	Slice lengthwise ⅛ inch thick. Reserve.

Sauce:

Olive oil	4 oz.	Heat the oil over medium heat and sauté the onions, green pepper, and the garlic until soft but not brown. Add the other ingredients. Simmer for 30 minutes. Reserve.
Onion, sliced thin	1 lb.	
Pepper, green, thin sliced	1 lb.	
Garlic, chopped	2 tsp.	
Tomatoes, plum, peeled, seeded	2 lbs.	
Basil leaves, fresh, chopped	4 tbsp.	
Parsley leaves, flat, chopped	2 tbsp.	
Thyme, dried	1 tsp.	
Salt and black pepper	to taste	

(Continued)

Olive oil	as needed

Rinse the eggplant to remove the salt. Pat dry with towels. Place the slices of eggplant and zucchini on a baking sheet that has been brushed with the olive oil. Brush more oil on top of the slices and place in a 400 degree F oven or under a broiler until browned. Turn slices once.

In a baking pan, place a layer of eggplant on the bottom. Cover with a layer of tomato sauce, then a layer of zucchini. Continue this process until all ingredients have been used. Save the best looking pieces for the top layer. Place in a 400 degree F oven for 10–15 minutes, or until most of the liquid has evaporated.

Served hot, this can be used as a base for grilled fish or meats, as a topping for omelets, or as the vegetable accompaniment. Served cold, it can be a component for cold salad plates or as an appetizer.

BRAISED FENNEL IN WINE   *Southern Italy*

Yield: 10–12 servings

This dish is a good accompaniment for simple fried dishes.

Sauce:

Olive oil	3 oz.
Onion, small diced	8 oz.
Garlic, chopped fine	2 tsp.
Flour	1 tbsp.

Heat the oil over medium heat and sauté the onion and garlic until they are soft. Sprinkle lightly with flour and mix well. Cook for a few minutes over low heat.

Tomatoes, peeled, seeded, and chopped	1½ lbs.
White wine, dry	8 oz.
Basil leaves, fresh, chopped	4 tbsp.
Salt and black pepper	to taste

Add tomatoes, wine, basil, salt, and pepper and mix well. Simmer for 20 minutes.

Fennel bulbs, medium	10	Remove stems and leaves. Carefully trim root end so bulb will not fall apart and cut bulb in half from the root end to the stem end. Cut each of the halves again in the same way. Add to the tomato sauce, cover, and simmer for 15–20 minutes, or until fennel is just tender. Use 3–4 quarters per serving, depending on size.
Basil leaves, fresh	as needed	Garnish with basil leaves.

LENTILS WITH PROSCIUTTO   *Northern Italy*

Yield: 10 servings

Olive oil	2 oz.	Heat oil over medium heat in a heavy-bottomed saucepan. Add the rosemary and prosciutto and sauté for a minute or so.
Rosemary leaves, fresh	1 tbsp.	
Prosciutto, sliced $\frac{1}{16}$ inch thick, then coarsely chopped	6 oz.	
Lentils	1½ lbs.	Add the lentils and mix. Add water or stock to cover. Simmer, covered, until lentils are tender.
Water or chicken stock	as needed	
Black pepper	to taste	When done, add a few grindings of pepper.

WHITE BEAN SALAD   *Ukraine*

Yield: 10–12 servings

Navy beans	2 lbs.	Soak the beans for 10–12 hours. Change the water once. Wash well and remove debris, if any. Place in pot large enough to hold the beans plus 2–3 inches of water above the level of the beans. Bring to a boil, lower heat, and simmer until beans are tender, about 45 minutes. Drain and reserve.
Water	as needed	

(Continued)

Sunflower oil	6 oz.
Sesame oil	2 tbsp.
Onion, small dice	8 oz.
Carrot, small dice	8 oz.
Garlic, minced	4 cloves

Heat the oils and sauté vegetables and garlic until just tender. Add the vegetables to the beans. Include the oil.

Mint leaves, fresh, chopped	3 sprigs
Lemon juice	2 oz.
Olives, black, Kalamata, pitted, chopped	10
Salt and white pepper	to taste

Add these ingredients and mix with beans and vegetables. Adjust seasonings and refrigerate for at least 4 hours. Before serving, bring to room temperature.

Serve as an accompaniment for grilled fish. It may also be used as a garnish for green, leafy salads.

SWEET-AND-SOUR PEARL ONIONS   *Northern Italy*

Yield: 10 servings

Onions, pearl	2½ lbs.

Drop onions into boiling water for 15–20 seconds. Drain, peel, and keep in ice water.

Butter	4 oz.
Sugar	3 tbsp.
Salt and pepper	to taste

In a large skillet, melt the butter over medium heat. Add the onions and toss to coat evenly with the butter. Add sugar, salt, and pepper.

Vinegar, red wine	8 oz.

Add vinegar and simmer, covered, for 15–20 minutes, or until the onions are tender.

Flour	2 tbsp.
Stock, beef	8 oz.
Sugar	to taste
Salt and black pepper	to taste

Remove onions and keep them warm. Dissolve the flour in the cold stock, then add to the pan liquids, stirring with a wire whisk. Bring to a boil, then lower heat and simmer for 5 minutes. Adjust seasonings.

Remove from heat. Prior to serving, combine the sauce with the onions and heat through.

JANSSON'S TEMPTATION   *Sweden*

Yield: 10–12 portions

Potatoes, boiling, peeled, sliced thin, or shredded	5–6 lbs.
Onions, sliced thin	1 lb.
Butter clarified	as needed

Hold the potatoes in cold water until needed. Sauté the onions over low heat in the butter until they are soft. Do not allow them to brown.

Light cream	1 qt. or as needed

Bring to a boil.

Anchovies, diced	8 oz.
Black pepper	to taste
Bread crumbs	as needed
Butter, melted	3 oz.

In a deep hotel pan, arrange layers of potatoes, onions, and anchovies until all ingredients have been used. The top layer should be potatoes. Add the hot cream and a few grindings of black pepper. The liquid should just cover the top layer. Sprinkle generously with bread crumbs. Pour melted butter over the top, cover, and bake at 350 degrees F for 30–45 minutes.* Remove cover and continue to bake until top is nicely browned and potatoes are tender.

Serve as part of a buffet hot food presentation. This can also be served as a late night snack accompanied by cheeses and crisp bread.

---

* Cooking time can be reduced if potatoes are blanched first.

CARAMELIZED POTATOES   *Scandinavia*

Yield: 10 servings

Potatoes, red, small, uniform size	30
Water	as needed
Salt	as needed

Peel the potatoes and cook in boiling, salted water until barely fork-tender. Drain and reserve.

Sugar	12 oz.
Water	4 oz.

Using a small heavy-bottomed saucepan, bring the water and sugar to a boil and simmer until sugar begins to turn dark brown.

Butter	8 oz.

Add the butter and heat until the butter is melted.

In a hotel pan large enough to hold the potatoes in a single layer, add the caramel mixture and shake the pan to ensure that the potatoes are well-coated. Keep in a warm oven until needed.

This dish is an attractive buffet item as well as a good accompaniment for roasted pork.

POOR MAN'S POTATOES   *Spain*

Yield: 10–12 servings

Potatoes, all-purpose, peeled, sliced thin	5–6 lbs.
Water	8 qts.

Bring the water to a boil. Place potatoes in a wire basket and lower into the water. When water returns to the boil, blanch the potatoes for a minute or less and place them immediately in iced water. Reserve.

Garlic, mashed to a paste	4 tsp.
Parsley leaves, flat, chopped fine	10 tbsp.
Salt and black pepper	to taste

Mix these ingredients thoroughly and reserve.

Olive oil	as needed

To prepare an individual serving, pour olive oil ⅛ inch deep in a skillet over medium to high heat. Drain, then towel-dry the potatoes. Place the potato slices in layers in the hot oil. When they begin to brown, turn them, lower the heat, and cover. Cook over low heat for 5–6 minutes. Turn and separate the potatoes once or twice. Just prior to serving, sprinkle the potatoes with 1 tbsp. of the garlic and parsley mixture. Toss in the pan and serve.

POTATOES WITH RED PEPPER SAUCE   *Spain*

Yield: 10–12 servings

Potatoes, new, red or white	4–5 lbs.

Select small, uniform potatoes. Boil, unpeeled, in a generous amount of water until tender. Drain and let cool. When cool enough to handle peel and cut in half. Reserve.

Sauce:

Peppers, red sweet, washed, halved, core and seeds removed	3 lbs.
Anchovy fillets	4 oz.
Cayenne pepper	½ tsp.
Black pepper	½ tsp.
Olive oil	2 tbsp.

Place the peppers, cut side down, on an oiled baking sheet and roast in a 400 degree F oven until the skins begin to char. Remove from oven, cover for 10 minutes, then peel the skins. Reserve. Place anchovies, cayenne, black pepper, olive oil, and reserved peppers in the bowl of a food processor and puree until very smooth. Adjust seasonings if necessary.

Olives, black (Kalamata or other brine-cured) pitted, chopped	12 oz.

Remove the pepper puree to a mixing bowl. Add the olives and mix well.

Place a pool of the pepper sauce on a plate and place the potato halves on top, cut side down.

Serve as an accompaniment for fish dishes. If served as a appetizer or first course, garnish the edge of the plate with a few slices of hard-boiled egg.

BAKED POTATOES WITH FRESH HERBS   *Southern France*

Yield: 10 servings

Potatoes, Idaho, scrubbed	10, 8–10 oz. each

Pierce the potatoes in several places with a sharp-tined fork. Bake at 400 degrees F for 1 hour.

Butter, whole	10 oz.
Parsley leaves, flat, chopped	4 tbsp.
Chives, fresh, chopped	4 tbsp.
Heavy cream	5 oz.
Salt and white pepper	to taste

When potatoes are cool enough to handle, use a sharp-tipped paring knife to remove an oval section approximately 1½ inches by 2 inches from the side of the potato that is the most irregular. Remove and reserve any pulp from this section, discard the skin. Remove all of the pulp from the remainder of the potato: reserve the shell. Mix the potato pulp with these ingredients and blend to a smooth consistency.

Return the potato pulp to the shells, using a large spoon or, for a more decorative presentation, pipe the mixture into the shells, using a pastry tube. Cover and reserve in a cool place, preferably not under refrigeration. If potatoes must be refrigerated, bring to room temperature before the next step.

Egg yolks, beaten	as needed
Heavy cream	as needed
Gruyère cheese, grated	as needed

Mix 1 part egg yolk with 2 parts cream. Brush on top of the potatoes. Sprinkle with grated cheese and place in a 450 degree F oven for 10 minutes, or until the potato is heated through and the top is lightly browned.

ROSTI POTATOES

Yield: 10–12 servings

Potatoes, all-purpose	5–6 lbs.

Cook potatoes in boiling water. When just fork tender remove from water and let cool completely. Peel potatoes and then shred them.

Butter, clarified	as needed
Salt	as needed
Water	as needed

To prepare an individual serving in a heavy skillet, heat butter over medium heat. Add potatoes (5–6 oz. per serving) and a sprinkling of salt. Turn the potatoes over a few times. Sprinkle with a little water and then compress the potatoes to form a pancake. Lower heat and cover. Cook until the potato has formed a light brown crust on the bottom. Invert potatoes onto the serving plate so that the brown crust is on top.

Variations: Goose fat or lard may be used instead of clarified butter. Fried bacon bits, lightly sautéed onion or grated Swiss cheese may also be added.

POTATO PANCAKES "REIBEKUCHEN"   *Sweden*

Yield: 10–12 servings

Potatoes, russet or Idaho	5–6 lbs.
Onion, diced fine	8 oz.
Eggs, beaten	6
Flour	6 tbsp.
Salt and white pepper	to taste
Nutmeg	to taste

Peel potatoes and store in cold water until needed. Grate potatoes and squeeze to remove the liquid. Add the onion, eggs, flour, salt, pepper, and nutmeg and mix well. This must be done quickly or the potatoes will discolor.

Cooking oil, vegetable or lard	to a depth of 1 inch

In a heavy skillet, heat oil over medium to high heat. Pancakes may be made any size. Drop potato mixture gently into the hot fat and fry until golden brown on one side. Turn once and fry the other side. When pancakes are done, drain on paper towels. Best eaten immediately.

Serve with applesauce, lingonberry, or cranberry preserves. May be used as an accompaniment for game or pork dishes or, in larger portions, as a luncheon entrée with a green salad.

POTATO DUMPLINGS *Hungary*

Yield: no. of servings depends on use and size of dumplings

Potatoes, all-purpose	5 lbs.

Boil unpeeled potatoes until fork-tender. Cool, peel, and rice or grate, using a fine grater.

Onions, minced	8 oz.

Sauté onions until light brown. Add to the potatoes.

Eggs	3 large
Flour	10 oz.
Semolina	10 oz.
Salt	1 oz.
White pepper	½ tsp.

Add these ingredients and, on a floured board, mix well to form a smooth dough.

Dumplings may be cooked in several ways. *For soups:* shape into individual balls and cook in stock or salted, boiling water. Cooking time depends on size of dumpling.

As an entree accompaniment: shape dumpling mixture into rolls about 5–6 inches long and 1½ inches in diameter. Cook in salted, simmering water for 20–25 minutes. These "rolls" may be reserved, then sliced and reheated in a steamer as needed.

The addition of chopped parsley or finely minced ham make interesting variations. For another variation: Sauté finely minced ham and onions. Add chopped, fresh dill and mix well. Form the dumpling mixture into balls about 2–2½ inches in diameter. Make a hole in each ball and insert some of the onion/ham/dill mixture. Close hole by pinching the dumpling mixture together. Reshape into ball and cook according to previous instructions.

WARM POTATO SALAD *Germany*

Yield: 10–12 servings

Potatoes, boiling	5–6 lbs.

Boil potatoes, skins on, until just fork-tender. Peel, slice lengthwise, then cut each half into slices ⅛ inch thick.

Bacon, diced	8 oz.	
Onion, diced	1 lb.	
White vinegar	8 oz.	
Stock, beef	8 oz.	
Salt and white pepper	to taste	

Sauté the bacon and onions until slightly browned. Add stock and vinegar and bring to a boil. Lower heat and simmer for 5 minutes. Pour over potatoes, mix gently, and season with salt and pepper.

Parsley, chopped	10–12 sprigs

Garnish with parsley.

SWEDISH BROWNED POTATOES   *Sweden*

Yield: 10–12 servings

Potatoes,* all-purpose	5–6 lbs.

Peel potatoes and cut into uniform size. Cover with lightly salted water and bring to the boil over high heat. Reduce heat to the simmer and cook until just potatoes can be pierced easily with a fork. Drain and return to low heat for a minute or two to evaporate all moisture. Reserve.

Butter, sweet	4 oz.
Bread crumbs	3 oz.
Salt	2 tsp.
White pepper	1 tsp.
Sugar	2 tsp.

Heat butter in a heavy skillet until it melts. Fry the bread crumbs until they are light brown. Add the salt, pepper, and sugar and mix thoroughly.

Reserved potatoes	

Add the cooked potatoes, and, shaking the pan, coat them on all sides with the bread crumb mixture. Continue this process until the potatoes are heated through.

---

* Small, peeled, and boiled new potatoes may also be used.

SPINACH ROMAN STYLE *Southern Italy*

Yield: 10 servings

Pancetta or slab bacon, very small cubes	12 oz.	Sauté the pancetta or bacon until the the fat has been rendered. Remove the sautéed bits and reserve.

Garlic, chopped	2 tsp.	Discard the excess fat and add the garlic, pine nuts, and white raisins, and sauté over low heat until the pine nuts begin to brown lightly. Let cool and reserve.
Pine nuts	3 tbsp.	
White raisins, soaked in water for 30 minutes	5 tbsp.	

Spinach, fresh, washed, tough stems removed	6–8 oz. per serving	To prepare an individual serving, melt the butter in a skillet large enough to hold the spinach. Dampen the spinach leaves and add to the pan, along with 1 tbsp. of the reserved pancetta mixture. Cover pan and cook until the spinach is just wilted. Toss well and serve hot.
Butter	1 oz.	

SALAD CAPRESE
Southern Italy

Yield: one serving

This is a simple salad, but one that is very attractive and delicious, providing that the ingredients are of top quality. Use very flavorful, ripe tomatoes that are in season. The mozzarella must be fresh, not the commercial, processed variety.

Tomatoes, sliced thick	4–5 slices	Alternate slices of the mozzarella and tomatoes.
Mozzarella, fresh, sliced thin	4–5 slices	

Olive oil	1 tbsp.	Whisk these ingredients together. Pour on top of tomatoes and mozzarella.
Basil leaves, fresh, chopped	2 tbsp.	
Wine vinegar	½ tsp.	
Salt and black pepper	to taste	

TOMATO AND PEPPER SALAD   *Morocco*

Yield: 10–12 servings

Garlic, chopped	2 tsp.
Olive oil	1 oz.
Tomatoes, plum peeled, seeded, and chopped	6 lbs.

Heat the oil and sauté the garlic over low heat until soft. Do not allow to brown. Add the tomatoes and simmer for 30 minutes.

Preserved lemon (see the recipe in the "Condiments" section)	1
Red pepper flakes	½ tsp.
Salt and black pepper	to taste

Remove and discard the pulp from the lemon, then chop the peel fine. Add the lemon peel and the red pepper flakes to the tomatoes and simmer for 5 minutes. Season with salt and pepper. Reserve.

Pepper, green, washed, halved, core and seeds removed	3 lbs.
Coriander leaves, chopped	3 tbsp.

Place the peppers, cut side down, on an oiled baking sheet and roast in a 400 degree F oven until the skins begin to char. Remove from oven, cover for 10 minutes, then peel the skins. Slice the peppers into thin strips and add to the tomato sauce. Simmer for 5 minutes. Remove from heat and let cool. When cool, add the coriander, mix well, and refrigerate for several hours before serving.

Serve chilled as a first course on a bed of lettuce leaves or as part of a group of appetizers.

TOMATOES WITH RICE AND PINE NUTS   *Greece*

Yield: 10 servings

Tomatoes	10 large

Remove the top of each tomato by cutting a cone-shaped section around the stem. Reserve the tops. Scoop out the tomatoes and reserve the pulp. Place tomatoes inverted on a rack and let drain.

(Continued)

Olive oil	4 oz.
Onion, diced	4 oz.
Rice, long-grain	6 oz.
Currants	3 tbsp.
Pine nuts	2 tbsp.
Mint leaves, fresh, chopped	3 tbsp.
Salt and pepper	to taste
Water	10 oz.
Reserved tomato pulp	

Heat the olive oil and sauté the onion until soft. Add the rice and continue to cook until the oil has been absorbed. Add the remaining ingredients and stir well. Cover and simmer until the rice is cooked, but still very firm.

Tomato juice	as needed
Olive oil	as needed
Sugar	as needed

Fill the tomatoes with the rice mixture. Cover each tomato with a reserved top, and place in a baking pan just large enough to hold them. Pour tomato juice to a depth of 1 inch on the bottom of the pan. Brush the top of each tomato with olive oil and sprinkle with a little sugar. Bake in a 350 degree F oven for 30 minutes.

Serve warm or at room temperature. May be used as the central item for a luncheon plate; as an accompaniment for grilled meats, fish, or fowl; or as an appetizer.

STUFFED TOMATOES WITH VEGETABLES   *Austria*

Yield: one or two per serving depending on size

Tomatoes	1 per serving

Make a 1-inch opening by removing the remainder of the tomato's stem. Using a small scoop, remove the seeds and most of the pulp. Salt the cavity lightly and invert on a rack to drain.

Potatoes	as needed
Carrots	
Peas	
Celery	
Pickles	

Cut vegetables (in any combination sufficient to stuff the tomatoes) into very small dice (except the peas) and blanch in boiling water until tender. (Other seasonal vegetables may be substituted.) Place in iced water and reserve.

Apples, peeled and diced	as needed
Mayonnaise	as needed
Lemon juice	to taste
Salt and white pepper	to taste

Bind the blanched vegetables and the raw apple with mayonnaise, which has been seasoned with lemon juice, salt, and pepper. Fill the tomatoes with the mixture and chill.

Parsley, fresh, chopped	as needed

Garnish with parsley and serve cold.

Serve 1 as an accompaniment for fish or meat dishes. Two make a nice luncheon dish. As a variation, it may be served hot: Use blanched asparagus tips, carrots, potatoes, peas, and mushrooms. Bind the mixture with a little béchamel sauce and sautéed onions. Top with grated cheese and place in a 400 degree F oven for 10 minutes, or until the cheese begins to bubble and brown.

DESSERTS

APPLE STRUDEL   *Austria*   Yield: 10–15 servings

Pastry:

Flour, bread	1 lb.
Salt	½ tsp.
Water	8 oz. (approx.)
Eggs, beaten	2
Butter, melted	2 tbsp.

Mix all these ingredients together and knead dough very thoroughly until it becomes soft and very elastic. The amount of water may vary, depending on the flour and humidity. Shape dough into a ball and let rest, covered, for 2 hours.

Filling:

Granny Smith apples, peeled, cored, sliced	4–5 lbs.
Sugar	8–12 oz.
Cinnamon	1½ tsp.
Raisins, sultana	8 oz.
Bread crumbs, sautéed in butter	10 oz.
Almonds, blanched, slivered	6 oz.
Lemon juice	1 lemon

Mix the sugar and cinnamon together. Mix this with the apples, making sure they are well coated. Add the remaining ingredients and mix thoroughly.

Light cream	as needed

On a floured tablecloth, roll the dough into as large a rectangle as possible. Flour your hands and place them, palms down, underneath the dough, in the rectangle's center. Gently stretch the dough out on the backs of your hands until you have a very thin dough of uniform thickness. Trim any thick edges and reserve in case patches are needed to repair any tears.

(Continued)

Butter, melted	as needed

Spread the apple mixture evenly over the surface of the dough, leaving a 4-inch border on 1 of the long sides of the rectangle and 2 of the shorter sides. Brush these edges with melted butter. Fold over the 2 shorter sides. Starting opposite the long, buttered edge, gently lift the tablecloth, causing the strudel to roll up like a jelly roll. Gently slide the strudel off the cloth and onto a buttered baking sheet. Brush with melted butter and bake in a 400 degree F oven for 45 minutes to 1 hour, or until golden. During baking, brush with cream 2 or 3 times.

Serve warm with a generous powdering of confectioner's sugar.

A SHORT PASTRY DOUGH   *France*

Yield: one 11-inch tart shell (8–10 servings)

Pastry shells may be filled with various fruit and/or cream fillings after baking. They may also be partially baked, filled, and then returned to the oven to finish. To prevent shells from becoming soggy, an apricot glaze or a thin coat of melted chocolate can be brushed on prior to adding the filling.

Flour, all-purpose	8 oz.
Sugar	1 tbsp.
Salt	¾ tsp.
Butter, sweet, chilled, in small pieces	6 oz.

Place the flour, sugar, and salt in the bowl of a food processor and blend by using the pulsing action 3–4 times. Add butter to flour. Pulse until the mixture has the texture of coarse crumbs.

Egg	1
Milk or water	1 tbsp.

Beat the egg together with the water or milk. With the processor running continuously, add this to the flour mixture. As soon as the dough forms a ball, remove it from the processor. Place the dough on a piece of plastic wrap and shape it into a flat disk about ½ inch thick. Wrap well and refrigerate for at least 1 hour before using.

Butter, softened	as needed

Lightly butter an 11-inch tart pan, preferably one with a removable bottom. Lightly flour a cold surface (marble is best), and roll out the disk into an even round (1½–2 inches larger than the tart pan).

Roll the dough up onto the rolling pin and transfer it to the tart pan. Gently lift the edges of the dough and press it into the pan, taking care not to stretch the dough. You may remove the excess dough by passing the rolling pin over the top edge of the tart pan. If you wish to make a thicker rim, trim the excess dough so that the overhang is uniform, then turn the excess dough under, making a double thickness of dough along the rim. After the dough has been turned under, place your thumbs on the inside of the rim and your index fingers on the outside of the tart pan. Gently compress the dough while pushing the dough upward along the rim of the tart pan to slightly increase the height of the rim and give the tart more depth.

Line the dough with aluminum foil and add enough beans to cover the surface to ½ the depth of the pan. Bake in a 375 degree F oven for 15–20 minutes. Remove the foil with the beans and continue to bake for another 5 minutes or until the bottom of the tart shell feels dry to the touch and is slightly browned. Remove from heat and let cool.

PALAÇINTA   *Hungary*

Yield: 10 servings

Flour, all-purpose	12 oz.
Salt	½ tsp.
Sugar	1 tbsp.
Milk	12 oz.

Combine flour, sugar, and salt. Add milk and mix until thoroughly blended.

Egg yolks, beaten	3 large

Add egg yolks to other ingredients and mix well. The batter should be free-flowing. If batter is too thick, add more milk; if too thin, add more flour.

(Continued)

Butter	as needed	Lightly butter a 6-inch to 10-inch skillet (nonstick, if available). Pour in just enough batter to cover the pan's bottom. Rotate the pan so that the batter is evenly distributed. Brown lightly on one side, turn, and brown lightly on the other side. When done, reserve in a warm place. Prepare all of the batter in this manner and set aside.
Apricot jam*	12 oz.	Mix small amount of brandy or liqueur with jam. Spread a thin layer over ⅔ of the pancake. Roll up, beginning on the side with the jam. Reserve until needed.
Brandy or liqueur	2 oz.	
Sugar, confectioner's	as needed	Prior to serving, heat the needed portion in a 250 degree F oven. Remove from oven and dust with powdered sugar. (Portion size will vary, depending on the pancake's size.)

* Chopped walnuts may be added to the jam.

CHEESECAKE WITH FRESH BERRIES   *Germany*

Yield: 10 servings

Pastry:

Flour, all-purpose	12 oz.	Place the flour, butter, sugar, and salt in a food processor. Using the steel blade, pulse 4 or 5 times, until the mixture has a mealy consistency. Add water and continue to process until the mixture masses. Remove and shape into a ball. Flatten this into a disk, dust with flour, and refrigerate, covered, for 1 or 2 hours.
Butter, chilled, cut in small pieces	10 oz.	
Sugar	2 oz.	
Egg yolks	2	
Salt	½ tsp.	
Water	4–5 tbsp.	

Filling:

Ricotta or farmer's cheese	1 lb.	Mix all these ingredients thoroughly.
Heavy cream	4 oz.	
Eggs, beaten	3	
Lemon peel, grated*	1 lemon	
Vanilla extract	½ tsp.	
Sugar	to taste	

Egg, beaten with 1 tbsp. water	1	Remove pastry from refrigerator and roll it out so it will line a 10-inch pie pan. Add the filling and bake in a 400 degree F oven for 35–40 minutes. After 15 minutes, glaze the top of the cake with the beaten egg. Pierce with a toothpick prior to removing from oven. If toothpick comes out clean, the cake is done.

Serve with a puree of seasonal fresh berries that have been sweetened to taste. Liquor of choice may also be added to further enhance the flavor.

* Alternative flavorings such as Kirsch or other liquors may be used.

YOGURT CAKE IN HONEY SYRUP   *Turkey*

Yield: one, 12-inch cake

Cake:

Flour, unbleached, all-purpose	12 oz.	Combine all these ingredients and mix well. Pour into a buttered, 12-inch springform pan and bake at 400 degrees F for 40–45 minutes.
Yogurt	12 oz.	
Baking soda	1 tsp.	
Sugar	6 oz.	
Butter	as needed	

(Continued)

Syrup:

Water	16 oz.
Honey	6 oz.
Sugar	4 oz.
Lemon, halved	1
Cinnamon stick	1, 4 inches
Cloves	10

Combine these ingredients and bring to a boil. Lower heat and simmer for 30 minutes. Remove the cinnamon stick and lemon halves. Raise heat to high and boil syrup until it becomes slightly thickened.

When done, pour the syrup over the cake and let rest at room temperature for 2–3 hours before serving.

LEMON TART   *France*

Yield: one, 11-inch tart (8–10 servings)

Short pastry (see the recipe at the beginning of this section)	1 recipe

(See the recipe for preparation of short pastry and preparation of tart shell. Complete up to and including the fourth step. Then, line the dough with a piece of aluminum foil large enough to cover the rim of the tart pan completely. Add enough beans to cover the surface to ½ the depth of the pan. Bake in a 375 degree F oven for 15 minutes. Partially lift the foil to determine if the shell is baked through. If not, bake for a few more minutes. Remove from oven and let cool. Remove foil and beans.

Lemons, washed	3
Eggs	6
Sugar	8 oz. or more, if desired

Grate the rind of the lemons and squeeze out the juice, taking care to remove all the seeds. Using a wire whisk, combine the grated rind, lemon juice, eggs, and sugar. Place in a double-boiler and cook, stirring gently, until the mixture begins to thicken to a custardlike consistency. (Do not allow this mixture to reach the boiling point or the eggs will congeal.)

Remove from heat and allow to cool completely. Whisk the custard a few times, then pour it into the prebaked pastry shell. Return the tart to a 350 degree F oven and bake until the edge of the crust turns light-brown and the top of the custard becomes glazed.

Cream, unsweetened, whipped	as needed

Serve with a dollop of the cream.

TART TATIN   *France*

Yield: 8–10 servings

Short pastry (see the recipe at the beginning of this section)	1 recipe	Hold in refrigerator until needed.

Butter, sweet	4 oz.	In a nonstick, 12-inch skillet, melt the butter, then add the sugar. Over low to medium heat, cook for 10 minutes, stirring occasionally.
Sugar	8 oz.	

Apples, tart, peeled, cored, quartered	3–4 lbs.	Arrange the apples around the circumference of the pan, core side up. Fill the center of the pan, following the same pattern. Place the apple quarters as close together as possible, because some shrinkage will occur. Continue to cook over medium heat until the sugar/butter mixture begins to thicken and caramelize. When the pan liquids become a medium-brown color, remove pan from heat and let cool for a few minutes. (The apples may be sprinkled with ground cinnamon at this point, if desired.)

Remove the dough from the refrigerator and let it warm up for 1–2 minutes. Roll the dough in a circle slightly larger than the skillet. Place the dough over the apples and tuck in around the edges. Work quickly so that the heat of the pan and its contents will not soften the dough.

Place the skillet in a 375 degree F oven and bake for 45 minutes, or until the crust is light brown.

Let tart cool for 5 minutes. Place a flat pie plate that is somewhat larger than the skillet on top. Invert the skillet, holding the plate in place, to unmold. If some of the apples adhere to the pan, remove them and put them in place on the crust.

Cream, unsweetened, whipped	as needed	Serve warm or at room temperature with the cream.

FLAN TART   *Portugal*   Yield: 8–10 servings

Dough:

Flour, pastry	8 oz.
Sugar	4 oz.
Butter, chilled, in small pieces	6 oz.

Place the flour and sugar in the bowl of a food processor fitted with a plastic blade. Add the butter. Mix, using the pulse action, until the ingredients have the texture of coarse crumbs.

Vanilla extract	½ tsp.
Egg, beaten with 1 tsp. water	1 large

Add the vanilla and the beaten egg and continue to mix until the dough forms a ball. Shape the dough into a flat disk, wrap in plastic, and refrigerate for at least 1 hour.

When ready to use, let the dough warm up a bit. Roll out on a floured board and fit into a 10-inch to 11-inch tart pan with a removable bottom. Cover with aluminum foil and weight down with beans or rice. Bake in a 350 degree F oven for 12–15 minutes. Remove the foil and the beans or rice. Reserve.

Flan:

Milk	8 oz.
Cream	4 oz.

In a heavy-bottomed saucepan over low heat, bring the milk and cream to a boil.

Butter, melted	2 oz.
Eggs	4 large
Sugar	3 oz. or to taste
Flour	1 oz.
Cornstarch	1 tbsp.
Salt	¼ tsp.
Lemon peel, grated	½ tsp.

Combine the remaining ingredients thoroughly. Gradually add the hot milk/cream mixture. Use a wire whisk, stirring quickly. Pour mixture into the partially baked tart shell* and bake at 350 degrees F for 40–45 minutes. Flan should be lightly browned.

---

* To fill the tart shell, pull the oven rack halfway out and place the unfilled tart shell on it. Use a ladle to fill the shell to the brim with the flan mixture, then gently push the rack back into the oven.

FLAN   *Spain*

Yield: 10 servings

Caramel:

Sugar	7 oz.
Water	2 oz.
Butter	as needed

Combine the sugar and water in a small, heavy pan over low to medium heat, stirring constantly. Cook until the sugar is honey-colored and the mixture has the consistency of thick syrup, about 8–10 minutes. Remove from heat and pour equal amounts into 10 oven-proof custard cups. Twirl cups to distribute caramel evenly. Spread a light coating of butter on the portions of the custard cups that are not covered by the caramel.

Flan:

Milk	1 qt.
Eggs	8
Egg yolks	2
Sugar	6 oz.
Vanilla extract	2 tsp.

Bring the milk to a boil. Beat the eggs, egg yolks, and sugar together. Add the hot milk, stirring quickly. Add the vanilla and mix well. Pour mixture into the custard cups, which have been placed on a rack in a baking pan. Fill the pan with hot water and bake in a 400 degree F oven for 30–35 minutes.

Test to see if done by inserting a toothpick or the tip of a small knife into one of the custards. If it comes out clean, the custard is done. Remove from heat, invert the cups in place on individual dessert plates, and unmold. If the flan is refrigerated, it may be necessary to run a thin knife around the sides or to immerse the cups briefly in hot water to unmold and release the caramel.

Serve as is or surround by a puree of fresh raspberries, strawberries, or other seasonal fruit.

COLD CHOCOLATE FOAM   *Northern Italy*

Yield: 10–12 servings

Chocolate, semi-sweet, in small bits	12 oz.

In a double-boiler, heat the chocolate until it melts.

(Continued)

Eggs, separated	8
Sugar	2 tbsp.
Coffee, espresso	½ cup
Rum	3 tbsp.

Using a wire whisk or electric mixer, beat the sugar and egg yolks until they thicken slightly and have a pale-yellow color. Add the melted chocolate, coffee, and rum.

Heavy cream	12 oz.

Whip the cream and fold it into the mixture.

Whip the egg whites to form stiff peaks. Gently fold into the mixture. Spoon into wine glasses or other suitable dessert glasses. Refrigerate for 4–6 hours before serving.

ORANGES IN ORANGE FLOWER WATER   *Morocco*

Yield: 10 servings

Oranges, navel	10 large

Select the best quality fruit. Peel oranges, removing all of the outer white membrane. Break the orange into sections, again removing all of the membrane. Place the orange sections in a glass bowl or stainless-steel mixing bowl.

Orange juice, fresh	8 oz.
Lemon juice, fresh	2 oz.
Orange flower water	5 tbsp.
Sugar, confectioner's	4–6 tbsp.
Lemon zest	2 tsp.
Cinnamon, ground	1 tsp.

Mix these ingredients together. When completely blended, taste and adjust the sugar and cinnamon, if necessary. Pour this mixture over the orange segments, mix lightly, cover, and refrigerate for several hours.

Almonds, toasted, crushed	as needed

To prepare an individual serving, place orange segments on a small, chilled dessert plate in an overlapping pattern around the plate's perimeter. Pour a spoonful or 2 of the orange juice mixture over the segments. Sprinkle some toasted, crushed almonds on top.

TAPIOCA PUDDING WITH FRUIT SAUCE   *Southern France*

Yield: 10 servings

Milk	1 qt.
Sugar	5 oz.
Butter	3 oz.
Salt	¼ tsp.
Vanilla extract	½ tsp.
Tapioca	5 oz.

In a heavy-bottomed saucepan, bring the milk to a boil over low heat, stirring. Add the butter, salt, and vanilla extract and mix thoroughly. Add the tapioca and cook for 10 minutes, or until the tapioca is transparent. This may be done in a double-boiler to avoid the possibility of scorching the milk.

Egg yolks, beaten	4
Egg whites, beaten stiff	4
Butter	as needed

Place the cooked tapioca in a mixing bowl and add the beaten egg yolks. Gently fold in the beaten egg whites, then pour the mixture in equal amounts into 10 lightly buttered ramekins. Place the ramekins in a baking pan with enough hot, not boiling, water to reach halfway up the sides of the ramekins.

Bake in a 325–350 degree F oven for 30 minutes. Test by inserting a toothpick in the center of 1 of the puddings. If it comes out clean, the tapioca is done. Let cool and refrigerate.

Fruit Sauce:

Raspberries, fresh*	1 lb.
Port wine	2 oz.
Sugar	as needed

Place cleaned fruit into the bowl of a food processor and puree with port wine or other liqueur of choice. Sweeten to taste.

Unmold the tapioca pudding by placing it in a little hot water briefly. Pour a pool of the fruit sauce on a dessert plate and place the unmolded pudding on top. Pour a small amount of the fruit sauce on top of the tapioca and let it drip down the sides.

* Any fruit sauce may be substituted. If fresh fruits are not available, stew dried apricots and puree with liqueur of choice. Add sugar to taste.

MELONS WITH ANISETTE   *Spain*

Yield: 10 servings

Ingredient	Amount
Melons (cantaloupe, honeydew, etc.), ripe	3 lbs.

Calculate the weight after removing the seeds and cutting the melon(s) into balls using a melon ball scoop. Any combination of melons can be used. Work over a bowl to retain as much of the fruit juices as possible.

Ingredient	Amount
Anisette	8 oz.
Sugar, confectioner's	to taste

Add the anisette to the fruit juices along with confectioner's sugar. Pour over the melon balls and toss well. Refrigerate for 3–4 hours before serving, stirring occasionally.

Ingredient	Amount
Orange slices, halved	as needed
Mint leaves, fresh	as needed

Serve in chilled goblets and garnish with orange slices placed around the perimeter of the glass and several spoonfuls of the anisette/fruit juice. Place several mint leaves on top.

APRICOT CREAM   *Turkey*

Yield: 10 servings

Ingredient	Amount
Apricots, dried	2 lbs.
Honey	8 oz.
Cinnamon stick	1, 4 inches
Lemon, halved	1
Water	as needed

Combine all ingredients in a heavy-bottomed saucepan with enough water to just cover. Bring to a boil. Lower heat and simmer for 1 hour, or until the apricots are very soft. When done, strain the liquid and reserve the syrup. Place the apricots in the bowl of a food processor and puree until very smooth. Add as much syrup as necessary to make a smooth, custard-like consistency. Let cool and reserve.

Ingredient	Amount
Heavy cream	1 pt.

Whip cream until stiff. Gently fold into the pureed apricots. Fill individual serving dishes and chill well before serving.

ORANGE CREAM   *Spain*

Yield: 10 servings

Eggs, beaten	10
Sugar	10 oz.
Lemon zest	2 tbsp.
Orange juice	20 oz.

Place the eggs and sugar in the bowl of an electric mixer and beat at medium speed until mixture is pale-yellow. Add the lemon zest and orange juice and blend thoroughly.

Place the mixture in the top of a double-boiler and cook over boiling water, stirring constantly, until the mixture thickens. Pour equal amounts into 10 wine glasses. Chill thoroughly before serving.

Orange peel, candied, cut in thin strips, or chocolate shavings	as needed

Garnish with candied orange peel or chocolate.

APPLE FRITTERS
Northern France

Yield: 10 servings

Batter:

Flour, sifted all-purpose	1 lb.
Eggs	2
Water or beer	16 oz.
Oil	2 oz.
Sugar	1 tbsp.
Baking powder	1 tsp.
Salt	1 tsp.
Nutmeg	to taste

Combine these ingredients and mix to a light, smooth batter. Adjust flour or liquid if batter is too thick or too thin. Batter should be flowing but not too thin. Reserve.

(Continued)

Apples, Granny Smith, peeled, cored, sliced into ¼-inch rings	10
Sugar	6 oz.
Cinnamon, ground	1 tsp.
Kirsch	2 oz.

Place apple slices in a glass container or stainless-steel container in a single layer. Combine the sugar and cinnamon and sprinkle on top. Sprinkle on a few drops of Kirsch. Make another layer and repeat this process until all the apples are used. Cover and refrigerate for 2 hours.

Drain the apples needed for service and dip into batter. Deep-fry at 350 degrees F for 4–5 minutes. When golden-brown, remove from fat and drain on towel. Serve warm.

These apple fritters may be served with a sprinkling of cinnamon/sugar or confectioner's sugar. They may also be served as an accompaniment for pork or veal entrées.

POACHED PEACHES WITH FRUIT PUREE   *Southern France*

Yield: 10 servings

Syrup:

White wine	16 oz.
Water	16 oz.
Sugar	8 oz.
Honey	2 tbsp.
Lemon, sliced	1
Cinnamon stick	1, 2 inches

Combine these ingredients in a saucepan large enough to hold 10 whole peaches. Over high heat, bring the liquids to a boil, stirring. Lower heat and simmer for 15–20 minutes.

Peaches	10

Select best quality, slightly underripe peaches with no blemishes. Plunge peaches into boiling water for a few seconds, then peel. Place the peaches in the syrup and poach gently, turning once. (The cooking time will vary depending on how ripe the peaches are.) Peaches should be tender but still firm.

Remove from heat and discard the cinnamon stick. Let the peaches cool in the syrup, then refrigerate.

Fruit Puree:

Strawberries*	1 qt.
Sugar	if needed

Place the strawberries in the bowl of a food processor and, using the steel blade, puree until smooth. Add just enough syrup to liquify the strawberries so that the mixture can be easily poured. Adjust for sugar, if needed. Refrigerate.

Strawberry	10
Mint leaves	as needed

To prepare an individual serving, cover the bottom of a chilled dessert plate with the fruit puree. Place 1 whole peach in the center of the plate. Garnish with a whole strawberry that has been partially sliced 3 or 4 times (leave it connected at the stem end) and opened like a fan. Place the strawberry on several large, fresh mint leaves.

---

* Substitute raspberries or any other fruit that would make a good color and taste combination with the peaches. Several fruits may also be combined. The puree flavor may be enhanced with a variety of fruit liqueurs.

PEARS WITH GORGONZOLA   *Northern Italy*

Yield: 12 servings

Pears, Anjou, peeled, halved, seeds removed	6

Pears should be unblemished and of uniform size. Using the tip of a sharp paring knife, make shallow "V" cuts to remove the hard stem portions remaining on each half. Remove seeds with a small melon scoop.

White wine	as needed

In a large skillet, bring enough wine to cover to a boil. Place the pear halves, cut side down, in a single layer in the skillet. Lower heat, cover, and simmer until the pears are tender. (Cooking time will vary depending on the ripeness of the pears.) When done, remove from heat and chill.

(Continued)

Gorgonzola	3–4 oz.
Butter, whole	2 oz.
Walnuts, crushed	2 oz.
Lemon juice, fresh	to taste

Blend these ingredients thoroughly. Place a small mound in the cavity of the pear. Chill until needed.

Sour cream or mixture of sour cream and sweet cream	as needed

Serve topped with a small amount of sour cream or combination of sour cream and sweet cream.

PEARS WITH BRANDY AND CREAM   *Northern France*

Yield: 10 servings

Pears, Anjou or Bosc	10

Select pears that are a bit underripe. Peel and halve pears lengthwise. Remove center core and fibrous stem parts. Cut each half into 3 slices and arrange them on the bottom of a small baking pan in a single layer.

Sugar	as needed
Pear brandy	as needed

Lightly sprinkle with sugar and brandy and place in a 350 degree F oven for 15 minutes.

Sugar	12 oz.
Eggs	6
Heavy cream	8 oz.
Flour	1 oz.
Salt	½ tsp.

Beat the sugar and eggs until they are slightly thickened and lemon-colored. Add the remaining ingredients and mix well. Pour the mixture over the pears and bake for about ½ hour or until slightly browned.

Cream, unsweetened, whipped	as needed

Garnish with a dollop of unsweetened, whipped cream.

Serve warm or at room temperature.

PEARS WITH ZABAGLIONE   *Southern Italy*

Yield: 10 or 20 servings (½ or whole pear per serving)

Syrup:

Ingredient	Amount
Water	8 oz.
White wine, dry	8 oz.
Lemon juice, fresh	4 oz.
Sugar	8 oz.
Cinnamon stick	2, 2 inches each
Cloves	1 tsp.

Combine these ingredients in a flat saucepan large enough to accommodate 20 pear halves in a single layer. Bring to a boil, then lower heat, cover, and simmer for 20 minutes.

Pears, Bosc, peeled, halved, seeds removed	10

Make sure pears are slightly underripe, uniform in size, and unblemished. Using the tip of a sharp paring knife, make shallow "V" cuts to remove the hard stem portions remaining on each half. Remove seeds with a small melon scoop. Place pears in a single layer and simmer, covered, in the syrup for 15–30 minutes, or until tender. (Cooking time will vary, depending on the ripeness of the pears.)

Remove the cloves and cinnamon sticks and let the pears cool in the liquid. When cool, refrigerate and reserve.

Zabaglione:

Egg yolks	8
Sugar	6 oz.
Marsala wine	8 oz.

In the top half of a double-boiler, off the heat, beat the egg yolks together with the sugar until eggs turn plate-yellow and the sugar is dissolved. Place the pot over simmering water. Add the Marsala slowly, stirring constantly, until the mixture becomes thick. Do not allow to boil. Let cool and refrigerate until needed.

Pour a pool of zabaglione onto a chilled dessert plate. Place 1 or 2 pear halves on top, cut side down. Glaze the top(s) of the pear halves with a spoonful or two of the syrup.

Cream, unsweetened, whipped	as needed

Garnish with a dollop of the whipped cream added just before serving.

STRAWBERRY SNOW   *Germany*

Yield: 10–12 servings

Strawberries, washed, stems removed	1 qt.
Egg whites	5
Heavy cream, whipped	4 oz.
Sugar	to taste
Kirsch	to taste

Puree strawberries in a food processor. Add egg whites and beat until stiff peaks are formed. Fold in whipped cream and flavor with sugar and Kirsch.

Using a pastry bag, pipe into wine glasses or other suitable goblets and chill.

BAKLAVA   *Turkey*

Yield: 30–40 pieces, depending on size

Walnut meats	1½ lbs.
Sugar	4 oz.
Cinnamon, ground	1 tsp.
Sugar	4 oz.

Using the pulse action on a food processor, chop the nuts to a medium-fine consistency. Add the cinnamon and sugar and pulse 3–4 more times to mix.

Butter, melted	as needed
Phyllo dough	1 lb.

Unfold the phyllo dough and place a damp towel on top to keep the dough from drying out. Remove 2 sheets and, placing a shorter side toward you, brush with melted butter.

Place several tablespoons of the nut mixture across the phyllo in a straight line nearest the edge closest to you. Roll 2 turns, jelly-roll fashion, then add another line of the nut mixture. Roll up completely and place on a buttered baking sheet that has a low lip to contain any butter that may accumulate during baking. Continue this process until all of the nut mixture and sheets of phyllo dough have been used.

Brush the rolls once again with melted butter.

Using a sharp knife, score the rolls diagonally in 3–4 places to mark the portions. Bake in a 350 degree F oven for 30–40 minutes, or until golden-brown and crisp. Reserve and cool.

Syrup:

Sugar	1 lb.
Water	20 oz.
Honey	4 oz.
Cinnamon stick	1
Lemon juice*	1 lemon

Mix sugar, water, and honey. Add the cinnamon stick and bring to a boil. Lower heat and simmer for 30 minutes. Add the lemon juice and simmer for another 5 minutes.

Pour syrup over the baklava. Cut pieces as needed.

A more traditional way to make baklava is to layer it in a baking pan. Start by placing 6–8 buttered phyllo leaves on the bottom of a 9-inch by 13-inch baking pan, then alternate the nut mixture with 2 buttered sheets of the phyllo dough per layer, reserving 6–8 sheets for the top layer. Before baking, score the top of the baklava to a depth of ¼ inch in a diagonal pattern to form diamond-shaped pieces for serving.

* Optional flavoring: Add rose or orange flower water to taste.

DOUGHNUTS WITH FRUIT SAUCE *Austria*

Yield: 10 servings

Doughnuts:

Milk, warmed	3 oz.
Yeast	¾ oz.
Flour, all-purpose	3 oz.

Dissolve the yeast in the warmed milk. Add the flour and mix to form a soft dough. Place in a warm place and let rest until double in bulk.

Milk	3 oz.
Flour	9 oz.
Butter, softened	4 oz.
Egg yolks, beaten	3
Rum	1½ tsp.
Lemon rind, grated	1 tsp.
Sugar	1 tsp.
Salt	¼ tsp.

Mix remaining ingredients, then add the yeast mixture. Place in the bowl of an electric mixer and, using the dough hook, mix until smooth and well blended. If needed, add a small amount of warm water. The dough should be dry and firm. Cover the bowl and place in a warm place until the dough has doubled in bulk once again.

On a lightly floured surface turn out the dough and divide into 30 equal pieces. Shape each into a small, round ball, then flatten each piece slightly and place on a floured tray. Cover and let rest until doubled in size.

(Continued)

Sugar, confectioner's	as needed

Deep-fry at 350 degrees F until golden-brown, turning once. Drain on towels and dust with confectioner's sugar.

Fruit Sauce:

Fruit of choice: (Raspberry, strawberry, mango, melon, kiwi, pear, apple, or other seasonal fruit)	approx. 20 oz. of fruit puree in any combination
Sugar	as needed
Liqueur of choice	as needed

Very soft fruits can be pureed without cooking first. Others, such as pears and apples, should be peeled, seeds and other tough fibers removed, then poached in water, sugar, and any other flavoring such as cinnamon or cloves. Puree fruits in a food processor. Add sugar and liqueur to taste. The purees should have the consistency of a pancake batter. If too thick, adjust with the poaching syrup, water, or a little white wine.

To serve, place 2 or 3 pools of fruit puree made from different fruits of contrasting colors on a large dessert plate. Place 3 doughnuts in the center and dust again with confectioner's sugar.

APPENDIX: HERBS, SPICES, AND OTHER FLAVORINGS

Herbs, spices, and other flavoring products play an important role in the preparation of foods throughout the world. Their purpose is to enhance the natural flavors of foods rather than to mask them. To do this with skill requires experience, imagination, and above all restraint. Herbs, derived from the succulent leaves of plants, are used either fresh or dried. Spices, which are the product of tropical plants' aromatic parts such as the root, fruit, bud, bark, flower, or seeds, are dried and then used whole or in a pulverized form. Ground or pulverized spices and herbs tend to deteriorate with time as the aromatic oils they contain evaporate. The ability of a spice or herb to impart the unique flavor desired will depend on a number of factors such as freshness, the manner in which they are employed, their relationship to the basic food products used, and the chef's taste preferences. Because of these variables, amounts given in recipes are suggested amounts. It is best to use the freshest possible products available and, whenever feasible, to grind them as needed.

Until modern times, spices were extremely expensive because their tropical origins made them difficult and costly to obtain. Herbs, on the other hand, which can be cultivated with great ease in many areas around the world, were more readily available and therefore less expensive. Today, every imaginable spice or herb is commercially available for culinary purposes throughout the world. It is safe to assume that in the countries and regions from which the recipes in this volume are derived, creative cooks use the fullest range of these flavor enhancers. Many traditional dishes, however, use particular flavorings only, which impart the characteristic taste associated with those food preparations. Following, are references to those spices, herbs, and other products that are most often associated with traditional dishes of particular countries or regions. Oils and other fats, as well as other products, are included because they too can play a distinctive role in a preparation's ultimate flavoring. First are listed the countries of Europe, then Russia and Scandinavia, and finally the Mediterranean countries.

ITALY

Herbs: Basil, Bay Leaf, Marjoram, Mint, Parsley, Oregano, Rosemary, Sage, Thyme
Spices: Cinnamon, Nutmeg, Saffron, Fennel Seed
Other Flavorings: Capers, Cream, Garlic, Grated Hard Cheeses, Wines, Olives, Pine nuts, Walnuts, Anchovies, Olive Oil, and Butter (used separately and combined), Dried Tomatoes

FRANCE

Herbs: Basil, Bay Leaf, Chives, Chervil, Marjoram, Parsley, Rosemary, Savory, Tarragon, Thyme
Spices: Allspice, Mustard, Saffron, Nutmeg, Fennel, Clove
Other Flavorings: Aioli (see the recipe in this book), Brandy, Butter, Calvados, Cider Vinegar, Crème Fraîche, Duck Fat, Garlic, Goose Fat, Graisse Normande (a mixture of fat and vegetable essences), Olive Oil, Peanut Oil, Rouille (see the recipe in this book), Shallots

CENTRAL EUROPE (AUSTRIA, HUNGARY, CZECHOSLOVAKIA, YUGOSLAVIA)

Herbs: Marjoram, Dill, Parsley, Tarragon
Spices: Caraway Seed, Cloves, Cinnamon, Nutmeg, Paprika (hot to sweet), Poppy Seed, White Pepper, Juniper Berries
Other Flavorings: Bacon, Beer, Butter, Cream, Chicken and Beef Fat, Dill and Parsley Butters, Goose Fat, Lard, Nuts, Onions, Preserved Fruits, Peppers, Whipped Cream, Wine, Sour Cream

GERMANY

Herbs: Dill Weed, Parsley, Sage
Spices: Allspice, Bay Leaf, Caraway Seed, Dill Seed, Ginger, Juniper Berries, Mace, Mustard Seed and Powder, Nutmeg, Paprika, Vanilla, White Pepper
Other Flavorings: Anchovies, Candied Fruits, Rendered Chicken and Goose Fat, Horseradish, Lard, Raisins, Rum, Vinegars, Sweet and Sour Flavors

RUSSIA, POLAND, RUMANIA

Herbs: Parsley, Dill Weed, Cilantro (Coriander), Mint, Marjoram
Spices: Allspice, Nutmeg, Peppercorns, Poppy Seed, Dill Seed
Other Flavorings: Wild Mushrooms (fresh and dried), Parsley Root, Celery Root, Dried Fruits, Lard, Sour Cream, Honey, Horseradish, Mustards, Butter, Pomegranate Juice, Kvas (a lightly fermented sweet/sour drink derived from dark bread or fruits), Sauerkraut, Pickled Vegetables, Lemon-flavored Sugar, Root Vegetables, Sour Cream, Sunflower Seed Oil, Peppers, Parsley Root, Celery Root, Tart Berries

SCANDINAVIA (NORWAY, DENMARK, SWEDEN)

Herbs: Dill Weed, Chives, Parsley
Spices: Allspice, Cardamom, Caraway, Chives, Dill Seed, White Pepper, Mustards
Other Flavorings: Cream, Horseradish, Goose and Duck Fat, Lard, Onion, Pickled Cucumbers and Gherkins, Sugar/Salt Mixture, Sour Cream, Vinegar

GREECE AND TURKEY

Herbs: Basil, Bay Leaf, Celery Leaves, Dill, Oregano, Parsley, Mint, Marjoram, Rosemary, Sage, Thyme
Spices: Aniseed, Cardamom, Cinnamon, Coriander Seed, Cumin, Nutmeg, Sesame Seed
Other Flavorings: Capers, Garlic, Grated Hard Cheeses, Honey, Latholemono (see the recipe in this book), Onion, Scallions, Olive Oil, Olives, Walnuts, Wine Vinegar

SPAIN AND PORTUGAL

Herbs: Basil, Bay Leaf, Coriander, Thyme, Parsley

Spices: Allspice, Cinnamon, Cumin, Chili Peppers, Dried Hot and Sweet Peppers (red and green), Nutmeg, Paprika, Saffron

Other Flavorings: Almonds, Bacon, Cured Ham, Hard Cider, Fruits, Garlic, Lard, Olive Oil, Pine Nuts, Raisins, Sherry, Walnuts

MOROCCO, EGYPT, AND THE MIDDLE EAST

Herbs: Basil, Bay Leaf, Coriander Leaves, Dill Weed, Marjoram, Mint, Parsley, Oregano

Spices: Allspice, Aniseed, Black Pepper, Cardamom, Caraway, Clove, Cayenne, Coriander Seed, Cinnamon, Clove, Cumin, Ginger, Nutmeg, Paprika, Saffron, Sesame Seeds, Sumac, Turmeric, "Ras El Hanout" (a mixture of thirteen or more spices)

Other Flavorings: Almonds, Chermula (see the recipe in this book), Fruits, Garlic, Harissa (see the recipe in this book), Olives (green and ripe), Onion, Olive Oil, Olive Oil Flavored with Hot Red Peppers, Orange Flower Water, Peanuts, Preserved Lemons (see the recipe in this book), Raisins, "Smen" (a butter cooked with salt and herbs)

SUGGESTED READINGS

Abdennour, Samia. *Egyptian Cooking: A Practical Guide.* Cairo, Egypt: The American University in Cairo Press, 1985.

Alexiadou, Vefa. *Greek Cuisine.* Thessaloniki, Greece: Vefa Alexiadou, 1989.

Algar, Ayla Esen. *The Complete Book of Turkish Cooking.* London and New York: Kegan Paul International, 1988.

Anderson, Jean. *The Food of Portugal.* New York: William Morrow & Co., Inc., 1986.

Andrews, Colman. *Catalan Cuisine—Europe's Last Great Culinary Secret.* New York: Antheneum, 1988.

Barrett, Judith, and Wasserman, Norma. *Risotto.* New York: Macmillan Co., 1987.

Beck, Simone. *Simca's Cuisine.* New York: Random, 1976.

Bertholle, Louisette. *French Cuisine for All.* New York: Weathervane Books, 1987.

Brizova, Joza. *The Czechoslovak Cookbook.* New York: Crown Publishers, Inc., 1965.

Brown, Karen. *European Country Cuisine—Romantic Inns & Recipes.* San Mateo, Calif.: Travel Press, 1987.

Bugialli, Giuliano. *Bugialli on Pasta*. New York: Simon & Schuster, 1988.

———. *Classic Techniques of Italian Cooking*. New York: Simon & Schuster, 1982.

Carrier, Robert. *A Taste of Morocco*. New York: Clarkson N. Potter, Inc., 1987.

Casas, Penelope. *The Foods and Wines of Spain*. New York: Alfred A. Knopf, 1988.

Chamberlain, Lesley. *The Food and Cooking of Russia*. Middlesex, England: Penguin Books, Ltd., 1988.

Cohen, Jon, and Scaravelli, Paola. *A Mediterranean Harvest*. New York: E. P. Dutton, 1986.

Derecskey, Susan. *The Hungarian Cookbook*. New York: Harper & Row, 1972.

Erturk, Ilyas. *Turkish Kitchen Today*. Istanbul, Turkey: Istanbul Matbaasi, 1969.

Escoffier, Auguste. *The Escoffier Cook Book*. New York: Crown Publishers, Inc., 1969.

Escudier, Jean-Noel, and Fuller, Peta J. *The Wonderful Food of Provence*. New York: Harper & Row, 1988.

Essen Wie Gott in Deutschland—Die deutsche Kuche von 12 Meisterkochen auf neue Art zubereitet. Munich: Wilhelm Heyne Verlag, 1987.

Fance, Wilfred J., ed. *The New International Confectioner*. Revised by Michael Small. 5th ed. London: Virtue & Co., Ltd., 1981.

Ghedini, Francesco. *Northern Italian Cooking*. New York: Hawthorn Books, Inc., 1973.

Goldstein, Joyce. *The Mediterranean Kitchen*. New York: William Morrow & Co., Inc., 1989.

Guermont, Claude. *The Norman Table*. New York: Charles Scribner's Sons, 1985.

Halverhout, Heleen A. M. *Dutch Cooking*. Amsterdam: De Driehoek, 1972.

Hazan, Marcella. *The Classic Italian Cookbook*. New York: Alfred A. Knopf, 1976.

———. *More Classic Italian Cooking*. New York: Ballantine Books, 1984.

Hazelton, Nika. *The Belgian Cookbook*. New York: Antheneum, 1985.

———. *Classic Scandinavian Cooking*. New York: Charles Scribner's Sons, 1987.

———. *The Swiss Cookbook*. New York: Atheneum, 1984.

Hess, O., and Hess, A. *Viennese Cooking*. New York: Crown Publishers, Inc., 1952.

Johnson, Hugh, Manjon, Maite, and Read, Jan. *The Wine and Food of Spain.* Boston: Little, Brown and Co., 1987.

Knight, Max. *The Original Blue Danube Cookbook.* Berkeley, Calif.: Lancaster Miller Publishers, 1979.

Kovi, Paul. *Transylvanian Cuisine.* New York: Crown Publishers, Inc., 1985.

Lang, George. *The Cuisine of Hungary.* New York: Atheneum, 1985.

Langseth-Christensen, Lillian. *Gourmet's Old Vienna Cookbook.* New York: Gourmet Books, Inc., 1959.

Lissen, Adrian. *Tapas.* New York: Gallery Books, 1989.

Luard, Elisabeth. *The Old World Kitchen.* New York: Bantam Books, 1987.

Machlin, Edda Servi. *The Classic Cuisine of the Italian Jews.* New York: Dodd, Mead & Co., 1981.

Middione, Carlo. *The Food of Southern Italy.* New York: William Morrow & Co., Inc., 1987.

More, Julian. *A Taste of Provence.* New York: Henry Holt & Co., 1988.

Nelson, Kay S. *The Eastern European Cookbook.* New York: Dover Publications, Inc., 1973.

Nordio, Jeanette Nance. *Taste of Venice—Traditional Venetian Cooking.* Topsfield, Mass.: Salem House Publishers, 1988.

Norman, Barbara. *The Spanish Cookbook.* New York: Bantam Books, 1967.

Ochorowicz-Monatowa, Marja. *Polish Cookery.* New York: Crown Publishers, Inc., 1958.

Olney, Richard, *The French Menu Cookbook.* rev. ed. Boston: David R. Godine, 1985.

Ortiz, Elisabeth Lambert. *The Food of Spain and Portugal—The Complete Iberian Cuisine.* New York: Antheneum, 1989.

Petrova, Nina. *The Best of Russian Cooking.* New York: Crown Publishers, Inc., 1979.

Root, Waverley. *The Food of France.* New York: Vintage, 1977.

———. *The Food of Italy.* New York: Vintage, 1977.

Sheraton, Mimi. *The German Cookbook.* New York: Random, 1965.

Souli, Sofia. *The Greek Cookery Book.* Athens: Michalis Toumbis Editions S.A., 1989.

Stubbs, Joyce. *The Home Book of Greek Cookery*. London: Faber & Faber, Inc., 1963.

Troisgros, Jean, and Troisgros, Pierre. *The Nouvelle Cuisine of Jean & Pierre Trois-gros*. Translated by Roberta Wolfe Smoler. New York: William Morrow & Co., 1978.

Tselementes, Nicholas. *Greek Cookery*. New York: D. C. Divry, Inc., 1950.

Uvezian, Sonia. *Cooking from the Caucasus*. New York: Harcourt Brace Jovano-vich, 1976.

Vada, Simonetta Lupi. *The Flavors of Italy*. Tuscan, Ariz.: HP Books, 1986.

Vergé, Roger. *Roger Vergé's Cuisine of the South of France*. Translated by Roberta Wolfe Smoler. New York: William Morrow & Co., 1980.

Viazzi, Alfredo. *Alfredo Viazzi's Italian Cooking*. New York: Vintage, 1983.

Volokh, Anne. *The Art of Russian Cuisine*. New York: Macmillan Co., 1983.

Wells, Patricia. *Bistro Cooking*. New York: Workman Publishing, 1989.

Wolfert, Paula. *The Cooking of South-West France*. New York: Harper & Row, 1983.

———. *Couscous and Other Good Food from Morocco*. New York: Harper & Row, 1973.

———. *Mediterranean Cooking*. New York: Ecco Press, 1977.

Wretman, Tore. *The Swedish Smorgasbord*. Sweden: Forum, 1983.

Yannoulis, Anne. *Greek Calendar Cookbook*. Athens: Lycabettus Press, 1988.

INDEX